The Cognitive Mechanics of Economic Development and Institutional Change

Allowing individuals and firms to specialise accelerates the pace of learning and leads to increased levels of knowledge across the board. However, for this to be truly effective, better communication is needed. Institutions are a serious aid to this process.

This book seeks to explain long-term economic development and institutional change in terms of the cognitive features of human learning and communication processes. The author links individual cognitive processes to macroeconomic growth theories, including economies of scale and scope, and to theories of institutional development based on asymmetric information in production processes and economies of scale in enforcement technology.

With considerable flair, Bertin Martens has applied the hot new area of cognitive economics to notions of growth and development, and has created a unique and impressive volume.

Bertin Martens is an economist at the European Commission, specialising in international economic relations and development aid.

Routledge Frontiers of Political Economy

The Cognitive Mechanics of Economic Development and Institutional Change

Bertin Martens

Routledge
Taylor & Francis Group

LONDON AND NEW YORK

First published 2004
by Routledge
11 New Fetter Lane, London EC4P 4EE

Simultaneously published in the USA and Canada
by Routledge
29 West 35th Street, New York, NY 10001

Routledge is an imprint of the Taylor & Francis Group

© 2004 Bertin Martens

Typeset in Sabon by Taylor & Francis Books Ltd
Printed and bound in Great Britain by Antony Rowe Ltd,
Chippenham, Wiltshire
British Library Cataloguing in Publication Data
A catalogue record for this book is available from the British Library

Library of Congress Cataloging in Publication Data
A catalog record for this book has been requested

ISBN 0–415–32633–8

Contents

Illustrations

Tables

Figures

Acknowledgements

This book has been in the making for many years, possibly ever since I started studying economics. Many people have helped me in the course of all these years to sustain my motivation, pull me out of deep gloom and continue this research project.

On the US side of the Atlantic, my thanks goes first and foremost to Douglas North, for his constant encouragement and prodding about the progress of this book. He arranged a fellowship that allowed me to take sabbatical leave from my duties at the European Commission and finally gave me the time to pull the various bits and pieces of this research together into a book. My thanks also to Paul Edwards, now president of the Mercatus Center at George Mason University. Mercatus not only provided financial support and a stimulating environment but, most importantly, the intellectual freedom to indulge in theories and thoughts way off the beaten track of mainstream economics. Thanks to Sayed Shariq and the Knexus Program at the Institute for International Studies, Stanford University, for plunging me into Stanford's intellectual whirlpool, and to Nate Rosenberg for engaging me as a fish-sitter, exactly the sort of quiet environment that I needed to pick up and rework some of the loose ends in this research project. Furthermore, the participants in the Social Change Project, a series of mind-freeing as well as mind-boggling work-shops on the cognitive and institutional origins of social change, presided over by Douglas North and financed through the Mercatus Center, provided some fresh thoughts and insights into a number of issues covered by this book. I am particularly grateful to Young Back Choi, Merlin Donald, Avner Greif, Timur Kuran, Chris Mantzavinos, Joel Mokyr, Vernon Smith, Kevin McCabe and Barry Weingast for their suggestions.

On the European side of the Atlantic, many people contributed know-ingly or unknowlingly to this book. I am most grateful to the multi-disciplinary research Centre Leo Apostel (CLEA) at the Free University of Brussels (VUB), in particular Francis Heylighen, who provided academic shelter and encouragement in times of intellectual need. The chaotic creativity of CLEA turned out to be fertile ground for the seeds of this multi-disciplinary research project. My thanks also to Marc xii *Acknowledgements*

Despontin and Frank Plastria at the Economics Department of VUB, who helped me to conceptualise knowledge. The Max Planck Institute for Research in Economic Systems in Jena was another safe haven that allowed me to work intermittently on this project in a very comfortable and stimulating environment, with support from Uwe Mummert, Thráin Eggertsson and Ulrich Witt.

I should not forget to thank the many participants at workshops and conferences where I presented bits and pieces of this work. They provided valuable feedback that prevented many errors and omissions: the Max Planck Institute in Jena; workshops at the University of Arizona in Tucson, New York University, George Mason University, the IRIS Center at the University of Maryland, the Knexus conferences at Stanford University, MERIT at the University of Maastricht, the University of Leuven, the University of New South Wales (Sydney), the University of Trento, and Bochum University.

The theory of economic development is part of the general problem of evolutionary change and its poor condition reflects the general poverty of the theory of dynamic systems. The plain fact is that *knowledge...is the only thing that can grow* or evolve, and the concept is quite crucial in any evolutionary theory. As far as matter and energy are concerned, we are subject to inexorable laws of conservation. In the case of energy, there is not even conservation; the second law of thermodynamics informs us there is constant...decay. It is only information and knowledge processes which in any sense get out from under the iron laws of conservation and decay....

Two processes may be distinguished here. The first might be called printing, in which a structure is able to reproduce itself by making a copy. Printing by itself, however...would merely fill the universe with copies of an initial structure. There must therefore be a second process to which we might give the name of organizing. Thus we can think of capital essentially as knowledge imposed on the material world by organizing...and...by a process akin to three-dimensional printing. In this view, consumption is essentially consumption of knowledge structures....

The recognition that development, even economic development, is essentially a knowledge process has been slowly penetrating the minds of economists, but we are still too much obsessed by mechanical models, capital-income ratios and even input-output tables, to the neglect of...learning processes which is the real key to development.

(K. Boulding, 'The economics of knowledge and the knowledge of economics', Richard T. Ely Lecture for the American Economic Association, *American Economic Review*, May 1966, pp. 1–13, my emphasis)

1 Introduction

This book aims to construct a plausible explanatory model of the emergence and co-evolution of economic systems and institutions that guide behaviour in human societies. The model revolves around cognition – the capacity of human beings to acquire and store knowledge, communicate it and use it for behavioural purposes.[1] The emergence of trade, or economic systems, is explained as an efficient form of communication of knowledge through embodiment in goods and services. Trade circumvents cognitive capacity constraints because, contrary to symbolic communication, the recipient is not required to process and store all embodied knowledge in his own mind. Furthermore, trade enables the emergence of specialisation – the asymmetric distribution of knowledge across groups of individuals. The book argues that specialisation has allowed human societies to overcome the limits on individual cognitive capacity and achieve rapid growth in knowledge, far beyond the possibilities of individual learning capacity. Specialisation and trade require institutional incentives, however, to allocate property rights to knowledge and handle the uncertainties generated by lack of knowledge of the traded goods. Society's ability to develop more powerful institutional incentives for specialisation and efficient exchange has marked the pace of cognitive and economic development. The evolution of many important organisational features in human societies, including production, markets, legal and political institutions, etc., can be interpreted in terms of a relentless search for ever more cognitive economy through more efficient handling of distributed knowledge.

More specifically, this book seeks to demonstrate the validity of two propositions:

- First, specialisation (or distributed knowledge) is a consequence of the search for cognitive economy. Since individual cognitive capacity is limited, any features of human society that help to relax this constraint carry an evolutionary advantage. Economic systems are such a feature because they generate cognitive economy through specialisation or the asymmetric distribution of knowledge over a group of individuals. The cognitive economy resides in the fact that not every individual has to acquire the same knowledge. Rather, we can make use of the specialised knowledge acquired by somebody else by trading our products for the products that embody his knowledge. As a result, specialisation has enabled human societies to achieve rapid growth in knowledge accumulation and storage capacity, far beyond the possibilities of individual learning capacity.

- Second, specialisation requires matching institutions in order to foster economic development. Institutions reduce transaction costs and regulate the residual uncertainties that are inherent to the exchange of specialised knowledge embodied in goods and services. They are a prerequisite for the efficient exchange of specialised embodied knowledge, which is necessarily a partial exchange only: the buyer does not possess all the knowledge that went into the production of the good. Society's ability to develop ever more efficient institutions, both in terms of individual property rights and collective decision-making, facilitates specialisation and marks the pace of economic development. Economic and institutional development run in parallel, and are both endogenous to the cognitive development of human societies.

The centrality of cognition

This is an essay in cognitive economics. The view that knowledge plays a central role in economic development is now broadly accepted, especially since the late 1980s. In 1988, Robert Lucas published a paper on 'The mechanics of economic development' (Lucas 1988). It triggered a wave of new research on economic growth that has become well known under the label of 'New' or 'Endogenous' Growth Theory. Lucas' aim was to endogenise the so-called Solow Residual, the unexplained variation in economic growth that kept popping up in empirical tests of neo-classical growth models. This residual was generally attributed to technological innovation, or changes in knowledge. Lucas suggested that this problem could be solved by introducing knowledge as an explicit production factor in growth models, alongside the conventional production factors of capital and labour. Despite the initial optimism surrounding these new models, they quickly ran into methodological problems, due to two specific properties of knowledge: non-rivalry and partial excludability. Partial excludability implies that it is hard to keep knowledge as an exclusive property of an individual or company; it can spill over to other economic agents. Non-rivalry implies that many users can use the same knowledge at the same time. Romer (1994) demonstrated that these two properties are difficult to reconcile with the diminishing returns or convergence requirement of the neo-classical mainstream economics paradigm. For a number of years, the endogenous growth school was torn between proponents and opponents of convergence, waging battle with an endless series of empirical tests of their models, without settling the issue. At the end of the day however, the concrete mechanisms through which knowledge plays a role in economic development remained by and large a black box. The debate in economic growth theory has gradually returned to its starting position in recent years. Accumulation of production factors in neo-classical growth models, including accumulation of knowledge, provides but a partial explanation for economic growth. Attention is focused once more on the unexplained Solow Residual – re-baptised as 'Total Factor Productivity' – that is widely recognised to be a major explanatory factor behind economic growth. At the same time, growth theory is back to square one in trying to open up the black box of Total Factor Productivity (Easterly and Levine 2000; Easterly 2001).

The view that institutions – humanly devised constraints on human behaviour – play a central role in economic development, and more specifically in Total Factor Productivity, has also gained wide acceptance in the last decade or so (Acemoglu *et al.* 2001; Rodrik *et al.* 2002; Sala-I-Martin 2002). This view goes back at least to North (North and Thomas 1973; North 1981), who argued that the quality of institutions determines the level of transaction costs that, in turn, affects economic efficiency. Modern institutional economics is a tree with many branches and twigs, with one common characteristic: all these schools of institutional economics examine how asymmetries in the distribution of information, or knowledge, affect economic performance. That is precisely what distinguishes neo-classical from neo-institutional economics. While the former generally assumes that (near-) perfect information is available in transactions at (near-) zero costs, the latter assumes positive information costs. Transaction cost economics looks at the cost of obtaining information required to conclude a contract or exchange (North 1990) and the potential costs of post-contractual uncertainty or absence of information (Williamson 1985). Incomplete contracts theory is based on quite similar principles, but focuses on the incentives embedded in a contract and the likely behavioural outcomes that they produce under imperfect information (Tirole 1999). Property rights theory examines how different allocations of this residual contractual uncertainty create different incentive structures. Modern organisation theory combines these different techniques to study incentives in large organisations or hierarchies where tasks are delegated and information is inevitably widely distributed across agents. Institutions – rules of behaviour – exist precisely because they are means to partially overcome these informational problems and the resulting uncertainties. While institutional economics is often associated with micro-economic applications at the level of individuals and organisations, a lot of these findings can be transposed to the macro-economic level. Its focus on incomplete and asymmetric information provides a useful starting point to study the role of information and knowledge[2] in economic growth.

Modern institutional economics has revealed the role that institutions play in the management of knowledge in societies. Institutions regulate the property rights on knowledge and the spill-over of knowledge between individuals – a very important issue in endogenous growth theory. Institutions also affect transaction costs and post-contractual uncertainties, and thereby play a vital role in enabling market transactions. Whereas markets exist to trade knowledge, whether or not embodied in goods and services, institutions exist to deal with the unknown aspects of the goods and services that are being traded and cause uncertainties. While macro-economic growth theory has focused on the volume of knowledge as a driver of economic development, institutional economics and its offshoots in organisation theory have focused on the asymmetric distribution of that knowledge, and the way in which that distribution is being managed through behavioural constraints – property rights, spill-overs, contracts to handle residual uncertainties, etc.

Economic institutions point to another key aspect of this book: the role of distributed knowledge – or specialisation, division of labour and division of knowledge[3] – in economic and institutional development. Against this institutional economics background, one can see why Lucas' (1988) attempt to solve the Solow Residual issue by integrating knowledge as a production factor in the growth model was too simple. He assumed that knowledge could be treated like any other production factor. That treatment becomes increasingly difficult to defend, not only because of the properties of partial excludability and non-rivalry that undermine the convergence requirement in neo-classical general equilibrium models, but even more so because the institutional implications of distributed knowledge management are not accounted for in this approach. In short, it is not just accumulation of knowledge that is important for economic performance; it is also the distribution of knowledge, and the way in which the problems associated with that distribution are handled by institutions. While there is by now a vast amount of literature that emphasises the importance of learning and knowledge accumulation in economic growth, very little has been written so far on the importance of distributed knowledge for economic growth, including the role that institutions play in the management of distributed knowledge. Despite the fact that distributed knowledge – or rather, the division of labour – figured prominently in the first paragraph of Adam Smith's (1776) *Wealth of Nations*, the book that signalled the start of modern economics, the concept rapidly disappeared in the course of the history of economic thought. This book argues that there are good reasons to revive it, though in a cognitive interpretation that differs somewhat from the interpretation originally proposed by Adam Smith. It will demonstrate why asymmetrically distributed knowledge is a crucial explanatory factor for the emergence and evolution of institutions. More importantly, it will show how the evolution of institutions is closely linked not only to the accumulation of knowledge, but even more so to the distribution of that knowledge across society. This book looks at institutions as endogenous outcomes of knowledge accumulation and distribution in society, not as rules of behaviour exogenously invented by social or political geniuses.

That brings us to the title and the purpose of this book. One can see how institutional economics and macro-economic growth theory, the main schools of thought in the economic growth debate of the last two decades, are slowly converging around (distributed) knowledge as a common driver for economic growth, or in a broader sense (distributed) cognition. This book seeks to further explore the role of knowledge, or cognition, as a common denominator of neo-classical and neo-institutional economic growth and development theories. It does not seek to produce a new and fully fledged economic growth theory, but rather to integrate into economics a number of concepts from cognitive science that may shed light on the nature and mechanics of distributed cognition, with a view to establishing a cognitive approach to economic development and providing the conceptual foundations for an integration of current economic growth and institutional economics theories into a single unified approach.

The wider picture

Above, I provided a first and purely economic reason why this book's focus is on cognition, namely that it is justified by recent developments in economic theory that point towards a convergence of growth theory and institutional economics around the common denominator of (distributed) knowledge, or cognition. However, there are at least two other reasons to put cognition at the core of an explanatory framework for the emergence and evolution of economic and institutional development in human societies.

The second reason is that a general theory of economic development of human societies should be capable of explaining the transition from pre-economic to economic societies, on the basis of a unifying concept that is present in both stages but underwent a change that explains the transition. I will argue in Chapter 5 that cognition constitutes such a unifying concept, and that changes in cognitive features of human behaviour – in this case communication features – can explain why economic systems and institutions emerged, and why they constitute an evolutionary (and cognitive) advantage for societies that have them.

The proposed model should be able to trace an uninterrupted line of cognitive, economic and institutional development of human societies, that stretches, say, from Olduvai Gorge in the Great Rift Valley, Tanzania (2.5 million years BC), to Palo Alto in Silicon Valley, California (2002 AD). While there is unlikely to be any significant genetic difference between the peoples that populate both valleys, there is an enormous difference in the knowledge sets that both peoples have at their disposal to cope with the threats and opportunities of their environment. This difference is not only due to cumulative learning across history, but more so due to differences in the organisation of knowledge storage and communication techniques in these societies, facilitated by institutions, and consequently differences in the degree of knowledge specialisation and the level of economic development. Silicon Valley is just the latest – and by no means the last – step in the cognitive development of primate societies.

The emphasis on the central role of cognition in the development of human societies, and cognitive continuity therein, implies that this book could be considered as an extension of the evolutionary epistemology tradition into the domain of the social sciences, and in particular into economics. Evolutionary epistemology (Hahlweg and Hooker 1989; Callebaut and Pinxten 1987) is an interdisciplinary school of thought that subscribes to the view that all cognitive evolution is just a continuation of biological evolution: all organic bodies are repositories of knowledge, even if they are not equipped with an active mind or with the ability to learn. Darwinian selection processes, with random mutations and selective retention, are also considered learning processes, though spread out over many generations rather than within a single lifetime. This results in accumulation of environmental and behavioural knowledge in genetic structures in living organisms. Organisms with central nervous systems have developed independent cognitive capacity: the ability to learn and adapt behaviour within a single lifetime, even at very short notice. Moreover, some animals are good at imitation and can thereby transmit knowledge between them. Human beings have done even better. We have developed symbolic communication systems that are a far more efficient means to transfer very complex knowledge, and even entire thought processes, from one individual to another. Finally, we have developed economic systems that allow us to transfer knowledge embodied in goods, so that the recipient can economise on his scarce cognitive capacity. There is no need for him to store all that knowledge in his own brain. He can simply make use of that knowledge in embodied form. However, this form of cognitive economy requires individual incentives to invest in learning and derive the benefits from it. That is where economic institutions that enable gainful trade come into play. I will argue in Part II of this book that both symbolic communication and exchange of embodied knowledge – trade and property rights – emerged as an evolutionary advantageous response to circumvent the limited cognitive capacities of human brains.

The third reason for the centrality of cognition is related to the quote from Boulding (1966) in the preliminary pages of this book. I have selected this quote because it provides a good starting point for this research and also because it connects two 'spheres' of the world: the physical world, governed by the first and second law of thermodynamics, that is often associated with economic production and exchange, and the cognitive world of knowledge, that counters the second law of thermodynamics – the entropy law – and is responsible for shaping and transforming the world, creating new order. Boulding (1966) points out that the quantity of matter and energy is for all practical purposes a constant, and energy is even subject to decay (rather than growth) as a result of the entropy law. As a result, it is somewhat difficult to see how mere production of goods and services, which requires matter and energy, could represent growth. The only thing that can grow over time is knowledge, our understanding of the world around us. We can use this knowledge to produce ever more sophisticated and complex transformations of matter and energy, via a process that he describes as the 'three-dimensional printing' of knowledge. However, a lot of knowledge may not be used for transformation and embodiment in matter, but rather for the transformation of the organisation of society, the way in which people behave and interact and to shape the institutions that guide human behaviour. (And some knowledge may of course not be used for any behavioural purposes at all and remain in a purely symbolic format.) At the time when Boulding wrote and pronounced these words, economists began to agree that knowledge accumulation is an important driver for economic growth. It took nearly four decades more for economists to begin to see that it also drives institutional change in societies, through the mechanism of distributed knowledge.

A summary of the main arguments

The book starts by taking a few steps back from the economic realm to examine some basic cognitive mechanisms that enable the accumulation and communication of knowledge in human societies. Cognition is not only about learning processes in the human brain, but also about external knowledge storage devices, asymmetric distribution of knowledge between individuals and the organisation of communication between them.

Part I of this book contains an overview of the relevant economics literature on economic growth (Chapter 2) and distributed knowledge (Chapter 3). It explores the uneasy relationship between (distributed) knowledge and modern economics. I do not present any new arguments. My only aim here is to prepare the ground for the cognitive and institutional arguments in Parts II and III. Knowledge itself is now widely recognised as an important variable in economic growth, but existing growth models have a hard time in handling the properties of knowledge. By contrast, the distribution of knowledge is not recognised as a relevant variable in mainstream macro-economic growth models. Only modern institutional economics theories implicitly or explicitly recognise that institutions exist in order to facilitate handling of asymmetries in the distribution of knowledge.

Chapter 2 presents an in-depth exploration of the arguments that were advanced above, at the start of this introductory chapter. It reviews in detail the role of knowledge in modern economic growth theory. The mainstream neo-classical Solow growth model deals with embodied knowledge only (in capital and labour) and therefore concentrates on factor accumulation only. That allows it to fit nicely within the constraints of the neo-classical economic paradigm, but results in poor empirical performance. Attempts in endogenous growth theory to include non-embodied knowledge in growth models ended in deadlock because the methodological problems created by the specific economic properties of knowledge (partial excludability and non-rivalry) could not be resolved within a neo-classical model. Partial excludability triggered an unproductive debate on convergence. Non-rivalry raised the more fundamental issues of non-convexity and economies of scale, both of which are incompatible with the neo-classical general equilibrium paradigm, but more in line with the empirical stylised facts of growth. The chapter concludes that traditional approaches to knowledge in economics are insufficient for a proper understanding of its role in economic development. It summarises a number of stylised empirical facts of economic growth, all of which point in the direction of increasing returns, rather than the decreasing returns that are at the root of the neo-classical paradigm.

Chapter 3 examines the role of distributed knowledge in modern economics. Early Classical economic writers such as Adam Smith (Smith 1776/1993) explicitly referred to distributed knowledge, or division of labour as he called it, as a key variable in economic development. That insight was unfortunately sidelined in the course of the history of economic thought. While Smith put the division of labour at the core of his economic theory, it rapidly disappeared and was replaced in the second half of the nineteenth century by investment in capital goods as the driving force behind economic development. One can easily trace how this finally led to the Solow model discussed in Chapter 2. There are very few models of division of labour or specialisation in the modern economics literature. Hayek (Hayek 1949) stands out as virtually the only post-war economist who deals extensively with specialisation and the communication problems that it entails. Some other authors have proposed models of division of labour, but mostly without an underlying concept of knowledge as such. Rosen's (1983) model is important because it introduces 'economies of scope', a key feature in a cognitive interpretation of specialisation, as will be shown in Part II.

Stigler (1976) argued that division of labour or distributed knowledge has no relevance for modern economics. My original contribution in this chapter is that I argue against that view and demonstrate how asymmetric, incomplete and imperfect knowledge have become key issues in modern institutional economics and organisation theory. A more thorough review of modern institutional economics is left for Chapter 8, however. The chapter concludes that distributed knowledge is still a relevant issue in modern economic theory, but that the link between more micro-economic models of asymmetric or distributed knowledge and macro-economic growth performance has not yet been made.

The train of arguments leading to my thesis starts in Part II. It reconstructs the cognitive mechanisms of human development from scratch, in order to explain the emergence of economic systems as a specific and advantageous step within the wider perspective of general cognitive evolution. It first proposes a definition of 'knowledge', based on bounded rationality or limited cognitive capacity, and derives the principle of cognitive economy: the search to extend cognitive capacity and lower its opportunity cost. It explains the origins of distributed knowledge in human societies: how and under which conditions it emerges from non-specialised societies, and how it affects further learning and knowledge accumulation. It then explores the conditions for the emergence of economic exchange, as a special and efficient form of knowledge communication in a system of distributed knowledge. It ends with the conclusion that distributed cognitive processing in the human brain is to a large extent responsible for economies of scope in learning, and thus for the emergence of specialisation in society.

The purpose of Chapter 4 is to define the subject of this research: what knowledge is and what drives learning or the accumulation of knowledge. I introduce several innovations in this chapter.

First, I present my own operational definition of knowledge, based mainly on the hypothesis of bounded rationality and on a few additional hypotheses regarding the link between knowledge and reality: the existence of causal relationships between events in the material world and imperfect perception of these causal relationships by cognitive agents. Individual cognitive capacity is scarce and learning thus has an opportunity cost. Learning is driven by the need to benefit from the opportunities and avoid the cost of challenges posed by the environment in which an individual lives. Knowledge increases the chances of doing so.

Second, in contrast to neo-classical and endogenous growth theories where knowledge remains a one-dimensional variable, my definition of knowledge allows me to identify two dimensions in knowledge: the degree of accuracy and the extent of variety in knowledge. I demonstrate in the next chapters that these dimensions are necessary to understand the underlying cognitive mechanics of specialisation. For a given cognitive capacity, a reduction in variety permits an increase in accuracy, which is a source of comparative advantage and the basis for economic exchange of knowledge. I propose a simple model that determines an optimal allocation of scarce cognitive capacity between accuracy and variety.

Third, I derive from the above the Principle of Cognitive Economy. When cognitive capacity is limited, cognitive processes have an opportunity cost. Any technological improvement that reduces this opportunity cost constitutes an evolutionary advantage. The chapter then illustrates how cognitive economy is realised at various levels, both inside and outside the human brain. Inside the brain this takes place through distributed internal representation of knowledge (bindings and categorisation theory).

Externally, symbolic representation generates an important cognitive leverage effect that gives human societies a competitive advantage over other primates.

Chapter 5 switches from the properties of individual cognition to the properties of cognition in a group. The purpose of this chapter is to show how economic systems, which exchange distributed knowledge in embodied form (goods), are more efficient in terms of knowledge accumulation and communication than systems which exchange knowledge in non-embodied forms only (through imitation and symbolic communication). Economic systems are a result of the evolutionary search for ever more cognitive economy.

The chapter starts with the well known Boyd and Richerson (1985) model of the cultural transmission of knowledge. The authors of that model intended to show that societies which are able to communicate knowledge could improve the 'fitness' of their population. They took the simplest form of communication, imitation, to prove their case. However, critics of the model (Rogers 1988) demonstrated that this is not the case, except under very restrictive conditions. I build on this model to show, first of all, that the principle of cognitive economy applies to communication in the form of savings in learning costs. Second, I trace the quantity and substitution effects that this price effect induces, and show that the model lacks incentives for learning and specialisation. Specialisation is eliminated by communication. Third, I re-interpret the model to demonstrate that the emergence of economic systems (trading knowledge embodied in goods and services) allows for true specialisation and constitutes an incentive for learning. I conclude that the evolutionary emergence of economic systems is a result of their cognitive advantage over the 'cultural' exchange of knowledge. Economic exchange of embodied knowledge constitutes an important source of cognitive economy because it requires only partial (truncated) transmission of knowledge between individuals in order to have full access to the knowledge embodied in goods.

After the emergence and comparative advantage of economic systems has been explained and linked to distributed knowledge in Chapter 5, Chapter 6 explores in more detail the cognitive mechanics of economic systems. I start from the simple individual cognitive equilibrium between accuracy and variety in knowledge, developed in Chapter 4, and examine how this cognitive equilibrium is affected when that individual is put in a group of agents with asymmetrically distributed knowledge. The group has a wider variety of available knowledge than the individual, which allows the individual to specialise and obtain access to a wider variety of knowledge through exchange of his specialised knowledge with other individuals. However, in order to keep specialisation, economic exchange under cognitive specialisation implies the exchange of 'truncated' or incomplete knowledge sets. This causes residual uncertainty in trade: the knowledge embodied in a good is only partially known to the buyer. Each individual must allocate part of his scarce cognitive capacity to the acquisition of common knowledge, just enough to enable communication with others but without transmission of the full knowledge content of goods. This requirement puts limits on the degree of specialisation. The model presented in Chapter 6 demonstrates how the allocation of scarce cognitive capacity between specialised and common knowledge is a function of the trade-off between *ex-ante* transaction costs and *ex-post* residual uncertainty in transactions. That trade-off, in turn, is determined by the quality of institutions – a variable that is kept exogenous in Chapter 6 but will be endogenised in Part III. Consequently, the degree of specialisation and the total volume of knowledge available in society are determined by the quality of institutions.

I have several original contributions in this chapter:

First, I provide a cognitive explanation for the mechanics of specialisation and transaction costs. While Adam Smith assumed that specialisation was self-evident, I show that the trade-off between variety and accuracy in knowledge, or the degree of specialisation, is affected by transaction costs.

Second, I show that the emergence of specialisation is firmly linked to institutions. This argument is often hinted at in the institutional economics literature but never really explored. The more specialisation, the more 'unknown knowledge' is being traded and the more need for regulation of the consequences of that unknown part through a system of allocation of residual uncertainty or residual rights – commonly called property rights. As such, trade and institutions are two sides of the same cognitive coin: the explicit and the implicit knowledge that is being communicated.

Third, I integrate two competing transaction costs concepts that have divided the new institutional economics (Coase-North versus Williamson) into a single approach, based on a cognitive interpretation of specialisation. Trading partial knowledge sets induces Coase-North *ex-ante* transaction costs because of the need to have at least a partial overlap in knowledge sets between specialised individuals. This entails opportunity costs, spending scarce cognitive capacity on acquiring that interface. The larger the overlap, and thus the higher the transaction costs, the better the acquiring party understands the knowledge it acquires and the lower residual uncertainty (Williamson's transaction costs).

Chapters 4, 5 and 6 offer a rather static view of the emergence of trade as an expression of the principle of cognitive economy and the advantages that it creates in terms of knowledge communication and accumulation. The objective of Chapter 7 is to present a more dynamic picture and re-connect the cognitive model of the previous chapters to economic growth theory. The model in Chapter 6 defined an equilibrium degree of specialisation, in function of transaction costs. However, it is unlikely that individual learning stops once this equilibrium specialisation point has been reached. That raises the next question: how does further learning affect that equilibrium? Does it increase variety or accuracy of knowledge, or both? Chapter 7 examines several (cognitive) mechanisms that continue to drive knowledge accumulation and economic development, beyond the specialisation equilibrium. It also seeks to link these mechanisms to the stylised empirical facts of economic growth, identified at the end of Chapter 2. These stylised facts point in the direction of increasing returns to scale, rather than the decreasing returns that are at the roots of the neo-classical paradigm. Chapter 7 presents a number of cognitive mechanisms that generate increasing returns to knowledge in a setting with distributed knowledge.

Chapter 7 starts by comparing Becker's (1964) static view of learning with a Schumpeterian view of monopolistic competition, and how that affects incentives for further learning. It demonstrates how the external environment of the Boyd and Richerson model is partially endogenised in a model with competitive markets: the knowledge acquired by others constitutes part of the environment. When learning by others accelerates as a result of cognitive economy, the pace of environmental change accelerates and forces all agents to allocate more scarce cognitive resources to learning.

This still leaves the question of the direction of further learning unanswered. Rosen's (1983) concept of 'economies of scope' is introduced to explain why further learning leads to further specialisation (accuracy), rather than acquisition of wider knowledge (variety). My original contribution here consists of giving a cognitive interpretation to the concept of economies of scope, linking it with the theories of cognition discussed in Chapter 4. The emergence of specialisation is linked to the distributed network structure of the brain. The basic neuro-physiological and cognitive mechanics of the brain generate economies of scope. That is what enables the occurrence of specialisation, not just learning or economic incentives to specialise.

I also propose a distinction between internal and external economies of scope. The latter provides a cognitive basis for complementarity of knowledge sets between specialists. It explains why specialists will cluster together rather than seek alliances with non-specialists, and thereby constitutes an explanation for the increasing returns that have been observed in the stylised empirical facts of economic growth in Chapter 2. Moreover, further specialisation increases the extent of the market for specialised skills: cognitive self-sufficiency decreases and more skills become marketable. While Adam Smith argued that the extent of the market determines the division of labour, I show that the reverse is also true: specialisation induces economies of scale in the extent of the market. Finally, I transpose the Fisher Theorem (Fisher 1930) from evolutionary biology to economics in order to explain why more specialised societies have higher knowledge growth rates. This does not necessarily translate into higher economic growth rates however. The cognitive economic model that I introduced in Chapter 6 kept institutional change exogenous.

However, as argued above, empirical evidence is increasingly pointing to the primacy of institutions as a determinant of economic growth. Explaining changes in Total Factor Productivity in growth models should therefore concentrate on explaining changes in institutions. The objective of Part III is precisely to endogenise institutional development in a model of cognitive economic development. Basically, Part III argues that the institutional architecture of society is endogenous to the volume of knowledge that it has absorbed and the degree of specialisation which this entails. It examines the dynamics of societal organisation and the institutional constraints that facilitate or inhibit further accumulation of knowledge.

The main objectives of Chapter 8 are to present a short overview of the relevant institutional economics literature, including definitions of basic concepts and to address the question of the emergence of institutions: what evolutionary advantage does it bestow on societies that have them? Institutions, the set of humanly devised rules that guide human behaviour, are defined as enforceable property rights, the positive and negative incentives attached to various behavioural options. Models that emphasise spontaneous emergence and enforcement of institutions start with Axelrod's (1984) Prisoners' Dilemma games. Repeated interaction between individuals can produce spontaneous restrictions on behaviour and move society from a Nash to a more Pareto-optimal behavioural equilibrium. My contribution to the debate here is twofold. First, I show why institutions that emerge through repeated interaction and decentralised enforcement cannot explain the emergence of anonymous trade, the typical mode of exchange between specialised individuals. Second, I demonstrate that such institutions are inefficient because of high transaction costs (monitoring, enforcement) and not robust against asymmetric power distribution between individuals. The chapter concludes that game-theoretic simulations of institutional emergence without central enforcement are not compatible with economic exchange of asymmetrically distributed knowledge.

Chapter 9 moves on to existing models of centrally enforced institutions (a state monopoly on violence) and presents an overview of the relevant literature. A centralised monopoly on violence produces more efficient institutional enforcement but carries the risk of expropriation by the ruler. I examine bottom-up and top-down theories of the emergence and evolution of states, and conclude that neither of these is entirely satisfying, mainly because the drivers of institutional change remain exogenous and often non-economic factors in the model. They are also difficult to combine with the transition from personal to anonymous trade (under specialisation). I then combine these models of central enforcement with a more recent class of conflict technology models that offer better perspectives, though they still lack some decisive features.

Chapter 10 is the central chapter of Part III. In this chapter, I combine some of the institutional enforcement mechanisms from conflict theory and the institutional economics literature (as discussed in Chapters 8 and 9) with those on the cognitive mechanics of specialisation (discussed in Part II). The combination of the two is a cognitive model that simultaneously produces endogenous evolution of institutions as well as economic production. Agents have a choice between production and conflict (violence) as a means to satisfy their consumption needs. I show that the actual choice depends on the state of knowledge about conflict technology and the distribution of knowledge about production technology. If conflict technology has weak economies of scale and is widely shared throughout society, a fairly egalitarian distribution of property rights is likely to emerge that induces weak individual production and learning incentives. A more asymmetric distribution of conflict technology is likely to result in monopolies on violence and expropriation of surpluses by rulers. However, as production technology (knowledge about production techniques) becomes more asymmetrically distributed, rulers are forced to give stronger incentives to producers, which inevitably entails a weakening of their expropriation capacity. Democratic free-market societies, and the corresponding institutional architecture of political and property rights systems, emerge only when conflict technology is highly concentrated in the hands of a single party ('the state') while information and decision-making on production processes is highly dispersed (specialisation). The confluence of these two informational states creates the optimal balance between power and strong incentives to accumulate further knowledge by individuals.

Part I
Knowledge and economics

2 The uneasy relationship between knowledge and economics

Nowadays, few people would disagree with the statement that growing knowledge, generated through science and embodied in technology, is a driving force behind economic growth. However, this has not always been so. For the most part of human history, technological progress was moving at such a slow pace that it was hard to see significant changes over a lifetime, even over several generations. Hard work, and especially luck, might have made a difference then in individual economic welfare, but not technological progress. In fact, the idea of widespread economic progress as such – growth, development, sustainable increases in production, income and consumption – was rather foreign to human societies until not so long ago, probably because there was not much sustainable progress to report on during a lifetime.

Even if most people today would agree that their daily lives are very much subject to economic development that is, to a large extent, driven by technological change, for many economists this is not an easy matter. Though they will most likely admit the existence of a link between knowledge and economic development in real life, economists hold widely differing views as to what that link looks like in economic theory. In this chapter, I examine what kinds of theories economists have developed about this link, how this fits the facts and where the problem areas are situated. It tells the story of the uneasy relationship between knowledge and economic science.

The role of knowledge in modern economic growth theory

Modern economic growth models are usually assumed to start with Harrod (1939), Domar (1946) and Solow (1956). Keynes (1936) had just published his *General Theory* that, for the first time, presented a macro-picture of economic systems and emphasised the concept of macro-economic equilibrium, though this may not necessarily coincide with a clearing equilibrium in all markets, notably labour markets. Harrod tried to give a more dynamic interpretation to Keynes' rather static theory of equilibrium between savings and investments (in capital goods). He introduces the term 'warranted growth rate'. To achieve a macro-economic equilibrium between savings and investments, the warranted rate of growth must be equal to the ratio of the savings rate and the capital/output ratio. Domar (1946) presented a similar model. Whereas Harrod and Domar assume only a single production factor, capital, Solow (1956) extended this approach and introduced the possibility of substitution between two production factors, capital and labour. He demonstrated how a long-run stable equilibrium growth rate could emerge if substitution between these two production factors was allowed. This Solow model ($Q = A f(K,L)$) assumes that output (Q) is simply a function of capital (K) and labour (L) inputs, and a constant A that captures all other factors that influence output. This has been the standard mainstream economic growth model for nearly half a century now. Together, the Harrod-Domar and Solow growth models are usually considered to be the starting point for modern economic growth theory.

The success of the Solow model in the economics literature is mostly due to the fact that it fitted very nicely into the theoretical micro-economic foundations of the neo-classical competitive markets paradigm. For instance, if a production function of the Cobb-Douglas type is used in the model, with production elasticity of each production factor smaller than one (diminishing returns to factor inputs) and the sum of production elasticities equals one (constant returns to the overall scale of production), then the production function is concave and a unique profit-maximising equilibrium exists. Moreover, in that case, the clearing price for factor markets (wages, profits) will equal marginal productivity of factors, in line with the Euler Theorem. In short, this type of approach yields general equilibrium in product and factor markets.

Its success cannot be ascribed to its empirical performance though. As Solow (1957) soon found out for himself, the model was not a good predictor of actual economic growth performance. An empirical test on US GDP growth time series showed that a third of the variation in economic growth rates could not be explained by variations in capital and labour. This unexplained residual soon became known as the Solow Residual. Griliches and Jorgenson (1966; 1967) made an attempt to attribute the residual to definitional and measurement errors, but their explanations were not deemed very credible (Denison 1967; 1969). It became only gradually accepted that the residual was due to technological innovation or changes in the state of knowledge, factors that were completely exogenous to the model and often summarised in a single exogenous constant, A. To make the model somewhat more attractive and endogenise part of the unexplained residual, that constant was often endowed with a time-trend, a growth rate that was purely a function of time, not of any other relevant economic variable. Romer (1994) remarks that no economist can seriously defend a model that defines knowledge as a simple exogenous time-trend. The relevance of knowledge is thus admitted but degraded to a second-rank variable, helpful to explain a 'residual' only. Making knowledge exogenous and dumping all cognitive activity into an exogenous black box, the constant A, is intellectually unsatisfying: a substantial part of growth remains unexplained. Some way of endogenising the growth residual had to be found.

Still, with hindsight, it is easy to understand why the variable 'knowledge' was ostracised from these neo-classical growth models. The Arrow-Debreu formalisation of the neo-classical competitive general equilibrium paradigm is based on the hypothesis of perfect information, or perfect knowledge of all prices and other characteristics of all goods and services traded on markets, now and in the future: knowledge is complete and freely available to any agent operating in the economy. This hypothesis clashes with the very concept of innovation. Innovation implies that future knowledge is not presently available (otherwise it cannot be 'invented' or 'discovered') and presently available innovation is not generally and freely dispersed in the economy – in which case it would cease to be a unique piece of knowledge.

Macro-economic growth theory remained in this unsatisfying state until the latter half of the 1980s, when the work of Romer (1986) and Lucas (1988) kick-started a new school of thought, known as endogenous growth theory or New Growth Theory. These theories are characterised by the quest to re-endogenise innovation and Solow's unexplained technology or knowledge 'residual'. Endogenous growth models explicitly introduce knowledge (or technology or human capital, or some other equivalent variable) as a production factor in growth models, next to capital and labour. Savings can be used to invest in knowledge and thereby generate innovation or new knowledge.

The idea of giving knowledge a prominent place again as an explanatory variable for the Solow Residual, and provide an endogenous explanation for the growth of knowledge, is now intimately associated with endogenous growth theory. However, the first attempts to produce an endogenous explanation for the Solow Residual probably date back to 1962, when Arrow (1962) presented his model of learning-by-doing. This paper is often considered as a precursor to the New or endogenous growth theories that emerged in the 1980s. It is certainly the first paper in the modern economics literature that tries to endogenise Solow's residual. Arrow showed how workers acquire new knowledge through learning-by-doing. This knowledge can be embodied in new vintages of improved capital goods with increased productivity. He treated knowledge accumulated through learning as a pure externality or a non-excludable public good (see below), the benefits of which are totally dissipated to all users of new vintages of capital goods. There is no monopoly rent from innovation or appropriable return to knowledge in Arrow's model, at least not for the inventor of new knowledge.

Another series of early precursors to endogenous growth theory is the so-called knowledge production function approach (Schneider and Ziesemer 1995), as represented for instance by Uzawa (1965), Phelps (1966) and Shell (1967). These scholars took a view exactly opposite to Arrow in the sense that innovation was treated as a fully excludable and privately appropriable good that is produced by one sector and sold to others. Recent endogenous growth models take a more middle-of-the-road position and allow for partial spillovers and excludability, for example Romer (1986), Stokey (1991) and Tamura (1991). Still, some do not admit spill-overs at all, for instance the neo-Solowians like Mankiw *et al.* (1992) and Nonneman and Vanhoudt (1996).

So right from the start of the endogenous growth literature, the introduction of knowledge as a production factor raised a new issue: how to treat this new production factor 'knowledge'? Is it an ordinary private good, something that can be bought and sold like any other good? Or is it more like a public good, with externalities and spill-overs that are hard to exclude? In other words, how to treat the excludability aspect of knowledge?

The characteristics of goods

Economists classify goods according to two characteristics: rivalry and excludability.

Rival goods can only be used by one person at the time; rivalry prevents other persons from using the same good at the same time. For instance, my fish and chips are a rival good: when I eat them, nobody else can eat them. Similarly, when I drive my car, nobody else can drive it at the same time; when I use my PC, nobody else can use it. Examples of non-rival goods are the Windows software on my PC: millions of people are using it at the same time, though the CD-ROM on which the software comes can only be used by one person (or computer) at the same time. Similarly, the novel that I read can be read by many people at the same time (non-rival), though the particular paper copy that I bought can only be read by one person at the time (rival). Clearly, rivalry is related to the natural characteristics of a good. Products based on material carriers are necessarily rival. Immaterial products, such as ideas and knowledge, are not rival – though they obviously need a material carrier to be communicated between persons. That material carrier itself is a rival good, however. For example, an economic theory is non-rival while the paper on which it is printed is rival.

While rivalry refers to the natural (material) characteristics of a good, excludability refers to legally imposed characteristics: the extent to which the use of a good can be effectively restricted to a single person or, alternatively, the extent to which persons can be excluded from the use of a particular good. In other words, excludability refers to the exclusivity of property rights on a good. Some goods can easily be made excludable; for others, enforcement of private property rights is more complicated. Food, cars, books, can easily be bought and sold privately, and it is fairly easy to guarantee exclusive use to the buyer. Air defence systems and law and order are hard to sell on a private market: if one person produces or buys it, all those around him can benefit from it too, thereby free-riding on the buyer's expense. Clearly, individuals will not be motivated in these circumstances to invest in such goods. Individuals will invest in fishing boats to catch (rival, excludable) fish but not in breeding (rival) fish in the (non-excludable) open sea.

Whether a good can be made excludable has a lot to do with the information characteristics and legal enforcement provisions concerning that good. For instance, until not so long ago, fish in the sea was basically a non-excludable good because it was hard to collect the information about who catches which fish. With modern computer and satellite technology, however, fishing boats can be equipped with instruments that measure each catch and relay this information directly to a supervisor who can keep track of excludable fisheries rights. This makes fish in the sea less of a public and more like a private good, provided the legal instruments are in place to enforce this excludability. Similarly, while software used to be relatively easy to copy and thus hard to make excludable, advances in information technology have made illegal copying more difficult. Globalisation of intellectual property rights laws also enhances excludability.

Table 2.1

	Rival	*Non-rival*
Excludable	*Private goods:* Food, houses, cars	Pay TV signals, a novel
Partially excludable		Windows software
Non-excludable	Fish in the sea	*Public goods:* Law and order, economic theories, air defence systems

The combination of rivalry and excludability characteristics allows us to define public and private goods. Public goods are both non-rival and non-excludable. Private goods are rival and excludable (see Table 2.1).

The (partial) excludability of ideas implies that they are somewhere in between pure public goods and conventional private goods. Ideas can become private goods only to the extent that exclusive property rights can be effectively enforced (through intellectual property rights, patents or simply secrecy). In other words, an idea is excludable when the owner of the idea has the effective monopoly over its use. As a result, the idea-monopolist can set a price above the marginal cost of production of the good that carries the idea (which is usually very small compared to producing the idea itself) and thus earn a monopoly profit, exceeding market equilibrium profit. That is what the Microsoft competition policy case is all about. Making ideas excludable through legal protection of property rights thus permits the effective exploitation of increasing returns to scale, caused by non-rivalry of ideas. It introduces a constraint in the market (through *de facto* or legal property rights) that prevents diffusion of an idea and ensures marketable value and monopoly rents.

The invention of the wheel, the transistor and the recipe for French fries are innovative ideas that have spread widely throughout the world. Unfortunately for the inventors, there are no exclusive property rights attached to these innovations and they are thus not excludable. The guy who produced the Microsoft Windows operating system on my computer took care, however, to acquire exclusive private intellectual property rights. Although these may not always be effectively enforced, they still generate a handsome revenue for him and constitute his monopoly rent – until, one day, he or his competitors invent a better operating system.

The monopoly rent issue immediately led to a new dispute among growth economists. Some placed a high premium on models that could endogenise innovation without undermining the neo-classical competitive equilibrium paradigm, including its perfect information hypothesis and decreasing returns to scale requirement. Naturally, they argued in favour of fully excludable knowledge. Other economists were more willing to abandon that paradigm and were willing to live with partially or even completely non-excludable knowledge. I discuss various schools of thought here, not necessarily in their chronological order.

How excludable is knowledge?

A first response – which I label as the 'neo-Solowian' response – to the 'residual' challenge consists of so-called 'augmented' Solow models that treat knowledge as an ordinary and thus excludable production factor. These models aim to enhance the empirical performance of the traditional two-factor (labour and capital) Solow model by adding one (Mankiw *et al.* 1992), two (Nonneman and Vanhoudt 1996) or more (Sala-I-Martin 1997) production factors. Mankiw *et al.* add knowledge as an explicit production factor to the model: human capital. This production factor covers all forms of knowledge that are embodied in the human brain. Various proxy indicators for human capital have been proposed, such as education levels or the skill level of the labour force. Nonneman and Vanhoudt (1996) add investments in research and development as an explanatory factor, as an indicator of knowledge that is not necessarily embodied in human brains but may reside in external carriers and products. At first sight, these human-capital-augmented Solow models look like an improvement. Indeed, knowledge is not necessarily embodied in (capital) goods only; it can also remain resident in the human brain or in various products of scientific research. Augmented Solow models also perform better in empirical terms than the traditional Solow model: the unexplained residual decreases substantially (Nonneman and Vanhoudt 1996). Apart from problems with finding good indicators of human capital, there is, however, a fundamental problem in these augmented models. Consider a growth model that aims to explain differences in levels of economic development across countries, like that of Mankiw *et al.* (1992). It assumes that physical capital goods are freely tradable across countries while human capital cannot move freely. Consequently, factor price equalisation will take place for capital goods, not for labour and human capital. However, as Romer (1995) pointed out, if the scarcity of human capital explains low incomes in poor countries, then scarce human capital (skilled labour) should fetch a higher price in developing countries than in developed countries and skilled labour should be moving from developed to developing countries. In reality however, we observe the opposite trend in migration of skilled labour. This indicates that skilled labour is better paid in developed countries, despite the fact that the supply of skills is relatively abundant compared to developing countries. Thus the theoretical assumptions that underlie the augmented Solow models do not match with the reality of factor price differentials across countries.

Another critique of the augmented Solow models, especially the heavily augmented ones that add many other presumed production factors to the model, is that they contributed to a degeneration of economic growth models into pure empiricism. Sala-I-Martin's (1997) paper, entitled 'I just ran two million regressions', illustrates the point. Augmentation has led to a new class of purely statistical macro-economic models. They are based on very large databases that contain as many variables as possible – that may or may not have anything to do with economic growth. One sets up a regression programme that tries out all kinds of model specifications on all these variables, and selects the (statistically) most promising results and labels them as 'growth models'. It is sometimes hard to qualify these as explanatory economic models. The computer may detect a statistical link, but does not provide an economic explanation for that link. For instance, what is the economic explanatory value of variables such as 'geographical region' and 'distance from the equator'? Sala-I-Martin (1997) asserts that he found more than sixty statistically significant variables to explain economic growth: is this an economic theory or pure ad-hoc casuistic?

To the extent that knowledge is a fully excludable factor of production and a normally tradable good, not subject to significant spillovers and externalities, endogenous growth models are simply models of human capital accumulation. This raises the question (Stern 1991) of whether endogenous growth theory is just a return to the human capital models of the 1960s and 1970s (for instance, Becker 1964). Those models already emphasised the importance of learning and knowledge accumulation for economic growth. Admitting full excludability of knowledge would simply reduce the neo-Solowian school to a non-event in economics.

Naturally, the neo-Solowians triggered a counter-reaction by economists who considered non-excludability or 'spill-over' and public goods aspects of knowledge to be more important. Private and excludable property rights are more difficult to design and enforce for knowledge than for ordinary private goods. Non- or partial excludability results in spill-overs or externalities and dissipation of benefits to other users who do not pay for that benefit. In line with the theory of public goods, this results in lower-than-optimal investment in knowledge, because the return for the producer would be lower than in the case of fully excludable property rights. In the extreme case, where excludability is non-enforceable, knowledge becomes a pure public good that is fully dissipated in externalities. Making knowledge (partially) excludable through enforceable intellectual property rights may reduce or even stop spill-overs and result in optimal investments in knowledge accumulation.

Most endogenous growth theorists nowadays tend towards the view that knowledge is indeed subject to some degree of spill-over and is therefore, at best, only partially excludable. However, some of them are still reluctant to dump the underlying neo-classical competitive equilibrium paradigm. To avoid this, they attempt to demonstrate the existence of (partial) non-excludability in an indirect way, still using Solow-type growth models that conform to the neo-classical paradigm. In the Solow model, the production factors (capital and labour, possibly augmented with others) are subject to diminishing returns, slowing down growth proportionally to the level of economic development. In other words: rich countries should grow slower than poor countries and growth rates should converge to a single level of income or productivity. Except, of course, if knowledge should grow faster in richer than in poorer countries, so that differences in knowledge growth would compensate for diminishing returns to capital and labour. In case of a high degree of spill-over of knowledge however, there can be little difference between the rate of innovation or knowledge accumulation across countries – and thus convergence should indeed be the case. So the entire ideological debate between neo-classical and not-so-neo-classical macro-economists became very much polarised around the convergence question.

The convergence debate

Convergence sparked a fierce debate in the macro-economics literature in the 1990s. There are three definitions of convergence (Sala-I-Martin, 1996, 2002). The first is called *absolute ß-convergence*: poor countries should be growing faster than rich countries because of diminishing returns. In the end, all countries should be converging to the same level of development.

It relies on the assumption that the only difference across countries is their initial level of capital stock. In reality there may also be initial differences in technology, institutions and population growth rates. This would result in different steady state outcomes rather than absolute convergence to a single point. This interpretation gave rise to a second definition, of *conditional convergence*. It predicts that the growth rate of an economy will be positively related to the distance that separates it from its own steady state: the further away from the steady state, the higher the growth rate. Conditional and absolute convergence coincide if economies have the same steady state. A third definition of convergence is called σ-*convergence*. This predicts that the rate of dispersion of per capita GDP among countries decreases over time.

Maddison (1991) shows both absolute and sigma convergence in a data set on the evolution of GDP per capita for thirteen rich countries since 1870, but his work covers only the rich countries. The Summers-Heston data set, with purchasing power parity estimates of GDP per capita for 110 countries from 1960 onwards constitutes a better starting point and points towards σ-divergence. It undermines absolute convergence but confirms that the rate of conditional *ß* convergence is around 2 per cent per year. Analysis of GDP per capita growth rates within regional groups (the OECD economies, the US states) has provided additional confirmation that this 2 per cent convergence rate is apparently a rather universal phenomenon (Sala-I-Martin 1996). Closer scrutiny of large samples has revealed the presence of 'convergence clubs' or sub-groups of countries that converge towards the same level (Durnlauf and Quah 1998). This explains why s-divergence and conditional *ß*-convergence occur at the same time. However, time series analysis over longer time periods still shows divergence (Pritchet 1995; Easterly and Levine 2002), even between convergence clubs. Some have argued that this is due to transitory growth performances (de la Fuente 2000). Others recognize that data and specification problems still blur the convergence debate (Sala-i-Martin 2002).

Easterly and Levine (2000) argue that the consensus evolves towards long-run divergence, though there may be pockets of conditional convergence. There are indeed some developing countries that have managed to narrow the divide with richer countries but there is little general evidence that the gap is narrowing. However, it is not clear whether this is due to excludability of knowledge, or to the presence of increasing (rather than decreasing) returns to production factors. Easterly and Levine (2000) attribute divergence to 'something else', which they call Total Factor Productivity. Total Factor Productivity becomes a basket of factors, ranging from technological progress and market structures to institutional reforms.

The neo-Schumpeterian school

A completely different and more micro-economic response to the challenge of the unexplained growth residual is the neo-schumpeterian school, sometimes also labelled the Evolutionary Economics school. This school was inspired by the work of Schumpeter (1934), who emphasised the role of entrepreneurial risk-taking and innovation in economic development. Schumpeter's ideas were re-cast in a more contemporary evolutionary approach by the seminal work of Nelson and Winter (1982) on evolutionary competition in economic systems. Next to Schumpeter, Darwin is never far away in these models: the most appropriate technological adaptation dominates the market, until an even more appropriate technology turns up. It draws a comparison between genetic competition in biological systems and competition between new pieces of knowledge, or innovations, in economic systems. It takes a more micro-economic approach and underlines the importance of innovative ideas to strengthen a producer's comparative advantage and monopolistic position on the market. Producers want to avoid pure price competition that erodes profit margins, by constantly searching for innovative ideas in products and production processes that give their products a competitive edge. Producers appropriate the monopolistic profits that their position generates but invest this in more innovation, in order to enhance their position and protect their competitive edge. These models allow for partial excludability of knowledge only because diffusion of innovations erodes monopolistic advantages. The extent and speed of technological diffusion and the concomitant erosion of monopolistic positions, determines the magnitude of monopoly rents. Even monopolists are never at ease because innovation never stops. However, path dependency of innovations may somewhat relax their position: innovations usually do not come out of the blue but build on previous technologies and ideas. As such, sub-optimal path-dependency may come to dominate markets. In the neo-Schumpeterian view, dynamic markets are characterised by monopolistic competition rather than pure neo-classical price competition. Pure price competition is a characteristic of markets that have become static, without much technological innovation. Note how well this neo-Schumpeterian model fits one of the most controversial technology and markets debates of recent years: the Microsoft competition policy debate.

The neo-Schumpeterians have produced a considerable volume of empirical work regarding the emergence and diffusion of innovations, innovation-oriented company, sector and government strategies. Most of their work is rather micro-economic and cannot easily be translated into a more macro-economic view. Like most innovation-oriented theories, it omits the consumer side of the economic equation. Instead of analysing the sources and characteristics of knowledge and learning, they treat innovation as a random phenomenon – inspired by random genetic mutations in biology – and implant a random innovation generator in a neo-classical model of the firm (see, for instance, Segerstrom *et al.* 1990; Aghion and Howitt 1992; Dosi and Nelson 1994). Innovations result in competitive advantages in the market that strengthen a firm's monopoly position, which may, however, be eroded by innovations in other firms. Innovation-based monopolistic competition of course leads to increasing returns to scale and the same non-convexity problems as discussed above. It is the non-rival nature of knowledge that causes this non-convexity: once invented, possibly at a high cost, an innovation can be copied, sold and re-used endlessly at very low marginal cost by the owner of the intellectual property right on the innovation. There is a lot of hesitation in the neo-Schumpeterian school in choosing sides in this debate. Some authors don't bother about the incompatibility problems of non-rival innovations with general equilibrium; others try to hide these incompatibilities and present their model as fitting fully into the neo-classical universe. Neo-Schumpeterian models also failed to come up with a more general economic theory of knowledge, learning and innovation, probably because they concentrated on the supply side of economics only. Classifying innovation as a purely random phenomenon, without roots in a theory of knowledge and its use in society, is intellectually not very satisfying. If all knowledge phenomena are random events, it becomes hard to tell a coherent story about the role of knowledge accumulation in the 'formatting' of economic structures and material embodiments. These hesitations and contradictions are not unique to the neo-Schumpeterian and evolutionary models of innovation, however; they go to the very roots of the most prominent school of thought in modern economics, endogenous growth theory.

Non-rival knowledge

According to Romer (1994), the entire convergence debate is but a digression from the main story behind economic growth theory. He points out that the essential economic property of knowledge does not reside so much in excludability problems, but rather in non-rivalry. While excludability and spill-over issues can be handled, at least partially, through various intellectual property rights arrangements, non-rivalry is a characteristic that is inherent to the nature of knowledge and cannot be attenuated in any way. Non-rivalry of ideas implies that an endless number of users can use the same idea without any additional cost or loss of benefits for the next user. By contrast, ordinary material goods and services are all subject to rivalry. For example, while many people can use the same Microsoft software (a piece of knowledge) as I do at this moment, no two people can use the same keyboard (a piece of matter) as I use at this moment. Producing new knowledge may require a high initial investment cost in research and development, but it can be applied endlessly at zero marginal cost thereafter. The micro-economic principle of diminishing returns no longer applies, and competitive equilibrium cannot be reached. Consequently, non-rivalry of the production factor knowledge implies that the production function is no longer homogeneous of the first degree anymore: the elasticity of output with respect to inputs is higher than 1. This creates a market structure issue, both for factor and product markets.

Non-rivalry has profound economic implications. In the case of conventional rival 'goods', the production function is homogeneous in the first degree (doubling of inputs results in a doubling of output) and returns to scale are constant. This mathematical property allows the application of Euler's Theorem (the value of output is entirely used to remunerate production factors according to their marginal productivity) and thus the existence of a competitive equilibrium situation in the markets for production factors, labour and capital. However, for non-rival knowledge, the degree of homogeneity would be above 1 and Euler's Theorem (factor remuneration according to marginal productivity) is not valid anymore. A one-off investment in research, for instance, can change overall output totally disproportionately to the investment cost. Romer (1990a) illustrates this with an example from the personal computer industry. A microprocessor manufacturing company can double its output of information throughput capacity by doubling all physical inputs in the computer manufacturing process and thereby produce twice as many PCs. However, the invention of a new microprocessor – a new idea – with twice the throughput capacity of previous models produces the same result, without increasing physical inputs. Consequently, returns to scale in innovation are increasing (the degree of homogeneity exceeds 1) while returns to scale in physical manufacturing are constant or even decreasing. Euler's Theorem no longer holds for the production of new ideas, and competitive equilibrium cannot be reached.

In an earlier paper on this issue, Romer (1990b) seems to suggest that we can live with that and that Ostroy (1984) provides a solution for this problem. Ostroy proposes to reformulate the Walrasian marginal productivity theory of distribution of value-added in terms of a no-surplus approach. Marginal productivity of production factors is replaced with marginal productivity of persons. Wage rates are determined through personal bargaining, rather than exogenously given as in the Walrasian model, and a commodity price is deduced from that bargaining outcome. This can result in price-setting, depending on the 'thickness' of the market, but it does not necessarily imply Pareto-inefficiency as long as a no-surplus equilibrium is reached, which is defined as a situation whereby no person can increase his wage without reducing somebody else's. Ostroy shows that a competitive equilibrium can be reached in theory, even with increasing returns to scale, but that its actual occurrence is unlikely. In fact, Ostroy reverses the logical of the Walrasian model and starts from wage bargaining first, which will in turn determine the price of the output to be produced, rather than taking the latter's market price as given. None of Ostroy's proposals seem to have found their way yet into concrete growth models. Most models stay well away from non-rival interpretations of factor inputs (and thus increasing returns) and there seems to be no clear-cut practical solution yet.

Monopolistic behaviour in goods markets, provoked by declining average production costs, is not a new issue in economics. It has been treated extensively in the literature, ever since the work of Robinson and Chamberlain on this topic. Modern growth theory has also dealt extensively with the issue, starting with Dixit and Stiglitz (1977) and Krugman (1979). See Schneider and Ziesemer (1995) for a survey. A fundamental problem in all these models with monopolistic market structures, both in product and in factor markets, is that Pareto-optimality is possible only under very restrictive conditions. None of these models has been able to generate a Pareto optimal competitive general equilibrium in the Arrow-Debreu sense. Consequently, the Pareto-optimality of the neo-classical paradigm remains elusive under conditions of increasing return, as generated by non-rival knowledge (Sala-I-Martin, 2002).

In a later paper, Romer (1994) acknowledges the full extent of this problem and, by implication, suggests that it will be hard to build a satisfying theory of economic growth, including knowledge as a production factor, on the basis of the neo-classical paradigm. The non-rivalry characteristic of knowledge basically contradicts the Walrasian competitive general equilibrium model that is so fundamental to modern neo-classical economics. It generates monopolistic market structures that create severe factor and goods markets closure problems, as pointed out earlier by the neo-Schumpeterians. Moreover, it questions the basic postulate of neo-classical equilibrium: perfect information. With knowledge being the fundamental source of (innovation in) production processes, it must be a scarce good and consequently cannot be treated as ubiquitous and freely available – as the neo-classical paradigm does. There can be no perfect information or knowledge. New Growth Theory introduces knowledge as a finite variable and thus necessarily imperfect. This enables a meaningful discussion of the concept of innovation. Neo-classical growth models cover only the rival material embodiments of knowledge – capital, labour and output – but fail to explain their origin in non-material knowledge. They therefore have difficulties in accounting for any changes in knowledge – innovation – and in the quality and number of rival goods. One of the most important merits of New Growth Theory is that it has introduced the idea that knowledge is a non-rival production factor, and its properties are to be distinguished from other production factors and commodities that constitute rival embodiments of non-rival knowledge.

The stylised empirical facts of economic development

The debate between all these schools of thought on macro-economic growth theory raged throughout most of the 1990s. The dust seems to have settled a bit around the turn of the millennium, and the time may be ripe now to take stock of the state-of-the-art of our knowledge of (the role of knowledge in) economic growth. Kenny and Williams (2001) summarise our knowledge about economic growth with the suggestion that we don't know much at all. The flurry of empirical testing of a wide variety of growth models, mostly on cross-section data on contemporary economies, has led to contradictory results. We do know something about growth now, if only that variables like investment, institutions and education, but also variables like war, religion and latitude, have some influence on growth in some situations. Most of these are long-term structural variables that are hardly influenced by policy-makers. In fact, contrary to short-term growth rates, long-term growth rates appear to be remarkably stable; growth rates half a century ago are the best predictors of growth rates today. But we are far from a universal model of growth. Kenny and Williams (2001) suggest that the search for universalism in empirical growth models is futile, especially when based on cross-section country data. A-historicism is a key problem in growth modelling, in their view. Such data sets would only yield a universal theory if the situation of all these countries were comparable and responses to changes in the determining factors of growth were universally the same, everywhere. That is unlikely to be the case. Economies are complex systems that may produce different reactions to the same impulse, depending on their internal state. As long as we do not have a good model of the internal state of an economic system, we can not possibly expect to be able to predict its response to an impulse. Besides, there is not much point in trying to do predictions with a model of the internal state of a single complex system, because complex systems, such as sectoral or country economies, are interrelated and responses depend on responses by other systems too.

Easterly and Levine (2000) are somewhat more positive and constructive about the present state of our empirical knowledge about economic growth. They derive five stylised empirical facts from a wealth of cross-section and time series data on growth:

- First, factor accumulation (human and physical capital) does not account for the bulk of cross-country variation in growth rates; something else – which they label Total Factor Productivity (TFP) – accounts for a substantial amount of cross-country differences.
- Second, there are huge and growing differences in per capita GDP across countries. Divergence, rather than conditional convergence, is the issue. Increasing returns to TFP is more consistent with divergence than decreasing returns and factor accumulation.

- Third, growth is not persistent over time; factor accumulation is much more persistent. This suggests that technology accounts for long-run changes, rather than factor accumulation.
- Fourth, all factors of production flow to the same places, suggesting important externalities and thus increasing returns for these focal points of attraction. Economic activity is highly concentrated in a few countries, and even regions within these countries.
- Fifth, national policies that enhance the efficiency of use of factors or alter the endogenous rate of technological change can boost TFP and accelerate growth.

Clearly, all these facts go against the accepted wisdom of mainstream neo-classical growth theory, as well as against the wisdom of the convergence-interpretation of endogenous growth theory. All these stylised facts point towards increasing returns to 'technology', or possibly to 'something else', which Easterly and Levine (2000) call Total Factor Productivity. What that something else is, is not clear: it is certainly not persistent factor accumulation, it has something to do with differential attraction, and it can be influenced by man-made policies, but that is about all we know. Easterly and Levine (2000: 2) recommend that 'a high priority should be placed on rigorously defining the term TFP, empirically dissecting it and identifying the policies and institutions that are most conducive to TFP growth'. This statement is very much in line with Kenny and Williams (2001) and probably the nearest that highly-respected economists will ever come to admitting 'we don't know what it is that causes economic growth, but we should continue to look for it'. That, in a nutshell, seems to be the present state of the art in economic growth theory.

More constructive conclusions can also be drawn from this set of stylised empirical facts and the growth theory discussions in the previous pages. First, economic growth has a lot to do with increasing returns to scale: divergence (rather than convergence) between country growth rates in the long run and divergence between regions (rich places attract more resources than poor places). The production factor 'knowledge', with its inherent non-rivalry and therefore increasing returns, looks like a good candidate to explain this feature. In any case, the Solow model and the neo-classical paradigm with decreasing returns are unlikely to make us much wiser in this respect. Second, though growth has something to do with investments in embodied knowledge (goods, human capital), it is also about unembodied forms of technology, or TFP, as Easterly and Levine suggest. It is likely to be driven by knowledge itself. Non-excludability and non-rivalry are important properties of knowledge, but other factors may be important too. We simply don't know at this stage and we can only find out by opening the black box of knowledge production and dissemination.

Though this chapter focuses on the role of knowledge in growth theory, it should be pointed out that in recent years the importance of institutions has come to the forefront, especially in long-term growth and economic development research. See for instance Acemoglu *et al.* (2001), Rodrik *et al.* (2002) and Kaufmann *et al.* (2002). Institutions are often interpreted as an important explanatory factor in TFP, though most institutional economists would not look at institutions from such a neo-classical angle. A more comprehensive discussion of what institutions are, how they affect economic development and what their relationship is with knowledge, is reserved for Chapter 8.

Conclusions

All the economic growth theories that we discussed in this chapter, including Solow, the neo-Solowians, endogenous growth theory and the neo-Schumpeterians, have a hard time dealing with knowledge. While they are fully aware of the importance of knowledge for economic growth and development, they have no proper way to capture knowledge as an economic concept, with properties that are different from those of other economic variables that represent embodied (and therefore rival and excludable) forms of knowledge, such as goods and production factors. One series of difficulties stems precisely from properties like partial excludability and non-rivalry of knowledge, that generate externalities and increasing returns to scale in monopolistic markets – and do not fit into the mainstream neo-classical economics paradigm. Knowledge provides economic systems with an escape route from entropy death, allowing them to make the transition from a 'reproductive' to an 'innovative' mode of economic activity. Existing economic growth theories have no way of coping with this systemic bi-modality. Neo-classical models are geared to handle purely reproductive entropy-increasing activities only. No wonder, then, that the stylised empirical facts of economic growth and development are so at odds with the theoretical models that are supposed to explain these stylised facts. Modern economic growth theory is in a quagmire.

At the root of these problems lies the inability of all these growth theories to substantiate a concept of knowledge and learning, or innovation. The production process of knowledge itself remains a black box. The implicit assumption seems to be that whatever way knowledge is produced in the human brain has no relevance for the economic process. It is only the final product, knowledge, that matters and not the production process itself. I hope to demonstrate in this research that this is a crucial mistake. The cognitive mechanics of learning processes, of communication of knowledge between minds and of embodiment of knowledge in material objects, do have profound implications for economic processes.

Modern economics has only a very limited toolbox at its disposal to analyse and describe the properties of knowledge: excludability and rivalry, increasing returns to scale. While these basic tools are no doubt useful, they do not permit a very sophisticated analysis of the role of knowledge in economic development. A larger, more versatile and refined toolkit is required. It should enable us to analyse a more complex relationship between knowledge and economic development. The construction of such a toolkit is the subject of Part II of this book.

The purpose of this research is to experiment with an entirely new line of reasoning, starting directly from cognitive processes in the human brain (including learning, knowledge, innovation, etc.) and to examine the conditions under which cognitive systems can generate economic properties, such as production, consumption, trade, prices, economies of scale, property rights, etc. From that perspective, goods are nothing but a specific form of external material embodiment of knowledge. Other forms of embodiment are possible too, including external symbolic representations and internal neuronal fixation in the brain. There must be an incentive to produce these embodiments, and each of these types of embodiments must have relative advantages and disadvantages. The search for a more comprehensive cognitive model of human behaviour, in a social setting, is the subject of this book. Economic behaviour is considered to be a subset of that more comprehensive model. This research is based on the assumption that a better understanding of the cognitive processes that underpin social and economic interaction will automatically bring us to a better understanding of economic growth and development issues.

3 The role of distributed knowledge in economics

Introduction

The previous chapter showed how the introduction of 'knowledge' as an explicit variable in modern macro-economic growth models generates all kinds of contradictions with the neo-classical competitive markets paradigm, mainly because of the special properties of knowledge: non-rivalry and partial excludability. These could be considered as distributional properties: they make it hard to contain knowledge to the person who produced it and facilitate spill-over or redistribution of knowledge to other persons. On the other hand, redistribution is never perfect. Some people produce knowledge through learning, others partially free-ride on these learning efforts and acquire this knowledge, but many do not acquire it at all. This results in an asymmetric distribution of knowledge. This chapter focuses on the asymmetric or unequal distribution of knowledge in society as another source of uneasy cohabitation between modern economics and knowledge.

Whereas the previous chapter examined how modern economic growth models cope with diachronic (i.e. across time) asymmetric knowledge distribution, the present chapter inquires how economics deals with synchronic asymmetries in the distribution of knowledge (i.e. at a particular point in time). Both constitute deviations from the perfect information assumption that underpins the neo-classical paradigm. With perfect information there can of course be no asymmetries in the distribution of knowledge.

The neo-classical and endogenous growth theories that we discussed in the previous chapter treated knowledge as a single-dimensional, cardinal quantity variable: it can only go up or down, just like the quantities of ordinary goods and production factors. The discussion on non-excludability and non-rivalry already showed that knowledge may have some other properties that are not really captured by this cardinal representation. The neo-Schumpeterians already took a step in that direction when they explicitly accounted for an unequal distribution of knowledge and the monopolistic market structures to which this gives rise. This points in the direction of asymmetrically distributed knowledge that is not fully shared between all agents who operate on a market – contrary to the perfect information assumptions of the neo-classical paradigm.

Since this is a book about economic development, the link between economic development and the distribution of knowledge may not be immediately obvious. But consider the following intuition. A striking difference between human societies in developed and developing countries is not only the level of economic affluence but also the extent to which people in these societies can replace each other. A typical village in a developing country, whether in Sub-Saharan Africa, Latin America or Asia, is still by and large an agricultural village, where people grow a few crops only. Most importantly, it implies that most people in that village are farmers, that they have very similar knowledge and can easily replace each other. Knowledge is not very asymmetrically distributed in such villages and the extent of specialisation or division of labour is rather low. By contrast, villages in developed countries have a wide variety of highly specialised people, holding very different knowledge sets; they cannot replace each other. There are engineers and accountants, social workers and computer programmers, lawyers and biologists. I cannot take over my neighbour's job and he cannot take over mine, at least not without a very substantial learning effort. Knowledge is very much dispersed in this affluent village. Only a few generations ago, these developed country villages were predominantly agricultural communities too, with some unskilled workers who worked in nearby factories. Farmers could replace each other fairly easily, and so could unskilled workers. Specialisation has enormously increased productivity, as Adam Smith correctly predicted. However, it has also had many other impacts that go far beyond productivity; it has changed the entire organisation of human society. Why has specialisation, or the division of labour, reached such advanced levels in highly developed countries, and in this period, and not elsewhere and earlier? This book assumes that the answer to these questions will provide an important key to explaining economic and societal development.

It is somewhat surprising that modern economic growth and development theories have no role for distributed knowledge – or specialisation or division of labour. This is all the more surprising since the opening shot in the history of modern economic thought, by Adam Smith (1776) more than two centuries ago, started by invoking the concept of distributed knowledge, in the very first paragraph of his *Wealth of Nations*. Here, I examine the role that distributed knowledge has played in the history of economic thought. I will offer some explanations for its disappearance in the course of that history. This will shed some light on the state of modern economic growth theory – discussed in the previous chapter – and clarify the historical roots of its uneasy relationship with knowledge.

Distributed knowledge appears under different guises in the history of economic thought and has been re-labelled several times: division of labour, specialisation, dispersed knowledge, asymmetric information. I consider these terms as synonyms here. In order not to lose track of it, an analytical definition is required, so that it can be more easily recognised if presented under different names. In this book, asymmetrically distributed knowledge or specialisation or division of labour, is defined as a cognitive state of society whereby individual knowledge sets among a group of persons do not fully overlap, so that knowledge is asymmetrically distributed across the group and no single agent has perfect (full) knowledge (or information).[1]

References to the concept of division of labour are rather scarce in the modern economics literature. An EconLit search on 'division of labour' reveals that it is mostly used in the international trade literature, where it is a synonym for specialisation among countries, without much of a conceptual or explanatory role.[2] Stigler (1976) pointed out that it has no significant explanatory role in modern mainstream economics, which could very well do without it.

This chapter presents a very short history of economic thought regarding division of labour or (asymmetrically) distributed knowledge. In the following sections I will distinguish between three schools of thought:

- The classical school, starting with Adam Smith (1776), who first used the concept of division of labour but without much reference to knowledge interpretations. In fact, there appears to be considerable confusion in the classical school regarding how the division of labour is supposed to work and its impact on society.
- Neo-classical or modern mainstream economics, based on the perfect information paradigm of general equilibrium theory, excludes the possibility of knowledge differentiation among agents. There have been several attempts, however, to reintroduce it, mostly under the guise of individual learning models.
- Modern Asymmetric Information economics that deliberately steps outside the neo-classical perfect information paradigm. This includes Hayek, the Bounded Rationality school of Herbert Simon and the institutional economics of Coase and Williamson.

The division of labour in classical economics

Adam Smith first expressed some of the basic principles of economics in his landmark *The Wealth of Nations*, a book that could be considered as the opening shot in the modern economics literature. He was probably the first to suggest that the combination of the pursuit of personal profit and competition between individuals was the engine behind economic growth and welfare. This idea is still at the heart of modern mainstream free-market economics. However, *The Wealth of Nations'* opening passage launches another fundamental idea as the centrepiece of economic thought: the division of labour.

> The greatest improvement in the productive powers of labour and the greater part of the skill, dexterity and judgement with which it is any where directed, or applied, seem to have been the effects of the division of labour.
> (Adam Smith, *The Wealth of Nations*, Book I, chapter 1, paragraph 1)

Smith insists on the crucial role of the division of labour, and identifies three advantages:

> First, to the increase of dexterity in every particular workman; secondly, to the saving of the time which is commonly lost in passing from one species of work to another; and lastly, to the invention of a great number of machines which facilitate and abridge labour, and enable one man to do the work of many.
>
> (Book I, ch. 1)

Furthermore, in the third chapter, Smith (1776) explains 'that the division of labour is limited by the extent of the market'. Taken together, these three well known statements in *The Wealth of Nations* constitute a landmark in the classical economics literature.

Two centuries after its publication, Stigler (1976) notes that the concept of division of labour, which constituted the centrepiece of Smith's economic reasoning, has virtually disappeared from economic theorising and plays no role whatsoever in present-day (mainstream) economics. In contrast, some other ideas from Adam Smith's book have successfully survived the history of economic thought: for instance, the principles of self-interest and competition are now universally recognised as the basic principles of economic dynamics. Stigler also concludes that we do not really have a theory of the division of labour in modern economics. More than twenty-five years later, this still seems to be a valid conclusion.

Smith himself may be partially to blame for this state of affairs regarding the division of labour. In the view of his first and most famous biographer, John Rae (1834), Smith was a flamboyant writer who aimed his books at a larger public than the specialists and scientists. As a result, his texts are often unclear and contain inconsistencies and difficulties of interpretation. It is therefore difficult to present a single formal model of Smithian economics, and we can, at best, try to capture the 'spirit' of Smith's economics in a range of models. Unfortunately, the division of labour and its role in economic growth is probably among the most ambiguous issues in Smith's writings – which may, indirectly, be responsible for the absence of a formal theory of the division of labour and for the disappearance of this subject from modern economics. Modern followers of classical economics have not developed any formal definitions and models of the division of labour. This is evident, for instance, from the comprehensive survey of classical or Smithian models of economic growth presented by Reid (1989). Even in formal Smithian or classical models of growth, such as those developed by Reid (1989), Barkai (1969) and Eltis (1975), the division of labour is never explicitly defined as a concept in its own right.

Here, I would like to trace three lines of reasoning by Smith's classical followers that have contributed to the disappearance of the division of labour from economic thought: the link between the division of labour and the extent of the market, the role of the division of labour in mechanisation, and the link between the division of labour and trade.

The division of labour and the extent of the market

Following Smith's lead on the role of the extent of the market, most modern classical economists capture the *effects* of the division of labour by incorporating a measure of 'the extent of the market' in their models. This is usually achieved by means of a production function where current production is not only a function of current levels of factor inputs, but also of production in the previous period. This introduces an increasing returns to scale effect as a result of learning over time: the higher production (over time), the higher the level of productivity. Such production functions are problematic, however, because growth becomes explosive.

By focusing on the effect of the division of labour rather than the division of labour itself, the division of labour loses its usefulness as a concept in its own right in modern classical economics. This interpretation of the division of labour shows that Smith, and the classical economists who came after him, mixed up economies of scale and economies of specialisation. While Smith may have had good reasons to do so, his modern successors probably put so much emphasis on the extent of the market because of strategic considerations in their continuing battle with the neo-classical school: increasing returns to scale result in monopolistic competition. Since the neo-classical school needs decreasing returns to scale (convexity) in order to achieve a competitive general equilibrium, classical economists' insistence on increasing returns to scale is a good strategy to undermine confidence in the existence of general equilibrium. Competition between these two schools of thought seems to have diverted the classical school's attention from their original subject, the division of labour.

Machinery and the division of labour

The above-quoted passage from *The Wealth of Nations* shows that Smith saw the invention of machinery as one of the three major advantages of the division of labour. When the range of a worker's tasks is gradually reduced through specialisation, the remaining simplified tasks lend themselves more easily to replacement by machines. This gave rise to another line of thought in the classical school that emphasised the link between the division of labour and technical progress, embodied in machinery. In that view, the degree of mechanisation of work – the capital/labour ratio in modern economic jargon – becomes an indicator of the division of labour. As a result, mechanisation slowly replaced the division of labour as an explanatory variable.

Charles Babbage (1835) developed Smith's arguments in his successful book *On the Economy of Machinery and Manufactures*. Marshall (1890) formalised the argument and slipped it into the neo-classical train of thought, where it was established as the centrepiece of production theory. He published the first edition of his *Principles of Economics* 114 years after Smith's *Wealth of Nations*, at a time when industrialisation was much further advanced and mechanisation was 'generally supposed' to be the driving force in industrial output growth. Marshall therefore did not hesitate to emphasise the third of Smith's three advantages of the division of labour, mechanisation, at the expense of the two others. This pushed the division of labour into the background: mechanisation became the driving force behind economic development, not specialisation. In the third edition of his *Principles* (1920), the division of labour is entirely explained as an organisational problem in the firm, the search for an efficient allocation of tasks among men and machines (Book 4, ch. IX).

Marshall does not fail to mention the role of the extent of the market either. He connects mechanisation, division of labour and extent of the market, the leading forces in late nineteenth-century industrialisation, in a single movement:

> the two movements of the improvement of machinery and the growing subdivision of labour have gone together and are in some measure connected. But the connection is not so close as is generally supposed. It is the largeness of markets...that leads to the subdivision of labour.
>
> (1920: 212)

From Marshall's capital-biased interpretation of the division of labour, it is but a small step to the Harrod-Domar and Solow growth models (discussed in the previous chapter) that link output to the capital/labour ratio. From there onwards, the concept of the division of labour became superfluous and could be abandoned by the neo-classical growth models that have dominated growth theory since the 1950s.

Lowe (1975: 421) admits that Smith's ideas on the link between the division of labour and machinery may seem somewhat strange to us, and attributes this to the fact that he saw machines as cooperative complements rather than competitive substitutes for labour. Brewer (1991) shows how this conception is completely in line with Smith's growth theory where capital accumulation is the driving force. The division of labour and technological progress followed automatically from such accumulation through the widening of the market. Brewer contrasts this view with John Rae (1834), who argued that capital cannot be accumulated indefinitely without new investment opportunities being created by technological progress or inventions – an argument that sounds very much like present-day New Growth Theory. Unfortunately, Rae's theories were never taken very seriously.

Trade and the division of labour: a chicken-and-egg problem

A third reason why the concept of division of labour slowly faded from view is related to Smith's somewhat muddled thinking on the relationship between trade and the division of labour. Modern students of economics know that trade is caused by the existence of comparative advantages, differences in productivity. Without comparative advantage, there can be no gainful exchange and the emergence of trade cannot be explained.[3] There can be no comparative advantage between identical individuals who produce the same goods at the same opportunity costs. Consequently, exchange is meaningful only when individuals specialise and differentiate their labour productivities for various tasks. Smith (1776), however, took quite the opposite view:

> The principle which gives occasion to the division of labour is...one of those original principles in human nature...that is the propensity to truck, barter and exchange one thing for another.
>
> (Book I, ch. 2)

In Smith's view, trade precedes the division of labour and is an exclusive constant in human nature. Animals don't barter but men do. He assumes that men are basically born equal, with a propensity to barter. Differentiation, comparative advantages and division of labour occur as a consequence of this propensity, in the course of lifetime and as a result of the professions and trades which they chose:

> The difference of natural talents in different men is, in reality, much less than we are aware of; and the very different genius which appears to distinguish men of different professions, when grown up to maturity, is not upon many occasions so much the cause, as the effect of the division of labour.
>
> (Book I, ch. 2)

Trade enables the emergence of the division of labour. Smith himself gives very few explanations on the emergence of the division of labour: why did it become such an obvious phenomenon in his times and his society and not earlier and in other societies? He linked its origin to the transition from agricultural to industrial societies because, in his opinion, agriculture gave few opportunities for specialisation:

> The nature of agriculture, indeed, does not admit of so many subdivisions of labour....It is impossible to separate so entirely the business of the grazier from that of the corn-farmer...the ploughman, the harrower, the sower of the seed, and the reaper of the corn, are often the same. The occasions for those different sorts of labour returning with the different seasons of the year, it is impossible that one man should be constantly employed in any one of them.
>
> (Book I, ch. 1)

According to Smith, the division of labour is thus a consequence, rather than a cause, of man's natural propensity to trade. Differentiation of talents among men born as equals, in turn, is a consequence of the division of labour, not a cause. Smith was just following the fashion of his time when he wrote *The Wealth of Nations*, and assumed *ex-ante* identical and equal individuals, endowed with a natural propensity to barter and trade. Smith's work was published in the same year as the American Declaration of Independence (1776) and just shortly before the French Revolution (1789) gave a decisive push to the ideas of *Liberté* and *Egalité*. These assumptions are not so acceptable anymore today. Human beings are born and raised in very different environments and learn different skills before they even start thinking about trade.

Smith's line of reasoning remained prevalent until Ricardo (1815) showed that trade is beneficial only when comparative advantages exist. Trade could not be prior to comparative advantages and could certainly not occur among equally endowed individuals. However, to explain the emergence of comparative advantages, Ricardo hesitated to do away with the equal-individuals hypothesis and preferred to attribute this to natural and cultural factors, such as climate that favoured wine production in Portugal and corn production in England. His retreat to an example from agriculture shows that the transition from agricultural to industrial societies was far from complete at the time he wrote: the corn trade was still at the centre of the economic debate. It also facilitated his task; he would have had a harder time in explaining comparative advantages in manufactures on the basis of natural and cultural factors.

By the mid-nineteenth century, Ricardo's sequence of the evolution of economic systems (first comparative advantages, then trade) had decisively replaced Smith's sequence (first trade, then differentiation and comparative advantages). However, economists after Ricardo, and especially after Marx, did not take this long-term perspective on economic systems, and concentrated on shorter-term phenomena such as prices, wages, profits and accumulation. They simply took specialisation and comparative advantages as exogenously given. By the end of the nineteenth century, the division of labour and trade were indeed part of the 'stylised facts' of society as the transition from a predominantly agricultural to a predominantly industrial society was well advanced.

Exit the division of labour (from economics)

Smith's view of the division of labour, as well as Ricardo's hesitations, are clearly cast in terms of the professions of their time: farmers, labourers, craftsmen, artists, philosophers and inventors. They are considered as the products of evolution in society at large, rather than the results of an economically and technically 'enforced' division of labour. A century later, when Durkheim (1893) examined the division of labour, the transition to manufacturing was far more advanced and men's natural propensities and equalities were no longer valid arguments. Durkheim lamented that even within a particular profession, it was impossible for a man to know everything there was to know and further specialisation became an unavoidable constraint on life.

By that time, the debate on the division of labour had moved to sociology, probably because Marx had drawn some unsettling economic and political conclusions from his own analysis of the division of labour in manufacturing. While Smith (1776) emphasised the productivity and income effects of an increasing division of labour, Marx underlined the alienation effects of the division of labour. Workers are estranged from the 'end product' of their production processes. Marx's ideas had sparked considerable social and political controversy by the end of the nineteenth century. Durkheim (1893) tried to pour oil on these troubled waters. He considers the economic effects of the division of labour as secondary, and instead analyses the impact on solidarity in society, trying to make a moralistic argument in favour of the division of labour. According to Durkheim, the division of labour emerges at a particular evolutionary stage in society, when mechanical solidarity is turned into organic solidarity, but this leaves the initial emergence of the division of labour still somewhat unexplained. He refers to slight initial 'natural' variations (environment, hereditary traits) that are further developed through rivalry, which basically brings us back to Smith and the 'learning-by-doing' theme. The emergence of trade-based corporatism (one trade per corporate body) is discussed extensively but his arguments neglect the company (many trades in one corporate body). Clearly, Durkheim's analysis of the division of labour avoids all economic references, presumably because he wanted to stay clear of the heated socio-political debate on the link between specialisation and alienation.

By the end of the nineteenth century, economists were happy to leave the subject of division of labour to sociologists. They had no use for it anymore in economics. The extent of the market, the capital intensity of production and exogenously given comparative advantages had pushed aside the need for the division of labour as an explanatory concept, though it left considerable gaps and unease in the economics toolkit, which made it hard to deal with issues such as technological progress.

The division of labour in modern economics

Yang and Ng (1993) note that the disappearance of the division of labour from the economics debate enabled Marshall (1890) to omit comparative advantages altogether from his market equilibrium approach. He artificially divides the world into pure consumers and producers, thereby forcing them to trade (by definition rather than by acquired and explained comparative advantage) in order to satisfy their objectives. This led to the neo-classical 'domestic' trade model that simply assumes that trade exists and that there is no need to explain its origin. Surprisingly enough, a crucial ingredient of economics, trade, is assumed to be an innate an unexplained element of economic systems.

Marshall's simplification of the economic world-view, without division of labour and comparative advantages, laid the foundation stones for the mainstream neo-classical general equilibrium model, formulated by Arrow and Debreu (1954). Production technology and consumer preferences is made exogenous and information is assumed to be perfect and homogeneously distributed: everything there is to be known is known to everybody. Knowledge, including its accumulation and distribution, thereby became an irrelevant variable. This set of assumptions basically excludes any change in knowledge, ideas or innovation in economic systems. From an information or knowledge point of view, the neo-classical model is extremely static. The Solow (1956) growth model finally translated this neo-classical world-view into a homogeneous production factor, 'labour', without any differentiation in the labour force and thus no division of labour. All workers have identical knowledge sets in this model. One wonders why they would trade at all.

As explained in the previous chapter, this model soon ran into problems, if not of a theoretical than at least of an empirical nature: an unexplained Solow Residual in growth regressions needed further explanations. The perfect information assumption stood somewhat at odds with the obvious facts of life and had to be relaxed. Attempts to re-introduce knowledge accumulation over time as a variable in macro-economic growth models and endogenise the Solow Residual, were discussed in the previous chapter. It was also explained how these attempts stood at odds with the underlying micro-economic general equilibrium paradigm and were, for this reason, unsatisfactory.

Apart from these macro-economic attempts to re-introduce learning and accumulation of knowledge, there are a few examples in the modern economics literature of micro-economic models that aimed to re-introduce individual knowledge differentiation (or distributed knowledge, division of labour) in economic models.

Arrow's (1962) 'learning-by-doing' model combines two of Smith's ideas: first, improvements in 'dexterity' or, in modern economic jargon, learning-by-doing; and second, invention of new machines or capital-embodied technological progress. In his model, workers learn by repeatedly doing the same tasks, which leads either to improvements in labour productivity and thus cost reduction (process innovation) and/or changes in the outputs that they produce (product innovation). If the outputs are machines, new vintages of machines embody this technological progress and increase labour productivity of the users. Arrow's is not a model of division of labour *strictu senso* because it does not distinguish between different qualities of labour within a set of workers. However, it does allow for workers' knowledge differentiation across time. All techno-logical progress is embodied in capital goods only, and results in higher productivity for new vintages of these goods. Arrow's model is still based on perfectly competitive markets; it does not allow appropriation of inno-vation rents in an imperfect market through price differentiation. This enables Arrow to circumvent the problem of non-rivalry of knowledge and the resulting increasing returns, discussed in the previous chapter.

Arrow's learning-by-doing approach plays a central role in the so-called New Classical models of division of labour, advocated by Yang and Borland (1991) and Yang and Ng (1993). Like Arrow (1962), they intro-duce learning-by-doing that gradually increases labour productivity and enhances comparative advantages. Contrary to Arrow, however, they assume complete embodiment of technological progress in labour rather than in capital goods. Comparative advantages are thus endogenously produced in the model. Quality and price differentiation in embodied knowledge explain the origins of gainful trade in this model. A major advantage of this approach is that it eliminates the artificial dichotomy between producers and consumers – introduced by Marshall – which forced them to trade to fulfil their objectives of utility and profit maximi-sation.

The weakness in this approach is that learning-by-doing alone is not a sufficient condition for the emergence of differentiation and (internal) comparative advantages from *ex-ante* identical individuals. If the rate of learning is the same for all agents, than there is no agent-wise differentia-tion in labour productivity and thus no differentiation in comparative advantages at the end of any time period.[4] Consequently, increasing returns to labour constitutes a necessary but not sufficient condition to explain the emergence of specialisation. Yang and Ng (1993) implicitly accept this criticism and try to circumvent it by introducing a second hypothesis, completely in line with Smith, namely that identical individuals *ex-ante* 'choose' a specialisation for which they accumulate increasing returns through learning-by-doing. Unfortunately, this turns the logic of their argument upside down: what has to be explained by the model (specialisation) is already assumed to exist in the initial hypothesis. At best, learning-by-doing and increasing returns to labour amplify the impact of the *ex-ante* specialisation 'choice'.

Another interesting model of the division of labour in the modern economics literature is presented by Becker and Murphy (1992). In their model, output production is a function of general knowledge and the extent of specialisation of workers across a given range of tasks that is required to produce the output. The model is very Smithian: the more workers specialise in a limited number of tasks, the higher productivity. Productivity can be negatively affected, however, by the transaction costs of coordination among workers, which increase with the extent of division of labour. However, Becker and Murphy assume that further subdivision automatically leads to higher output productivity. There is no underlying behavioural model to explain why smaller task sets imply the higher their productivity. Productivity gains from specialisation are assumed to exist, not explained. This is at best an implicit model of the division of labour: only the number of workers varies, not their individual skills set. There is no variation and differentiation in individual labour productivity.

Edwards and Starr (1987) provide an explanation for increasing output with specialisation, or 'economies of specialisation'. They argue that economies of specialisation are a special case of economies of scale. Economies of specialisation can only occur if there is indivisibility in skills (set-up or learning cost) that causes non-convexities the more use is made of that skill. If non-convexities did not occur, there would be no advantage in specialisation. Adam Smith's statement that the division of labour is limited by the extent of the market would be false in that case; whatever the extent of the market, there would be no point in specialisation. This is true both for on-the-job learning-by-doing and for off-the-job formal learning. Both involve opportunity costs (lower-than-maximum productivity) that can be considered as fixed investment or set-up costs that can be written off over the entire scale or use of the acquired production skills. We will return to this argument of 'economies of specialisation' in Chapter 7, under the more appropriate label of 'economies of scope'.

Rosen (1978) presents a model of worker specialisation and task substitution in production processes, based on a truly differentiated labour force with distributed knowledge and specialisation among workers. Workers are distinguished according to their comparative advantage at a particular task, out of a fixed task set that constitutes a production process. Rosen shows how the autarky frontier (every worker performs all tasks to produce his own output) is the lowest level of efficiency while total specialisation pushes output up to the efficiency frontier. As such, it is one of the first models to formally demonstrate that specialisation enhances economic efficiency and increases knowledge absorption in an economy.

Rosen's is an optimisation model where the key question revolves around the optimal degree of specialisation between workers, given a number of technical constraints. It does not provide a functional explanation for the existence and role of the division of labour in economic processes. That changes in Rosen's (1983) second paper on the division of labour. It is among the very few papers in the modern economics literature that attempt to explain the emergence of the division of labour in terms of incentives for specialisation. He casts the emergence of specialisation in a contemporary increasing-returns-to-learning format. In view of its central importance, I will refrain from further explanations here and return to it in detail in Chapter 7.

A brief return to Adam Smith is warranted here. Rosen's (1978; 1983) models' demonstration of the advantages of specialisation in a single set of non-separable tasks reflects, to a certain extent, Adam Smith's intuition that there is no need to pursue two different jobs if one gives you greater satisfaction and recognition than the other. This so-called 'fourth argument' in favour of specialisation (Rosenberg 1976), presented only in Smith's *Lectures on Rhetoric and Belles Lettres* (1762) and not in *The Wealth of Nations*, has become a key issue in most of the recent literature on the division of labour. Indeed, preference for specialisation in one job is the issue of the division of labour.

Several authors have attempted to formalise Smith's argument in favour of specialisation in one activity. Full-specialisation in one activity is a central hypothesis in the New Classical models of Yang and Borland (1991) and Yang and Ng (1993) discussed above. Ippolito (1977) accepts this principle as self-evident, without formal proof. He calls it 'Smith's rule'. Wen (1994) has formally proved the validity of this argument. However, Baumgardner (1988) shows that increasing returns in production is not a sufficient condition to arrive at a one-producer-one activity solution. He counterbalances increasing returns to scale with rapidly increasing demand elasticities. This is a return to Smith's argument concerning the extent of the market and its effects on limits to specialisation. Market conditions may not be favourable for full specialisation. The degree of specialisation then becomes an empirical question, striking an optimal balance between demand elasticities and returns to scale in production.

Concludingly, it can be said that modern models of the division of labour either follow the Smith (1776)-Arrow (1962) line of reasoning based on learning-by-doing, or they follow the Smith (1762) argument concerning the advantages of full specialisation in one job. The New Classical models of Yang and his associates mix both approaches. Some models simply postulate the existence of economies of specialisation (Becker and Murphy 1992; Rosen 1978) without going into their origins. Rosen (1983) is exceptional in that he tries to explain the emergence of specialist knowledge from more general knowledge. All of these models stand somewhat at odds with the perfect information and decreasing returns to scale assumptions that underlie the neo-classical general equilibrium paradigm, though they do not really step out of the constraints of that paradigmatic straitjacket. For that purpose, we need to turn to the recent wave of economic theories that, implicitly or explicitly, do away with perfect information and switch to asymmetric information assumptions, that is: asymmetrically distributed information or knowledge within a group of agents.

Hayek on the division of labour

No review of the role of distributed knowledge in modern economics can be complete without a discussion of the Austrian School, and particularly Hayek's contribution in this regard. For a survey of Hayek's work, see Caldwell (1997). Indeed, the well known Mises-Lerner controversy on the possibility of centralised socialist planning in the 1930s revived all the issues related to distributed knowledge, at a time when mainstream neo-classical economics was about to dump the subject as irrelevant. Mises and Hayek rejected the possibility of central planning because of the insurmountable information problems involved. That debate led Hayek to a more thorough analysis of the economics of knowledge and information, that culminated in his paper on 'The use of knowledge in society' (Hayek 1945). He observed that the amount of knowledge available in society is far too large to be 'known' by a single individual. Individual knowledge absorption capacity is necessarily limited. As society progresses, knowledge gets more dispersed and the division (asymmetry) of knowledge increases, leading to increased mutual dependence on each other's knowledge. This is precisely the same starting point as the bounded rationality and imperfect information literature of several decades later. In that sense, Hayek could probably be considered as one of the earliest precursors of modern bounded rationality and asymmetric information theories in economics – although he did not mention these terms.

Hayek remarks that, if we possess all relevant information regarding preferences and the means of production, the question of constructing the most optimal economic outcome is not an economic question anymore but purely a question of logic and mathematical calculation. Calculating optima with perfect information is not the economic problem. Rather, the economic problem in Hayek's view is finding out how to organise best the limited amount of information that economic decision-makers can handle. In other words, the central issue in economics is not a scarce resources allocation problem; it is a problem of allocation of scarce knowledge and information about resources. This is so because

> the knowledge of the circumstances of which we must make use never exists in concentrated or integrated form but solely in dispersed bits of incomplete and frequently contradictory knowledge.
>
> (Hayek 1945: 519)

Central planning assumes that all this knowledge can somehow be centralised. Competitive market processes leave all that knowledge at the level of decentralised individuals. His early writings reflected the view that market prices acted as the sole coordinating mechanism between individuals with asymmetric knowledge sets. Market prices convey all the necessary information between individuals to achieve coordination, according to Hayek. Since that necessary information is compressed into just a few bits of information – the price – the price mechanism constitutes an important source of cognitive economy. Rather than an individual having to run around to find out what is happening with a particular good, he can just look at its price to make his decisions. We will show in the course of this research that Hayek's belief in prices as the coordination mechanism in a distributed knowledge setting is somewhat simplistic and certainly incomplete; several other 'coordination' components come into play.

His later work assigns such a coordinating role to norms, rules and institutions too. Although Hayek probably did not read Coase (1937), or was not inspired by that paper, he comes close to neo-institutional economics in his later writings, long before Coase's theory of the firm gave rise to the voluminous neo-institutional literature. He failed to see the problems of moral hazard and opportunistic behaviour in asymmetric information situations, though, preventing his further advances in institutional and contract theory. That can not be held against him though: asymmetric information models emerged only three decades later (Jensen and Meckling 1976). Hayek never worked out any formal definitions or models of his concepts, which enabled his critics to label his work as 'fuzzy'.

From the point of view of this book, Hayek's most important contribution to modern economics is not only that he kept alive the discussion regarding distributed knowledge, or the division of labour, but also that he interpreted this in an asymmetric information context. Adam Smith and the classical economists right up to Marshall had never got to that point. Indeed, Hayek sees scarce information processing capacity as the key issue in economic decision-making and societal organisation. In this respect, the Austrians stand in contrast to the neo-classical competitive markets paradigm that assumes that competitive markets will result in a single market price for a good. Hayek argues that a single price means absence of competition because buyers will not be able to distinguish anymore between different offers.

In a way, this research is meant to do justice to Hayek's insistence that distributed knowledge is the key to understanding economic systems and economic decision-making. Part II starts with an enquiry into the nature of knowledge and human cognition, and gradually develops the idea that a high degree of distributed cognition is very typical for human societies, and has led to the emergence of economic systems as well as essential economic institutions such as private property rights. I will argue that modern societies and their economic and institutional systems cannot be properly understood without invoking the properties of distributed knowledge systems.

Modern schools of thought on asymmetrically distributed knowledge

Bounded rationality

I cannot conclude this brief overview without at least a reference to a few schools of thought in modern economics that are more or less explicitly based on distributed knowledge. They can all be situated under the flag of asymmetric and/or imperfect information economics. Their origins can be traced back to the work of Herbert Simon on bounded rationality (March and Simon 1952). Simon explicitly based his research on human decision-making on the assumption that individuals, however intelligent they are, have a very limited information processing capacity and consequently are only able to grasp a very small part of total available information or knowledge in the world. Simon's work was partly a reaction against rational choice theory, a cornerstone of neo-classical economics. In Simon's view, people rarely behave as rational calculators, searching for the most optimal solution to a problem. In most cases, they do not have the necessary information, or the necessary information processing capacity, to do so. People usually follow some existing behavioural rules and standards, and mostly get pretty good results out of that (see Conlisk 1996, for a survey).

Clearly, the flag of bounded rationality and asymmetric information covers an area that is very similar to distributed knowledge. All these theories are based on the idea that agents in an economy hold different information sets and none of them is perfectly informed – and this corresponds exactly to the generic definition of distributed knowledge that I proposed in the introduction to this chapter. Agents are specialised in various sub-sets of information, and this gives them a comparative advantage over others and enables them to gainfully trade these informational advantages, packed in the goods and services that they produce and sell.

New Institutional Economics

It is easy to see how bounded rationality decision making theory made key contributions to modern institutional economics. The term 'institutional economics' covers a wide range of schools of thought and methods. It includes several varieties of transaction costs economics, from Coase (1937; 1960) to North (1990) and Williamson (1985), as well as various branches of organisation theory, including property rights (Grossman and Hart 1986) and incomplete contracts theory (Tirole 1999), and its analysis of organisational design (Holmstrom and Milgrom 1991; Aghion and Tirole 1997). This is not the place to explain the details of each of these schools. Interested readers are referred to more general handbooks of institutional and organisational economics (for instance, Furubotn and Richter 1998; Masten and Williamson 1999; Laffont and Tirole 1993).

All these schools of institutional economic thought have a common characteristic: they examine how informational problems affect organisational performance, though from different angles. That is precisely what distinguishes neo-classical from neo-institutional economics. While the former generally assumes that (near-)perfect information is available in transactions at (near-)zero costs, the latter assumes positive information costs. Transaction cost economics looks at the cost of obtaining information required to conclude a contract or exchange (North 1990) and the potential costs of post-contractual uncertainty or absence of information (Williamson 1985). Incomplete contracts theory is based on quite similar principles but focuses on the incentives embedded in a contract and the likely behavioural outcomes that they produce under imperfect information (Tirole 1999). Property rights theory examines how different allocations of this residual contractual uncertainty create different incentive structures. Modern organisation theory combines these different techniques to study incentives and delegation of tasks in large organisations or hierarchies. Institutions – rules of behaviour – exist precisely because they are means to partially overcome these informational problems and the resulting uncertainties. Bilateral contracts, general laws and informal agreements ensure that some of these are kept within acceptable limits. However, they can not create a risk-free world, and we have to live with these residual uncertainties in our daily activities, including in the delivery of foreign aid.

Chapter 10 of this book applies the techniques of one branch of modern neo-institutional economics, namely principal-agent or agency theory. Principal-agent theory starts from the simple observation that modern organisations are usually hierarchically structured, with principals giving instructions to agents. Principals in a company, a club or a public administration, cannot take all decisions and carry out all tasks themselves. They need to delegate at least part of the work to agents. While the principal appropriates the benefits (and costs) of the task, the agent receives a reward – a wage, a stock option, a promotion, etc. – in return for carrying out the specified tasks. Delegation implies that the principal does not have full knowledge about the activities of the agent; knowledge is asymmetrically distributed within an organisation. If he wanted to have full information and monitor every aspect of the agent's activities, he might as well carry out the delegated tasks himself; there would be no gain from delegation. Delegation may result in two types of problem. First, the agent may deviate from the instructions given by the principal and carry out the delegated tasks in such a way that this advances his own interests, rather than those of the principal. This is called moral hazard. Second, at the time of reaching agreement with the principal, the agent may have access to information inaccessible to the principal, and may manipulate this information in ways that run against the principal's interests (as when sellers of second-hand cars are more likely to offer low-quality cars for sale, or when counterfeit money drives out good, as classically described in Gresham's Law). This is called adverse selection. Both problems lower the return from the task for the principal, compared to the return under perfect information.

To conclude: New Institutional Economics is clearly based on the concept of asymmetrically distributed knowledge. Since institutions have become a key explanatory factor in long-term economic growth, it is obvious that distributed knowledge should also play a central role in explaining growth. Unfortunately, that sort of argument has not got much of a hearing ever since Adam Smith put the division of labour at the centre of his economic theories. This research aims to put the concept of distributed knowledge back in its rightful place. However, the cognitive arguments that will be used in the remainder of this research would have probably sounded unfamiliar to Adam Smith.

Part II

The principle of cognitive economy

4 Knowledge and the principle of cognitive economy

As explained in the Introduction, the objective of this research is to develop a new approach to economic growth and development which revolves around the concept of (distributed) knowledge – a theme that is common to both economic growth theory and institutional economics. The purpose of this chapter is to define what knowledge is, what drives learning or the accumulation of knowledge, and why the principle of cognitive economy is so important in that drive.

If knowledge is going to be the focus of our attention, than we'd better start by defining what we are talking about. Many books and papers in the social sciences, including in economics, regularly use concepts like information and knowledge and assume that these are intuitively clear. Endogenous Growth Theory made knowledge the centrepiece of its models but never attempted a definition of knowledge. While this may be acceptable for ordinary applications, I prefer to introduce more explicit definitions because the applications that we are going to explore in the next chapters are not so ordinary. Rather than going into endless epistemological debates, I approach the subject from an information theory point of view. Moreover, this definition of knowledge will be connected to our knowledge of how the brain works. I start from neuro-physiological mechanisms in the human brain and link these to a categorisation theory of cognition.

That will pave the way for an investigation into the role of symbolic communication in cognitive development. Communication is a necessary ingredient of distributed knowledge in society. In this chapter, we stick to simple communication channels like imitation and symbolic communication. In the next chapter, another and potentially more important communication channel will be discussed: trade in goods and services. All communication channels share a key characteristic: they reduce the volume of cognitive activity required to acquire knowledge and thereby reduce the opportunity cost of learning. The resulting savings in information processing capacity are an important advantage for any agent equipped with limited information processing capacity. This will lead us to the principle of cognitive economy: cognitive devices that achieve more compression of information and more efficient communication of these compressed packages constitute an economic advantage. Most of the discussions in this and the next three chapters will revolve around these devices and the conditions for achieving cognitive economy.

Information, learning and knowledge

In this section, I define the basic concepts of information, learning and knowledge that are going to be used throughout this book, including an exploration of the implications of these definitions. I am not going to make any attempt to summarise the theories and debates in epistemology, the study of knowledge. Libraries have been filled with books on epistemology, and just about every conceivable thought and interpretation has been discussed at length. Most studies in cognitive social science seem to avoid the subject, though, probably because of the intense debate and lack of common ground in epistemology. That is an unsatisfactory situation from a social science point of view. Also, it need not be so, because simple models of knowledge exist that allow us to approach at least the basic issues. The purpose of this section is to present an operational definition of knowledge, taking inspiration from modern information and complexity theory, and cognitive science. I am fully aware that any possible definition will immediately run into criticism from one branch or another of the wide range of schools of thought in epistemology. I make no attempt at avoiding or countering that criticism; on the contrary, I will present the counter-arguments myself.

Human beings, like most other animals, have the capacity to detect information signals emitted by their environment through their sensory organs: eyes, ears, nose, tongue and nervous cells spread out all over the body. A fundamental starting point for a cognitive approach to societal development is that human beings are endowed with a limited capacity to process the information that reaches their sensory systems. We can process only a small fraction of audio-visual and senso-motoric information that reaches our brain. A person may be super-intelligent and have the information processing capacity of a supercomputer, still there are limits to his individual information absorption capacity, far below the amount of information emitted by the environment which, for all practical purposes, is virtually infinite. This is the starting point for the literature on bounded rationality, originally initiated by Simon and March (1952). This school of thought emerged as a reaction to the claims of rational choice theory that human beings are capable of fully rational behaviour. Bounded rationality claims that, because of inherent limits on human information processing capacity, full rationality is not an option in most choice situations in ordinary life. Most choices are made with a very limited set of information that contains a partial and incomplete description only of the actual situation. Bounded rationality has by now become sufficiently well known in economics and social science in general, and needs no further explanation here (see Conlisk 1996, for a survey).

A consequence of bounded rationality is that human beings are not permanently optimising their entire range of behavioural options. First, because they do not have all the necessary information to calculate a fully rational response, and second, even if the necessary information were available, they would not be able to cope with that volume of information (perfect information is infinite). Hence individuals seek shortcuts to overcome these information constraints. Rather than attempting a rational recalculation of their entire situation, individuals rely on experience, behavioural responses learned in the past, possibly in similar but not identical situations, that are extrapolated to the new situation; or they rely on beliefs and assumptions, vague ideas that are simply assumed to be true. Choi (1993) explains this process of assembly of various bits and pieces of more and less reliable 'knowledge'. No decision can be taken without full cognitive closure, that is knowledge on all relevant possibilities and options. However, since we cannot possibly acquire real cognitive closure, 'imaginary' pieces of knowledge are brought into the picture to achieve closure. Choi labels these as 'paradigms and conventions'. These are devices that supply acceptable approximations of reality that result in satisfactory, though not necessarily optimal, outcomes.

Since knowledge links an external situation to an internal state of mind, it provides the basis for a behavioural response to that external situation. Often, the distinction between knowledge and behaviour is dropped, however. Whether or not knowledge actually results in behaviour, is not the issue. In the bounded rationality literature, knowledge is equated with 'routines' or 'algorithms', the set of behavioural options from which a cognitive agent can choose his actual behaviour. In subsequent sections in this chapter, the correspondence with neuronal 'bindings' in the brain and 'categorisations' in the mind will be explored.

It is important to understand how these routines or knowledge sets emerge from raw audio-visual and other sensory information that is perceived by the human body, and what they imply in terms of information processing capacity. To explain the processing of information into knowledge, we start from a number of assumptions about the external environment in which humans operate:

1   A dynamic reality exists outside the human mind. It emits a virtually infinite amount of information. There are causal links between events in reality. Events are not random and can be understood by exploring the chain of causality that caused them.

2   However, full knowledge of reality requires an infinite amount of information. Any finite amount of knowledge about reality is only approximate.

3   Because human agents are physically finite, their information processing capacity is necessarily finite too. Consequently, whatever the amount of information available, human knowledge of past and present states of reality is necessarily approximate only.
4   Another consequence is that reality is not fully predictable. Any prediction of future states is inherently approximate.

From a philosophical point of view, these assumptions trigger a whole lot of questions and criticism. The first assumption goes against the prevailing postmodernist view that we construct worlds in our minds only and that there is no guarantee that such a world does indeed exist in 'reality' separate from our minds. It also clashes with some theories in quantum physics that propose non-deterministic events. I am aware of these contradictory theories but will not take them into account here. Like any theory or piece of knowledge, the theory proposed in this research is necessarily imperfect and an approximation only. I hope to demonstrate in the next chapters that these approximations are good enough to explain a number of cognitive phenomena at the individual and societal level that we are interested in.

The second assumption is based on Prigogine's (1987) exploration of the sources of our ignorance or imperfect knowledge about reality. In statistical thermodynamics, probability 'enters the scene in order to account for our ignorance of the true microscopic evolution of a given system' (65). He uses the example of tossing a coin. If we have infinite information about the initial conditions, a computer will be able to predict the outcome with probability 1. However, any amount of information less than infinite will produce a prediction with probability 0.5 only.[1] Whatever our degree of knowledge of the initial conditions becomes irrelevant then, as long as it is not perfect. It is only within the limits of infinite precision that a computer can get rid of probabilistic concepts and give the exact outcome.

Another example of the imperfect and approximate nature of our knowledge is the calculation of the circumference of an island. At first sight, it is easy to walk around an island with a measuring instrument and simply measure the circumference. If we look at it in more detail, the method is not so obvious. We would have to define the exact limit of the island, the line on the beach that constitutes the border. Do we simply measure the distance between two benchmark points or do we follow the curvature of the beach between these benchmarks? We could try to fine-grain the measurement and follow all the small bends in the beach line. Going down to the atomic level, we would have to follow the curvature of the atoms. The more precise we want to be, the longer the circumference. An island that measures just a few kilometres by walking along the beach may thus reach a circumference of hundreds of kilometres if we take into account the slightest curvature in the sand, and may become virtually infinite in circumference if we go down to the atomic level. In short, the circumference of an island is not well defined.

The second assumption also introduces a distinction between information and knowledge. This forces us to define both concepts, explore how *knowledge* is extracted from information through learning processes, and what learning is all about in terms of information processing. In line with Gell-Mann (1995), I define *learning* as the process of discovery of regularities in an apparently chaotic stream of information emitted by the external environment. The information content of a signal is the number of distinctions that can be made in the signal. If no distinctions can be made, there is no information. The simplest form of distinction is binary code, used in computers. The 0–1 binary distinction is the minimum amount of information required to make a distinction. A single bit code, say only 1's, would not be able to make distinctions in a string of information. More elaborate systems exist: the decimal system identifies ten discrete states; the Latin alphabet identifies twenty-six discrete states. In our daily environment there are innumerable classifiers of distinctions.

Simply memorising all information or distinctions in a stream of information would not only occupy vast memory spaces but would also fail to identify links between events. The identification of regularities enables compression of this information stream into a smaller volume of information. That compression process is called learning, and the output of learning is called 'knowledge', i.e. a set of regularities discovered in the external environment that can be used for behavioural purposes, to respond to the threats and opportunities in that environment.

For example, you observe a stream of information about the distinct states of the sun during the day: rising above the eastern horizon in the morning, climbing in an arc across the sky towards its zenith in the south and then descending towards the western horizon, ending in nightfall. If you observe it long enough, you will discover that this is a regular pattern in the sun's behaviour. It is not necessary anymore to learn each position of the sun at every moment of the day; 'knowledge' of the regularity in this behaviour will enable you to tell the sun's position at any moment of the day. A look at your watch will be enough for you to predict where, approximately, it will stand. Thus compressing strings of observations into regularities not only permits information economies but also, and more importantly, forecasting of events. Events become more predictable and therefore less uncertain.

The degree of compression of an information set, or the knowledge content that has been extracted from that set, can be measured by the concept of complexity. Gell-Mann (1995: 56) defines the effective complexity of a routine (or knowledge set) as 'the length of a concise description of the...regularities identified' by an agent in his observations of the external environment. In the sun's orbit example, the observer replaces his lengthy set of many observations, with an orbit trajectory between the eastern and western horizon. That trajectory description can be far shorter than the set of many observations. As a more abstract example, consider the following string of thirty binary digits: 101101101101101101101101101101. An observer could store that string in his memory. However, it is much easier and shorter to memorise that the string consists of ten times '101'. The effective complexity of that string would increase (for the same length) if it appeared as follows: 101101101101101101101101111111. Now the regularities can only be reduced to 'eight times "101" plus 6 times "1"'. This is a longer description; the effective complexity has increased and it requires more knowledge, and therefore more information processing in the brain, to fully describe the string. Still, both these descriptions allow an observer, when he is confronted with part of the string, say the first four digits, to accurately predict the remainder of the sequence of bits. Regularities thus facilitate forecasting. On the other hand, if the string of thirty binary digits were fully random,[2] it could not be compressed at all into a regularity. There, the shortest description would be the string itself. That description cannot be further compressed. One could describe it as 'thirty random bits', but there is no guarantee that the same string would be replicated if thirty random bits were generated; on the contrary, it would be very unlikely.

The third assumption simply draws a conclusion from the first and second assumptions, namely that cognitive agents cannot have perfect knowledge of events, not even of a single 'event' or change of state, because the amount of information required to get a perfect understanding of that move is infinite, as Prigogine (1987) demonstrated. Loasby (1999) adds several other reasons for the inherent incompleteness of human knowledge, apart from limits to human cognition, including the insufficiency of inductive reasoning as a proof for the validity of our arguments, the interdependence of human behaviours that makes it impossible to accurately predict future states of the world and, in general, the nature of complex systems in our world that makes external observation an unreliable basis for prediction. These arguments are of a more epistemological nature. Their foundations could be brought back to underlying bounded rationality argument.

As a consequence of this third assumption, learning processes are of a stochastic rather than a deterministic nature: the relationship between events is learned with a degree of 'coarse graining' of information; a reasonable approximation of possible relationships is the best an agent can achieve. Further 'fine graining' requires more observation of regularities and thus time spent on learning. This is costly because it uses scarce information processing capacity, capacity that could be used for other purposes.

This above example of bit-string compression focused on a sequence of information of finite length, and very short length at that. Reality emits a virtually infinite string of information bits, and we would not even attempt to identify all the regularities in that set. We seek to extract a not-too-complex knowledge set out of the observations, a set that is sufficiently accurate to allow us to go around without being too precise to clog our mind with useless details, so as to save scarce information processing capacity for other purposes. How accurate we want it to be and what sort of other purposes we have in mind depends very much on the environment in which we operate. The next section explains the trade-off between accuracy and variety in knowledge.

Loasby (1999) concludes that if we accept this bounded rationality approach to human learning and behaviour, we should also accept two consequences. First, economics must necessarily start from incomplete knowledge rather than the perfect information or perfect knowledge that underpins the neo-classical economic paradigm. Arrow's extension of the neo-classical paradigm to situations of uncertainty does not really solve that issue because it is limited to parametric uncertainty: uncertainty that allows nevertheless for the calculation of probabilities of possible events which, in turn, requires some sort of historical-statistical database on these events. But since we are discussing absent information here, Knightian uncertainty comes into the picture: we don't know what we don't know and therefore can not parameterise these unknown variables. A second and even more important consequence is that economics is not so much about organising scarce physical resources, as is often claimed in economics textbooks, but first and foremost about organising scarce cognitive capacity: how to organise human behaviour in the face of the inherent incompleteness of knowledge and consequently the inherent Knightian uncertainty that humans are faced with? Incomplete knowledge and uncertainty result in the principle of cognitive economy – the search for ever more economic use of scarce human cognitive capacity. We will show in this and the next chapters that this becomes a driving force in the evolution of human societies, and a powerful explanatory principle for many organisational features in human society, including the emergence of economic exchange itself. But let us first return to the purely cognitive aspects of human knowledge and behaviour.

Knowledge and environmental adaptation

Following the more qualitative assumptions regarding the properties of knowledge and the descriptions of how it works that were explained in the previous section, I develop in this section a more rigorous approach to knowledge, rooted in connectionist or neuronal network models of cognition.

At the level of an individual brain or artificial neuronal network, knowledge could be considered as a 'set' of nodes, connected through neuronal links. This sort of set-up can easily be translated in graph theory concepts.[3] The knowledge set H can be defined as a graph with k nodes (2

$\leq k < \infty$) and q unordered lines that link pairs of nodes. The elements of the knowledge graph H are the pair-wise links between neuronal nodes.[4] The pair-wise connection requirement implies that no line can be a loop around a single node and every node must be connected to at least one other node. We add the additional constraint that no more than one line can exist between any pair of nodes. Consequently, k and q are related variables. In the case of a neuronal network with $k \geq 2$ nodes, the number of links in H, q(H), varies between a lower limit q_L of $(k-1)$ pairs of connections (the minimum number that ensures that all nodes have at least one pair-wise connection) and an upper limit q_U of pair-wise connecting links (when all possible pair-wise connections are made). When $q = qU$ the graph H is called a *complete graph*. Because of the requirement that $k \geq 2$, H can never be an empty set. When $k = 2$, then $q = 1$ and the lower and upper limit coincide at 1: H contains only one pair.

In a theoretical setting, the elements of a knowledge graph would be individual neuronal links. In practice, for a specific piece of knowledge in a human brain, containing billions of neuronal nodes and links, it will not be possible to go down to the neuronal level to define a knowledge set. For instance, it is virtually impossible to identify the set of neuronal links involved in the word 'car'. It will therefore remain a conceptual definition. At a more empirical level, proxies will have to be developed at a higher level of integration of neuronal links into elementary (or more comprehensive) knowledge concepts. For instance, words could be used as proxy for individual knowledge concepts in a language knowledge set. A specific language knowledge set, for instance for the French language, could also be considered as a subset of total knowledge stored in an individual agent.

These higher-level knowledge concepts can be introduced as subgraphs of H. A graph G is a subgraph of H if $\forall k,q \in G: k,q \in H$. To distinguish between subgraphs in an overall knowledge graph H, we introduce the concept of *connectivity* (Harary 1969: 43). The connectivity λ of a graph H is the minimum number of lines that have to be removed in order to disconnect one (or more) subgraphs from it. Obviously, the higher λ, the more subgraphs can be disconnected in H and the more fragmented H becomes. Setting the level of connectivity becomes a tool for defining knowledge concepts in H. Note that if H(k,q) is a complete graph (when $q = q_U$), disconnection is impossible, unless $\lambda = q$ lines are removed, which annihilates the knowledge set because no node will have a connection anymore. Note that connectivity and subgraphs can be compared to neuronal 'bindings' and 'categorisations', discussed further on in this chapter.

The qualities of the knowledge graph H can now be described in terms of two variables: coverage or variety and accuracy or coarseness (Gell-Mann 1995). Variety refers to the number or the range of different types of events covered by the knowledge set, or the probability that a randomly selected event is covered by the knowledge set. Accuracy refers to the probability that a particular event can be accurately predicted on the basis of that knowledge set. Since knowledge is a concise description of reality, it can never be fully accurate. There is always a margin of uncertainty. Knowledge makes events more predictable (though never certain), it reduces uncertainty. In economic terms, knowledge permits an agent to avoid the cost of threats and reap the benefits of opportunities. The more knowledge, the more resources or income an agent can derive from his environment.

However, we should not only evaluate the resource mobilisation or income generation potential in terms of the total knowledge that an agent holds. We should also look at the composition of his knowledge set in terms of accuracy and variety. That composition determines the extent to which he can respond appropriately to threats and opportunities that occur in his environment.

Variety could be defined at several levels. At the nodal level, the number of nodes (k) included in H could be a measure of the variety of knowledge covered by H. This may be theoretically satisfying but individual nodes do not correspond to recognisable knowledge concepts in reality. For that purpose, a higher level of amalgamation will be required, combining a set of nodes into a meaningful knowledge graph and identifiable piece of knowledge. The higher the connectivity criterion (for lines or nodes), the more the overall knowledge graph will be fragmented into subgraphs of knowledge. For example, an individual's knowledge graph can be λ-connected so that λ disconnects knowledge of language from, say, knowledge of car mechanics. When λ is increased to $\lambda'>\lambda$, knowledge can be further subdivided into different languages. At a $\lambda''>\lambda'$, a single language is further subdivided into knowledge of grammar and vocabulary, or the number of words available in the vocabulary becomes identifiable. The connectivity criterion λ can thus be used to identify the number of subgraphs I in H so that: $\forall\, i \in [0,I]$: $h_i \subset H$ and $\forall\, i \neq j$: $h_i \cap h_j = \varnothing$, with $\partial I/\partial \lambda > 0$. That number of subgraphs, or the ratio I/H for a given λ, is a measure of variety in H.

Note that this definition of variety in knowledge and the existence of subgraphs in an overall knowledge graph, circumvents the question of continuity versus discreteness in knowledge elements or subgraphs. Subgraphs, as identified through a criterion of connectivity, are discrete sets with empty intersections with other subgraphs. At the same time, they remain connected and ensure continuity with other subgraphs at a level of connectivity that lies outside the λ-dependent definition of the subgraph.

Accuracy of a given knowledge graph H, or any subgraph of H, can be measured by the density of the links between the nodes of H. Absolute density $D(H) = q$ while relative density $d(H) = (q - q_L) / (q_U - q_L)$. The latter measure is more appropriate since it is independent of k, and thus independent of the size of the disconnected subgraphs in H (or the level at which variety is defined).

The combination of accuracy and variety properties of a knowledge graph enable us to define the 'volume' of knowledge in H, or v(H),[5] as the product of variety and accuracy or v(H) = I d(H). Volume can expand both by increasing variety (the number of subgraphs) and by increasing accuracy (the density of links between nodes in a subgraph).

The above approach allows us to give more concrete content to the choice between accuracy and variety in individual knowledge sets. The more variety the agent seeks to incorporate in his knowledge set, the better he is able to cope with a wide range of possible events in his environment, and thus the higher his income generating capacity. However, variety is subject to diminishing returns. Because of inherently limited information processing capacity, more variety implies less accuracy. The more accurate an agent's behavioural routines are, the better he will be able to cope with some events and thus the higher his income generating capacity. Again, accuracy is subject to diminishing returns. If he concentrates on improving the accuracy of just a few routines, he will not have sufficient variety to face a wide range of possible events and his income generating capacity will decrease again.

For a given upper limit on total volume of individual knowledge, max v(H), the choice between I and d(H) becomes an optimisation problem. An agent aims to maximise his income or resource availability (R) or minimise the uncertainty (uC) associated with his behavioural responses to environmental events. His objective function takes the form $R^{-1} = uC = f(I^{-1}, d(H)^{-1})$. R and uC are negatively correlated, and so are uC and H, by definition. Both variety and accuracy in knowledge are positively correlated with resource mobilisation capacity, or negatively correlated with uncertainty reduction: the more accuracy and/or variety in knowledge, the better the agent can deal with the events in his environment, drawing benefits from opportunities and avoiding the cost of challenges, and thus reducing uncertainty. Moreover, I assume that both are subject to decreasing returns: $\partial R / \partial d(H) > 0$ and $\partial^2 R / \partial^2 d(H) < 0$, and likewise for the variable I. Decreasing returns will allow us to define a unique equilibrium allocation between accuracy and variety.

uC is minimised subject to a capacity constraint I d(H) $\leq$ max v(H). This is a standard economic optimisation problem, comparable to utility maximisation under a budget constraint. The optimisation problem is pictured in Figure 4.1. The horizontal axis represents the volume of knowledge, v(H). It is constrained to the right by the knowledge capacity constraint, max v(H). The more scarce knowledge is allocated to the acquisition of accuracy, the lower uncertainty. But at the same time, allocating more knowledge to accuracy reduces the potential variety that can be covered and therefore increases uncertainty again. The optimal allocation is somewhere in between the extremes. Because of diminishing returns, the shape of the uC-curve is convex. The optimal allocation of limited information processing capacity between variety and accuracy acquisition is achieved

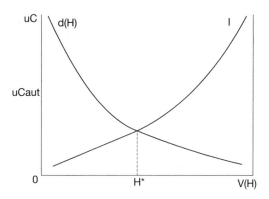

Figure 4.1 Accuracy versus variety in knowledge

when $\partial uC/\partial I = - \partial uC/\partial d(H)$, represented by H* in Figure 4.1. A smooth and convex relationship between uC and H ensures the existence of a unique uncertainty minimisation equilibrium.

Note that Figure 4.1 applies to the situation of an individual cognitive agent, living in full cognitive autarky, without the possibility of communicating or exchanging knowledge with other agents. He can only rely on his own cognitive devices to face the challenges and exploit the opportunities in his environment. The cognitive autarky condition will gradually be relaxed in the next chapters, where various means of communication are added to the model.

Agents have no objective method to determine *ex-ante* the equilibrium composition of their knowledge set. Any position they chose to take on the accuracy-variety continuum is necessarily subjective. The only real test is an *ex-post* comparison of performance among individual agents. Agents can learn from experience and adjust their knowledge composition accordingly. Achieving equilibrium becomes an evolutionary trial-and-error process (Alchian 1950).

Let me illustrate this trade-off between accuracy and variety of knowledge with an example. Consider a city street map. The scale of the map is an indicator of the amount of detailed information that it provides. A perfect map would provide as much information as possible about the city. Therefore, a perfect map would have scale 1:1. At that scale, the map contains all possible distinctions in the cityscape, from street shapes to each brick on the pavement. Apart from the fact that such a map would be hard to handle, it is useless: you might as well look at the city itself in that case, rather than use a map. A less perfect map, at a scale of, say 1:1000, would inevitably lose some degree of detail and may cause you to miss out on some points of interest in the city or lose your way. However, it is of practical value, as long as it does not lose too much detail. A street map at scale 1:1,000,000 is about as useless as a map at scale 1:1 because it would reduce the centre of any major city to the size of a pinhead. There is no information (no distinctions by street) in that map because the city is just a single point on that map. Clearly, in order for information to be useful, it needs to be somewhere in between totally perfect and totally imperfect. Human beings strive for the appropriate degree of compression of information and maps are flexible compression instruments. However, it is hard to know *ex-ante* how precise knowledge of city streets needs to be. Walking through the city, we may be confronted with an orientation decision for which our map is not accurate enough. At that point, we wish – too late – that we had bought a more precise map. Maps compress the observed distinctions (information) in a cityscape into regularities (pavements, streets and all items in that street are compressed into a simple straight line) that are hopefully sufficiently detailed to serve their purpose. Maps contain more than just a set of information; they structure that information and indicate causal relationships. They contain knowledge that allows the user to forecast events: if I follow street A until the next crossroad and turn right, I will end up in street B.

Note that the equilibrium between accuracy and variety is explained here in the context of a single agent, living in autarky. Cognitive agents can actually do far better in terms of survival probability and uncertainty reduction than the above simple model allows them to do. In the next chapter, I will explain how life in social groups may fundamentally alter this equilibrium, pushing agents towards maximum accuracy and minimum variety in their knowledge set while increasing their survival probability at the same time. That is made possible when specialisation emerges. Just to lift part of the veil and whet the reader's appetite, a slight extension of the map example will illustrate the importance of social cooperation. When your map happens to be insufficiently detailed for a particular orientation decision, you may either remain stuck in your knowledge autarky equilibrium, or you can ask passers-by for more information. Chances are that they have acquired a specialised knowledge set about neighbourhood streets, more precise than your map, because they live or work there. Exchange of information between the passer-by and you may solve your problem. In the next chapter, this trivial example will be cast in a more rigorous knowledge exchange model. That will shift the question of the optimal composition of individual knowledge, away from the accuracy-variety trade-off and towards the appropriate degree of specialisation.

In this section, I introduced the 'environment' as a determining factor in the composition of individual knowledge. This brings us back to Darwinian fitness and selection principles. Before we close this section, it should be pointed out that the amount or volume of knowledge in itself is a bad indicator of fitness or adaptation. Rather, it is the appropriate balance between an individual's knowledge set – including its composition – and the information emitted by his environment, that constitutes a measure of fitness. Consider the following two examples.

First, lions hunting antelope on the African savannah. Success in hunting depends on information, the lion's ability to track antelope and the antelope's ability to detect the lion. Both species have developed knowledge and behavioural routines for these purposes, through genetic selection as well as phenotypic learning. The environmental equilibrium between the two species is a function of their knowledge sets. Suppose we disturb this equilibrium by equipping the lions with remote sensing equipment that enables them to know exactly where and when antelope are to be found. As a result, hunting becomes much more efficient and risks extinguishing the antelope species, thereby extinguishing the lions as well, by starvation.

A second example: the fitness of stock traders. Tirole (1986) shows how stock trading can only be the result of imperfect or incomplete information. If all traders had perfect information, all information regarding the value of a stock would be priced into the market and no profitable deal could be made anymore. It is only because traders have imperfect information and because that information is asymmetrically allocated among traders (they all have different pieces of information), that they hold different perspectives on the value of a stock, so that subjectively gainful deals can be made – which may turn out to be not that gainful at all. The stock-trading example rejoins Prigogine's (1987) example of trying to predict the outcome of tossing a coin. Only when infinitely precise information about the initial conditions is available can the outcome be predicted with certainty. The slightest imperfection is sufficient, however, to reduce the chances of a correct prediction to 0.5. Similarly, with stock markets, infinitely perfect information about the stocks and companies is required (something that even the companies themselves do not have); the slightest deviation from this perfection is sufficient to set stock markets in motion. It also explains why stock market trading is often called 'speculation': traders speculate that something will happen, without having sufficient information to assess the veracity of their speculations.

In a way, the antelope-hunting example is a simple extension of Tirole's (1986) 'no trade theorem': lions with perfect information about the position of antelope would, in the long run, destroy their own gainful opportunities. The relative population ratio of lion to antelope would rapidly increase and, ultimately, result in the extinction of both species. These examples show that increased accuracy of knowledge may actually be a disadvantage: it may destroy opportunities and reduce fitness because knowledge results in a modification of the environment itself.

The internal representation of knowledge

So far in this chapter, I have presented an information-based definition of knowledge and learning and showed how the composition of knowledge is related to environmental factors. We still haven't explained how knowledge is represented in the brain, and how these representational systems affect the way knowledge is accumulated, organised and transmitted. The next two sections focus on internal representations of knowledge, inside the (human) brain. Thereafter, a section will be devoted to external or symbolic representations.

Any theory of cognitive development at the macro-level of human societies has to be consistent with the principles of individual human cognition and neuro-physiological processes at the micro-level of the human brain. For this reason, we first have to descend to this micro-level and examine the theories and evidence here. There are many theories of knowledge representation in the brain. Rummelhart and Norman (1988) classify these in four categories and present an overview of each:

- The most frequently encountered representational systems are propositional and knowledge is represented by formal logical statements.
- Analogical representational systems present a direct correspondence between the world and its representations.
- Procedural systems see knowledge representation as an active process.
- In distributed knowledge[6] systems, the world is not represented in discrete places in the brain but instead distributed over a large set of representing units, each representing a piece of a large amount of knowledge.

It is not my intention to discuss all these theories and categories in detail. Rather, I propose to pick out one system that suits the purposes of this research and see how much mileage we get out of that choice. While there are strengths and weaknesses in each of these representational systems, my hypothesis is that distributed knowledge representation models fit best with the concepts and theories that are the subject of this book. The arguments in favour of this hypothesis will gradually become clear below. I first examine how distributed knowledge representation systems conform to (a) the basic neuro-physiological evidence regarding the functioning of the brain (in this section) and (b) the structural characteristics of knowledge assembly, as seen from the point of view of categorisation theory (next section).

External information impulses are perceived by the sensory organs and produce neural activation that is transmitted to neural networks in the brain (audio-visual, smell and taste, other nervous system signals produced by mechanical and temperature activation of neurons). But how do these isolated strings of information impulses become structured sets of knowledge? How does the nervous system extract the regularities from the information set and process these into behavioural routines? For instance, how do we associate the visual perception of a speed limit sign with the behavioural response 'look at the speedometer' for other visual input and possibly an additional 'push the brake' behavioural response?

In neurology this is known as the problem of 'binding': how different neural impulses get combined into a coherent process of information gathering, processing and behavioural response, possibly supported by recalls from memory. Traditional theory assumes the existence of points in the brain, the so-called multi-modal cortices, where integrated representations of a fragmented reality are achieved. They integrate the multitude of sensory signals into a coherent picture. This view suggests that perception depends on a unidirectional process, starting close to the sensory input regions and moving up along cascades of integrative cortices that produce gradually more integrated views from the incoming information signals and extract more complex knowledge from these signals. Integration – knowledge, pictures of the world – is achieved at discrete locations in the brain. There is some anatomical evidence in support of that view. Neuronal structures do radiate from the primary sensory cortices via multiple stages towards the inner lobes of the brain. Neurons farther away from the primary sensory cortices have larger receptive fields than those nearer to these cortices.

Damasio (1989a; 1989b) rejects the idea that a single site in the brain could integrate fragmented signals. He replaces the unidirectional process with a recursive, iterative and decentralised model. Evidence from his patients with damaged brains showed that damage to higher order cortices does not inhibit integrated perception. Hence integration is achieved in a more decentralised way. According to Damasio's theory, meaningful integration is achieved by multi-regional retro-activation of widespread fragment records. This suggests, first, that perceptual experience depends on neural activity in multiple regions activated simultaneously in the brain, rather than in a single region. Second, that activity occurs nearer to the sensory input and behavioural output cortices, rather than in the inner brain regions. Convergence zones bind fragmented records of sensory and motor activity, at different levels. Some bind fragments into entities; others bind entities into events and sequences of events, etc. The typical feature of convergence zones is to register combinations of components in terms of temporal and spatial coincidence or sequence. This is the central issue in cognitive processing.

In Damasio's view, the physical characteristics of an external object are recorded in separate constituent ingredients, each of which is the result of cognitive mappings at a lower scale. Integration of these ingredients into more abstract cognitive concepts corresponds to criterion-based conjunctions of characteristics. Similarly, events and sequences of events consist of inter-temporal conjunctions of characteristics. Perceptual reconstruction (or memory re-activation) is achieved by retro-activation of fragmentary records of sensory inputs, in multiple regions and as a result of feedback activity from convergence zones that reconstitute the bindings between these fragments. The success of such a recall operation depends on attention, the critical level of activity in each of the activated regions below which consciousness cannot occur (Damasio 1989a: 27).

One can easily see how Damasio's de- and re-constructivist perspective fits in with the theory of knowledge extraction from information streams, presented earlier in this chapter. Incoming information signals are deconstructed into ingredients that correspond to distinctions within the information set. Ingredients are reconstructed into overall pictures and more abstract concepts through retro-activation of the ingredients, spread out over a variety of regions in the brain and not stored in a central place. Integration of fragments of 'thought' into higher levels of abstraction is achieved by the binding of these fragments on the basis of correspondences in activation patterns. These correspondences allow the brain to extract regularities within and across sets of activation patterns. By associating these regularities, the brain can extract 'knowledge' from apparently chaotic information streams.

Damasio's perspective also fits with the distributed knowledge representation approach. Knowledge is not located anymore at discrete places in the brain but rather spread out over a range of places. To re-activate a particular piece of knowledge, all these places in the brain need to be activated. Rummelhart and Norman (1988: 571) label such systems 'super positional memories' and attribute the following properties to them:

- Different memory structures are superimposed upon one another (rather than being stored independently of one another).
- Any given memory structure must be represented across a large number of storage elements (rather than having a unique address that specifies where to retrieve it).
- They are resistant to damage.
- Information within the memory system is directly affected by other material; storage interference is a common source of error.
- Retrieving information from a super positional memory is like detecting a signal in noise; the signal-to-noise ratio is important.
- When a known signal is presented, the system responds by amplifying the signal; when an unknown signal is presented, the system dampens it.
- When a signal similar to a known signal is presented, the system responds by distorting the presented signal towards the known signal.
- When a number of similar signals have been stored, the system will tend towards the central tendency of the set of signals, whether or not there has been a signal that corresponds to this central tendency.

- When part of a known signal is presented, the system responds by filling in the missing parts of the signal.

Note the last property: it will be a key element in the explanation of external representations, once we come to that subject in the section after next.

This list of properties gives some idea about how distributed memories work, but more precision is required to get an operational memory or representational model. Rummelhart and Norman refer to research on associative memories, as a specific type of super positional or distributed memory. Associative models discriminate between positive and negative links between units in a distributed network. Positively linked units excite each other when one is activated; negatively linked units inhibit each other when one is activated. Connectivity matrices can be constructed that exhibit the positive and negative strengths of links between various patterns of unit links. The activation of one unit in this matrix by means of an input signal results in an activation pattern that 'represents' the knowledge associated with that signal. These models bring us to the question of the concrete organisation of knowledge or representations in the human mind.

The internal representation of knowledge: categorisation theory

This is where categorisation theory comes in. The categorisation theory model of internal knowledge representation can best be explained in modern computer software jargon as a relational database. Categorisation theory assumes that the information streams flowing into the brain from the sensory organs (the 'entries') are broken down according to the attributes of the phenomena that are being perceived. Modern databases can handle a virtually unlimited number of entries, but each entry has a limited number of predefined attributes, the 'fields' in the entry sheet. Categorisation theory models can also handle an unlimited number of perceptual (audio-visual and other sensory) entries, but each of those has an unlimited number of possible attributes, 'fields'. Also, the fields are not predefined but emerge from an analysis of the various properties or attributes of the perceptual entries. Attributes that look like already known things are stored in the corresponding category; attributes that don't look like anything known are stored in a new category or 'field'. As such, the relational database is asymmetric in the composition of its fields. For example, the view of a red sports car can be decomposed in red, sleek, fast, car. The sight of a blue pickup truck can be decomposed in blue, bulky, slow, spacious, car. The two views share the intersection of the attribute 'car'. Other attributes are shared with many other objects: red/blue objects, sleek/bulky objects, fast/slow objects. It is this categorisation of attributes of sensory-motoric experiences that constitutes the foundations of categorisation theory. Categories are not necessarily exactly and clearly defined. Fuzzy logic is likely to prevail in most cases. Categories do not necessarily correspond to natural attributes, but neither are they fully artificial; they can be both. The perceived world is already structured in some ways and categorisations will correspond to these structures (Rosch 1978). For example, objects normally fall to the ground and not in any other direction. Apples are green, red or yellow, not purple or blue. On the other hand, the morphological limits to our sensory systems also impose structures onto the perceived world: we cannot see the inside of material things, cannot detect their atomic structure, etc.

One can now begin to appreciate the reasons why I chose to follow the path of distributed knowledge representation models and, concomitantly, categorisation theory, to describe the actual storage and retrieval mechanisms for internal representations of knowledge in the brain. These models have some interesting properties (Rummelhart and Norman 1988; Rosch 1978) that fit nicely with the definition of knowledge presented earlier:

- Categorisation theory fits well with the model of distributed knowledge representation in the brain: knowledge is not localised in discrete parts of the brain but spread out over a variety of places. Only the reactivation of patterns of attributes can reactivate a piece of knowledge.
- It fits well with the definition of knowledge as an extraction of complexity from a stream of raw data inflows. Fragmented input signals into the brain can be considered equivalent to raw data streams, information streams containing 'distinctions'. What the brain does is extract the regularities from this information stream, that is map the attributes of these distinctions.
- Categorisation theory and distributed representation are compatible with the idea of partitionable knowledge. Attributes are detailed and identified up to a level of fine-graining of knowledge that satisfies the beholder. If there is a need to identify further distinctions (more detailed information), the holder of a piece of knowledge can build on his existing less refined dataset and add further attributes to it, without destroying the existing data set. It just requires the identification of additional attributes. This property will turn out to be very useful in the context of increasing division of labour and specialisation (see Chapter 6).
- The flip side of partitionable knowledge is fuzziness: no borderline or distinction is complete and exactly defined. Categorisation theory allows for that fuzziness. This corresponds with assumption 3 in the list at the start of this chapter, that finite knowledge is necessarily approximate.

- Categorisation theory also enables us to distinguish between less and more abstract knowledge. The degree of abstraction is a function of the level of integration of attributes. Higher levels of abstraction are representing a further compression of the original sensory data input stream, obtained through further identification of regularities (or shared attributes) that are extracted from the original raw data stream.
- Another property of categorisation models of internal knowledge representations is that, regardless of how we organise things in our minds, the necessity to share these structures with other people will necessitate a common simplifying structure (Freyd 1983, mentioned in Rummelhart and Norman 1988: 575–6). This property will come in handy in Chapter 6 where we discuss the nature and origin of transaction costs.
- Last but not least, categorisation induces cognitive economy (Rosch 1978). Because objects in the world have many common features, classifying objects according to these features saves memory and scarce cognitive processing capacity. Representations for a red car, red shoes and red paint will economise on scarce cognitive capacity by sharing the attribute 'red'. There is no need to register that attribute three times. Also, representations for a red car and a blue car will not be completely separate memory storage points: they overlap in the 'car' attribute.

A metaphor from modern information technology could again be used to illustrate the principle of cognitive economy: file sharing. There is no need for every representation to be memorised in the brain with its own full set of attributes. Attributes can be shared between representations and the only thing is to make sure that every representation can be reconstructed with all its attributes through the appropriate hyperlinks.

The last property of distributed knowledge categorisation systems – cognitive economy – is probably one of the most important properties, and certainly one that we are going to encounter repeatedly in this book, in other cognitive features of human societal development. Cognitive economy is the red line of thought that runs through all products and societal characteristics that humans have produced. It explains why external symbolic representations emerge (next section), why communication is such an important aspect of learning (Chapter 5), the cognitive economies that can be realised through production and trade of goods (Chapter 6) and the establishment of property rights institutions (Chapter 10).

Connectionist versus modularity concepts of knowledge

The preceding sections may give the impression that I am resolutely following a purely connectionist track in my approaches to knowledge, looking at the mind as a *tabula rasa*, with its content and structure fully determined by the environment only and not by any evolutionary adaptive features that have been absorbed into its underlying genetic structure. The latter approach is known as the modularity theory of mind.

The mind is certainly not a *tabula rasa*, and there are consistent and predictable patterns of localisation of types of information processes in the mind. What these modular patterns actually are and whether they are genetically determined and 'hardwired' is another matter, however. This research is not meant to innovate in the domain of cognitive science. So I stick to existing interpretations that keep a middle-of-the-road position between hardcore connectionism and modularity theory. In fact, these labels become fairly meaningless if one follows the line of reasoning of Karmiloff-Schmit (1992) and Elman *et al.* (1996). These authors examine the underlying neuro-scientific evidence and try to match this with a theory of cognitive development. Using the term 'innate' for cognitive outcomes that are strictly gene-based, and 'learned' for all other outcomes, is not very useful. A more careful analysis of the genetic development process of the body may provide some clues regarding the role of genes and environment in producing cognitive and behavioural outcomes.

First, genes are not discrete in their location and effects. A single gene complex may be spread out over a variety of places on DNA strings. These gene bits interact with each other. The same set of genes can produce an array of different outcomes, depending on their interaction with each other and with the molecular and cellular environment in which they are located. This explains why, despite the fact that all cells in a body contain the same genetic material, there are different cell types and many more cell functions in the morphology of the body. Elman *et al.* (1992) distinguish between mosaic development, whereby cells develop independently of each other, according to their own timetable without waiting for information signals from other cells, and regulatory development, whereby the type and speed of development is regulated through cell interaction. Complex human bodies rely considerably on the latter type of development. They define the term 'innate' as referring to 'aspects of brain structure, cognition and behaviour that are the product of interactions internal to the organism' (23). Such innate constraints on cognitive development may be the result of pre-wired cortical micro-circuitry, architectural constraints at a higher level than micro-circuitry, or chronology constraints as a result of gradual learning itself.

Second, the relationship between genome and phenotype is highly non-linear. The linear relationship between body size and the volume of genetic material that exists for small organisms, breaks down in more complex organisms. Instead, increasing complexity is driven by regulatory mechanisms at molecular, cellular and higher levels, rather than at the genetic level only. Morphological development is not fully specified by genes anymore, but through these interactive regulatory processes that occur during development. This may help to explain why, for instance, chimpanzees and humans differ in 1.6 per cent of their genes only, while there are considerable differences in their morphology and behaviour that can not be accounted for by this 1.6 per cent of their gene pool. Elman *et al.* explain this switch to regulatory mechanisms by constraints on the amount of genetic information that can be safely stored in a single cell.

Third, a consequence of this interactive view of development is that subsequent specification and modularisation of the brain appears to be an outcome of development rather than a cause. Modularisation occurs in the course of development, not before development. Experiments with transplantation of brain tissue, for instance, show that the brain is rather plastic, especially early on in the development process when tissue can easily be transferred to other functional locations and adopt the functional aspects that are required for the new location. Even at later stages in development such transfers are feasible, though it may take more time and be less efficient. New wiring can be established in the adult brain, or old patterns of connectivity can be converted. Elman *et al.* (1996) argue against Pinker's idea that children are born with a 'language gene'. However, they concur that once the language modules in the brain have been wired up in the course of cognitive development processes, it is much harder to modify its contents (and switch from English to Chinese, for instance). This view is of course not new; developmental psychologists, such as Piaget, have long ago proposed it. But neuro-science has only recently discovered the mechanisms that underpin this developmental approach.

Last but not least, a major reason for choosing the connectionist approach in this research is, as Elman *et al.* (1992) point out, that it allows us to explain the phenomenon of partial knowledge, the state in between full and no knowledge – a key feature of the definition of knowledge presented in the previous section. If the innate or modularity view of knowledge were driven to an extreme, then every piece of knowledge would be located in a particular place in the brain; knowledge would become a discrete object. In the circumstances, it would be hard to define what we mean by partial or incomplete knowledge: either an idea is there or it isn't. By contrast, in connectionist distributed knowledge systems, whereby a piece of knowledge is spread out over a network of connecting neuronal nodes, the density and extent of the network may affect the accuracy or fine-graining of a particular piece of knowledge. For this reason, I consider the connectionist approach to be more fruitful for the study of distributed knowledge – both inside the brain (as will be discussed in the next section) as well as outside the brain through specialisation among human beings (discussed in the next chapters).

Symbolic storage and communication of knowledge

So far, we have focused on internal knowledge representation systems, inside the human brain. But what about external representation systems? According to Zhang (1997; 2000), studies of external representation systems started only recently, probably because it was (wrongly) assumed that external representations were merely stimuli to the mind and that not much insight into the workings of the mind could be gained from their study. Zhang demonstrates that external representations are not simply passive stimuli but constitute active and intrinsic ingredients in many cognitive processes. Indeed, knowledge is generated through the interwoven processing of internal and external representations.

How the perception of external representations facilitates the establishment and recall of bindings in the brain and categorisations in the mind, can easily be understood in the context of distributed representation systems. External representations (outside the brain) facilitate categorisation and bindings in at least three ways:

- By providing an external facilitation device for memory storage and recall, the perceived representation reactivates latent bindings in the brain. Even if the corresponding bindings do not exist any longer in the brain or have faded to a very low level of activation that inhibits recall ('forgetting'), the external representation can help to re-create them. Seeing the bill on my desk reminds me that I need to pay it.[7]
- Through external bindings that were not internally established: external representations can be manipulated in such a way as to generate new bindings that did not exist in the brain but can be imported as a result of the perception of that manipulation. When I see two of my colleagues in an intimate embrace in the street, a new categorisation is established in my mind: the two are in love. While I might have come to that same categorisation if I had paid more attention to their behaviour in the office, the perception of the external representation 'embrace' is sufficient to establish that link.
- By facilitating the copying of bindings that exist in the mind of one person to the mind of another person: external representations are communication devices that help the emitter to transfer a set of mappings and categorisations from his mind to the mind of a recipient, who did not previously have this particular mapping (though he should have a set of lower-level mappings on which to build a more integrated mapping). I am unable to speak Chinese, but by pointing to food and to my stomach I can signify to a Chinese that I am hungry.

This latter is probably the most important function of external representations, for it opens up the possibility of transmission of bindings from one mind to another. Brains cannot be in direct contact with each other;

there is no direct synaptic link between my neurons and yours so that my neurons could activate yours, or vice-versa. We need a medium to transmit activation patterns from one brain to the other. External representations are that medium: they link brain activation patterns to specific external artefacts that can be perceived by others.

At this stage, we need to introduce an important distinction within the class of external representations. Not all external representations are equally efficient in these three functions; some do far better than others in terms of memory storage and recall, and manipulation and communication of knowledge. The theories of distributed internal representation systems discussed above allow us to say something meaningful about the efficiency of external representations, and to define the properties of a class of external representations that is especially important in the context of this book: symbolic representations.

Normally, external representations stand for themselves. A picture of a car represents that car; when I see a drawing of a tree it represents a tree. In that case, the symbolic representation (signifier) represents itself (signified). This type of symbols are often called 'icons' (Deacon 1997). Signifier and signified are one and the same thing. Some things, however, may have connotations with, and actually represent, other things: the car may represent a rich and comfortable lifestyle (depending on the type of car), the song may recall memories of a love affair, and my face in the mirror reminds me that I'm getting old. Here, the signifier may still signify itself but also other things: it becomes a 'symbol' of something. There is a gradual shift away from the signified object towards other objects, concepts and categories. That shift is made possible because our distributed knowledge representation system has established links between the object and other attributes that are not normally associated with that object. When the signifier and the signified become totally disconnected and all attention shifts from the signifier to the signified, we call these external representations symbolic representations, or symbols: representations that represent something else than themselves.

For example, when I see the European flag, I hardly think of a piece of blue cloth. In my mind, it signifies far more complex things like memories of my work at the European Commission, a unified vision of a political Europe that stands above the nation-states, a geographical area between the Urals and the Atlantic ocean, a large area full of linguistic diversity, etc. In short, that flag triggers a whole range of bindings and sets in motion a whole train, or even many trains, of thought, depending on the circumstances in which I see it. The flag is a relatively simple piece of cloth that contains little information (distinctions) as such; it is easy to perceive, in the blink of an eye. But as a symbol it allows me, with that blink of an eye, to reactivate a large number of categories and attributes in my memory. I could reactivate these without the flag as well, but it would take more time and conscious cognitive effort to do so. The flag facilitates the reactivations of categorisations in my mind. It is an informationally simple signifier that activates an informationally complex set of significations.

The flag example illustrates why symbols are so important. It has to do with the principle of information economy, mentioned above as one of the important principles in categorisation theory. With non-symbolic external representations (things that stand for themselves), the complete object needs to be perceived by the viewer in order to get all the information about that object. With increasing discrepancy between the signifier and the signified, only some of the attributes of the signified need to be present (in the form of a signifier) in order to reconstruct the other attributes. Remember the last item in Rummelhart and Norman's (1988) list of properties of distributed knowledge systems: 'when part of a known signal is presented, the system responds by filling in the missing parts of the signal'. That is the role of symbols in the economics of scarce human information processing capacity. When I see the European flag, it recalls many complex geographical, cultural and political concepts.

A signifier cannot stand in as a symbol for something else if that signifier is informationally more complex to perceive and understand than the signified. In that case there would be no point in having a symbol; it would be easier to bring in the signified object itself. Symbols emerge only where there are good reasons of cognitive economy to do so. Remember the map example at the beginning of this chapter. A map is a symbolic representation because the signifier (the map) stands for something else (the signified = streets in a city). There is no point making a map with a scale of 1:1; it would be informationally as complex as the city itself and would not simplify the task of finding our way about the city. Informationally less complex maps, at higher scales, do facilitate that task. Flags are informationally efficient because it is virtually impossible to bring the entire country to a person in order to physically show what you mean. If flags and maps had not been invented, it would be informationally much harder to convey to a person the concept of a country or state.

The further the signifier and the signified divert from each other, the more abstract symbolic systems become and the more they can refer to specific properties that are hard to convey through look-alike 'iconic' representations. For instance, properties like quantity or temperature can only be presented in an abstract symbol where the signifier is only nominally related to the signified. Five apples can be represented by five representations of apples, or by the symbol '5' (which is not at all related to apples) followed by a single apple. The abstract symbol allows many manipulations that would be hard to achieve with the five representations of apples. This shows how informational improvements in symbolic systems affect our ability to manipulate them, and hence their efficiency in helping us to leverage our limited information processing capacity.

Deacon (1997) demonstrates how language offers another step towards enhanced cognitive efficiency in the use of symbols. Language manipulates symbols (words) according to rules of syntax that determine the ordering of symbols and also refine their precise meaning. That syntactical order allows the reader of a message to infer more information from the ordered set of words than he could derive from an unordered set. This way, the same stream of symbols or information bits (words) supplies a higher knowledge density without actually requiring more information processing capacity.

These cognitive mechanisms of symbolic knowledge transmission between internal and external representation systems, for a single individual, can easily be transposed to communication between individuals. There are a number of conditions, however, for interpersonal communication to be successful. First, the communicating parties should fully share the categorisations and attributes of the primary symbols that are used in the communication. Partners who do not understand each other's language and symbols cannot communicate efficiently: the signifiers become meaningless (without a signified) or do not refer to the same signified, which results in distorted communication. Second, the recipient needs to absorb all the higher-level categorisations and linkages that the emitter embedded in the communicated set of symbols, in order to 'learn' and absorb the communicated knowledge into his own knowledge set. These conditions reveal the limits to the informational efficiency of symbolic communication. Whatever the informational efficiency of the symbol set that is used for knowledge communication, the recipient needs to copy the communicated knowledge of the emitter into his own brain, i.e. reconstitute all categorisations, attributes and linkages, in order to use that knowledge. This reduces specialisation in society (emitter and recipient share the same knowledge) and imposes a cognitive opportunity cost on the recipient's scarce information processing capacity.

Fortunately, humankind has developed an even more efficient means to transfer knowledge between persons than communication: production and trade. How this works, why it is more efficient than symbolic communication and what its societal consequences are, will be explained in the next chapters. Just for a moment, try to imagine how the world would look like if symbolic communication were the only means to transfer knowledge: we would all have to study medical books and follow courses in medicine in order to cure our own diseases; we would have to sit through a mechanical engineering course in order to build and repair our own cars, TVs, computers and washing machines, etc. Knowledge would be communicable, but not the behavioural outputs that embody this knowledge into material goods and services. That is what economic systems, and indeed most of societal organisation, are all about.

The cognitive leverage effect of symbolic systems

In this section I focus on a number of illustrations of this cognitive leverage effect of symbolic systems, as well as criticism of this view.

Zhang and Norman (1994) and Zhang (1997; 2000) demonstrate how variations in the informational efficiency of external symbolic representation systems affect the difficulty of performing cognitive tasks. A typical example is the Tower of Hanoi task, whereby three objects of different size can be put in three different locations. The task consists of putting them all in a single place in increasing size order, with the lowest number of moves and subject to three rules: only the largest object in a place can be transferred, an object can only be transferred to the place where it is largest, and only one object can be transferred at the same time. Zhang (2000) demonstrates how these tasks are facilitated if the physical qualities of the objects already internalise some of the rules. For instance, three sizes of coffee cups can only be placed on each other from smaller to larger; there is no need to make the last two rules explicit. Hence there is no need for players to devote part of their scarce cognitive capacity to verify compliance with this rule; that speeds up implementation of the task.

A more interesting example from Zhang (1997) consists of the expansion of knowledge categorisation systems from a single to multiple dimensions. A single 'category' dimension allows nominal classification of objects only: they either belong to the same or to a different category. Adding a 'magnitude' dimension allows for a more sophisticated ordinal classification: smaller, larger, etc. Adding the 'interval' dimension enables cardinal classification: two, three, four, etc. Finally, adding an absolute zero to the cardinal classification permits the calculation of ratios: twice as big as, etc. This example shows the informational importance of the invention of numeric (cardinal) classification systems, especially with the invention of the number zero. Without numerical symbols, symbolic systems could at best convey ordinal rankings. Even within numerical systems, there are various degrees of information efficiency (Zhang and Norman 1994). Polynomial systems (like Arabic numerals) are more efficient because the number of symbols required to encode a number is proportional to the logarithm of the number to be encoded. Differences in symbolic representation also affect cognitive handling, not only in terms of the difficulty of reading and writing, but also the handling of formal manipulations, such as addition and multiplication tables.

However, Hutchins' (1995) seminal study of human cognition and the use of external cognitive devices in navigation has led him to reject the leverage effect. He (153–5) disagrees with what he calls the 'commonplace to speak of technology, especially information technology, as an amplifier of cognitive abilities'. In his study, technology includes all kinds of navigation instruments that produce symbolic representations of real physical situations, like position and speed. He sides with Cole and Griffin (1980) who claim that the appearance of amplification is a mistaken perspective because it considers the cognitive product or output of tools only. When the perspective is shifted to the process that goes on, it turns out that tools break down the human cognitive computation process into a different set of components, including different interfaces with the human mind. Tools modify the entire process and transform the task at hand into a different set of cognitive problems. None of the original component cognitive abilities has been amplified by the use of any tools. Hutchins concludes that 'the computational power of the system composed of person and technology is not determined by the information processing capacity of the tools used but by the role the technology plays in the composition of a cognitive functional system' (Hutchins 1995: 155).

Hutchins' (1995) vivid description of the role of human cognition and technology in the navigation of ships illustrates his point. All kinds of modern navigation instruments have fundamentally altered the way in which navigation is conducted, requiring new roles, knowledge and organisational set-ups for those involved in the navigation process. His comparison of modern Western navigational methods with those of Pacific islanders who travel long distances between islands without any instruments, underscores his point. The islanders also use navigation methods that require cognitive computation, though of a very different nature. Still, the end result is the same: both methods ensure that a ship leaving point A arrives at point B. It is fairly meaningless to compare the amount of computation involved in both navigation methods, and hard to claim that modern Western navigation reduces the amount of human computational involvement.

At first sight, Hutchins' comparative navigation methods example indeed appears to invalidate the role of symbolic information processing as a means to reduce the workload of human cognitive interfaces. However, a more careful look casts doubt over this interpretation. For instance, Hutchins specifically mentions that navigation tools avoid human algebraic reasoning and arithmetic and produce results that are more directly and visually interpretable. This is a clear example of reduced human cognitive workload. Another aspect of this question is that different navigation methods are not comparable in the extent of detailed information that they produce. The output of a navigation method is not only a shipping route from point A to point B, it also includes the precision of position and course determination. In that respect, Polynesian navigation, the US Navy's 'manual' methods and computerised GPS navigation are not comparable. For a given route between two points, GPS navigation provides considerably more computational detail and precision. So we should limit the comparison to comparable things, such as using a slide rule to compute an outcome or doing the same computations with a calculator, or doing them by hand. In that case, the reduction in cognitive workload, for a given degree of precision or detail, is an inescapable conclusion. A more extreme example will illustrate this point. One can imagine a GPS-assisted computer entirely taking over the navigation process, without human involvement – and indeed ships that do so already exist. There, the reduction in human computational input is obvious. These considerations lead me to stay in line with Zhang's (1997) interpretations and reject Hutchins' critique of the cognitive leverage role of symbolic systems.

5 Communication and distributed knowledge

The previous chapter focused on individual information processing and knowledge representations. I discussed the nature of knowledge, its representation inside the brain, and external representations. Since the information processing capacity of the human brain is inherently limited, cognitive economy turned out to be the guiding principle in storage and processing of knowledge representations. Internally, cognitive economy is realised through distributed representation and a categorisation approach to storage of knowledge. Externally, cognitive economy is achieved through the use of symbols that shift representation from an informationally complex signified subject to a less complex signifier. Additionally, symbolic systems provide cognitive relief because they enable external storage and processing of information.

The present chapter switches from individual knowledge processing to communication of knowledge between individuals. Since direct contact between brains is not possible, external representations, such as material artefacts and symbols, are a necessary condition for communication of knowledge between individuals. The emergence of communication induces a very important change in learning and knowledge accumulation: knowledge can now be transferred from one person to another. Individual learning is no longer the only source of knowledge. Furthermore, it enables the emergence of distributed knowledge or specialisation between individuals. From there, it is but a small step to economic systems and institutions – but that is left for subsequent chapters.

Here, the principle of cognitive economy will allow us to examine what the advantages are that communicable knowledge bestows on societies and on individual knowledge carriers. I use the Boyd and Richerson (1985) model (abbreviated as B&R) to investigate this issue. B&R assumed that 'cultural' transmission through a simple communication channel like imitation could improve the overall fitness of a society because it is less costly than individual learning. However, Rogers (1988) proved that this was not the case. Boyd and Richerson (1995) responded to Rogers with a model that does allow for improved fitness, but under restrictive conditions only. I will build on this model, and stretch it beyond its original purpose in order to show that knowledge communication does indeed help to increase the total volume of knowledge in human society (a quantity effect on knowledge) because communicated knowledge induces cognitive economy in learning. However, the advantages of knowledge communication through imitation and symbolic means remain limited, because there is no true specialisation or asymmetrically distributed knowledge in society: every time a piece of knowledge is communicated, it reduces specialisation between the emitter and the recipient. For specialisation to be effective, knowledge should remain asymmetrically distributed after communication, and society needs to provide incentives for individuals to invest in learning and gain from the transmission of learning to others.

This analysis will pave the way for a discussion of the emergence of trade and institutional systems in human societies – subjects that will be touched upon towards the end of this chapter and left mostly for detailed discussions in the chapters that follow. I demonstrate in this chapter that (a) the emergence of distributed knowledge was made possible by communication systems (imitation-based as well as symbolic) and even more so by production of goods and exchange of knowledge embodied in goods, i.e. by economic systems; and (b) economic systems are but a continuation of the search for cognitive economy in the storage and transmission of knowledge. These conclusions will pave the way for a more general conclusion, towards the end of this book, that the organisational features of society are endogenously determined and a function of knowledge accumulation.

Dual inheritance and the relative cost of acquiring knowledge

The seminal work of Boyd and Richerson (1985) was originally developed as a means to break free from the strictly Darwinian tradition whereby all behavioural traits can be transmitted through biological (genetic) inheritance only. That does not allow for horizontal transmission of knowledge between individuals. B&R introduce a dual inheritance model: behavioural knowledge can be transmitted both through genes and through communication – which they call 'cultural' transmission. Their purpose was to prove that societies that utilise cultural means of transmission or communicated knowledge have an evolutionary advantage (in terms of knowledge accumulation) compared to societies that do not have this facility. B&R use the very simplest form of knowledge communication: imitation. The model[1] distinguishes between two sources of knowledge from which an individual can draw: they can learn from others' behaviour through (low-cost) imitation or they can study the environment themselves, derive knowledge from that study (the high-cost extraction of regularities from an apparently chaotic stream of information). Imitation or culturally transmitted behaviour includes knowledge that is easy to observe and replicate and does not involve significant cognitive activity by the recipient. All knowledge that requires significant cognitive effort by the recipient is classified as individual learning.

In terms of the cognitive model presented in Chapter 4, individual learning encompasses the full works of cognitive processing: detection of a flow of information emitted by an environment, processing of this flow in order to extract the regularities (compression of information into knowledge) and store them as categorisations and their attributes (possibly in symbolic format, another form of information compression), retrieval (decompression of symbols) and use for behavioural purposes. Social learning – or imitation – on the other hand means that the regularities have already been extracted by other individuals and turned into behavioural routines; the imitator simply observes the behaviour and copies it into his or her memory. There is no cognitive processing (compression and decompression) involved.

Successful imitation is subject to the WYSIWIG ('What You See Is What You Get') condition: all relevant knowledge should be completely reflected and observable in behaviour. If observable behaviour represents only part of (or none of) the knowledge used in that behaviour, then imitation is useless. For example, I can observe a car mechanic handling all kinds of tools in particular ways to repair my car. But simply copying his behaviour may not help me out of trouble next time it breaks down. The car mechanic uses a lot of knowledge about cars that is not externally represented in his observable behaviour, to determine the course of his actions. Clearly, behaviour does not fully reflect knowledge in this case. He may be able to demonstrate how to remove the oil plug and change the oil, but not why and when to do it. As long as imitation is a reasonable approximation of WYSIWIG, it works. The further we are removed from that condition and the more underlying knowledge becomes important, imitation may rapidly reach the point where it becomes pointless. For instance, I may listen to a person who speaks a foreign language, register the sounds, and try to imitate these sounds, without understanding their meaning. In this case imitation without the underlying knowledge of these symbolic expressions is clearly pointless. In the case of symbolic representations, the signifier does not signify itself but something else; so, imitating the signifier as such is pointless behaviour. I shall continue to assume, as we have done so far in this research and for the purpose of this chapter, that the information available through behaviour (external knowledge representations) is a true reflection of the knowledge (internal representations) that goes into that behaviour. In the next chapter, that assumption will be relaxed: various forms of (de-) compression will be introduced and their impact on the transmission of knowledge will be analysed.

Hence, as long as we stick to the WYSIWYG condition, imitation implies copying of external knowledge representations that are identical to the internal representations. In that case, imitation is indeed a less costly way of acquiring knowledge than learning because it avoids the cognitive operations of compression and decompression.

But a cheaper option for knowledge acquisition is not necessarily the best. B&R (1985) launch an analysis of the costs and benefits of individual versus social learning. They concentrate on the revenue implications of sub-optimal behaviour, not on the opportunity costs of individual learning in terms of scarce individual cognitive capacity (or bounded rationality). In fact, B&R are not explicit about the sources of learning costs. One can only surmise from their explanations that costs are due to lost income opportunities (time taken off from productive activities for individual learning) or to errors in individual learning (regularities may be wrongly identified, random errors in storage and retrieval may occur, and drift or biased selection criteria in the recipient's mind may result in erroneous learning). The underlying assumption seems to be that cognitive capacity is scarce and thus entails an opportunity cost. In fact, the very concept of learning implies that knowledge is not available at zero cost and that processing of information into structured knowledge requires the use of scarce cognitive capacity. Social learning avoids (some of) these costs through direct imitation of other persons' behaviour. A 'cultural' population can thus adapt to new environments at a lower opportunity cost than an 'a-cultural' population, where each individual must learn his own behavioural patterns. This 'cognitive cost' interpretation paves the way for a cognitive economic model where relative costs between individual learning and social imitation play a crucial role, not in the selection of behaviours as such but in the selection of methods to acquire behaviours.

Since B&R are not very explicit about the sources of learning costs, it is worth examining in greater detail the origins of these costs, including their cognitive interpretation in accordance with the mechanics of learning processes explained in Chapter 4. Let us start by taking a look at the potential sources of opportunity costs in learning. Consider a simple learning-by-doing process whereby an agent ('Robinson Crusoe'), who starts from zero knowledge, gradually enhances his skills and increases his productivity in a particular task by repeatedly doing it. This generates the logistic learning curve shown in Figure 5.1. There is no opportunity cost of learning here because there is no alternative use of the agent's cognitive capacity; he has no other knowledge and can only do this task. His learning process follows a curve that is by definition at his maximum productivity level. Now, consider the introduction of a second individual to this environment ('Friday') who has already mastered that same task. His productivity is at maximum level, i.e. he holds the best knowledge of the task (the horizontal line in Figure 5.1). If that task is simple enough to be copied through imitation, then Robinson Crusoe can simply imitate Friday and reach the maximum productivity level in a much shorter time than individual learning would allow. If Robinson nevertheless chooses to follow his own individual learning path, he incurs an opportunity cost (the shaded area in Figure 5.1).

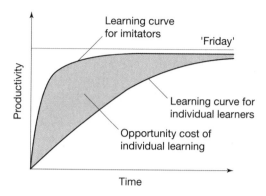

Figure 5.1 The cost of learning

In the case of individual learning, the learner needs to analyse the information flow from his task environment, establish all the bindings between the various activated regions of the brain, or work out the categorisations involved and their various attributes and connections. Repetition of tasks in learning-by-doing facilitates that cognitive process: with every repetition, the learner will become more aware of the behavioural intricacies of the task. In the case of imitation, the learner 'reverse engineers' these bindings by imitating the behaviour of the prototype agent, thereby inducing the bindings in the brain that go along with the behaviours involved. However, it does not require original analysis of the environmental information inflow. We can very well imitate somebody's behaviour and achieve similar outcomes without understanding why particular actions are required. For instance, I know that I should add yeast to the flour when baking bread, because I observed my grandmother doing so. However, I have no idea what the underlying chemical processes are that make yeast turn flour into bread (neither had my grandmother). Still, I do it and it works perfectly well. If I had to establish this series of tasks that leads to the production of bread all by myself, through trial and error and experimenting, it would probably have taken me a lifetime to find out about the yeast.

The above is true provided that the environment remains unchanged over the relevant time period. Now assume that the environment changes during the learning process. First, the productivity of imitated behaviour declines rapidly. What may have been perfectly suitably behaviour at time t = 1 may be totally out of date and dysfunctional by time t = n. The productivity of imitators declines over time (the declining slope in Figure 5.2), depending on the rate of environmental change. Second, individual learning curves will be less steep because the environment changes during the learning process: learners are aiming at a moving target. A learner's productivity is unlikely to reach the maximum level because there are always some changes in the environment that reduce the effectiveness of learned behaviours. Still, contrary to imitation, individual learning keeps up to some extent with changes and manages a fair level of productivity. This results in a lower opportunity cost of learning in a changing environment; it actually turns into a benefit once individual learning produces behaviours that exceed the productivity of imitation (the shaded area to the right in Figure 5.2). This cost-benefit analysis of learning versus imitation, in a changing environment, reflects the situation in the standard B&R model. Below, we will discuss another version that shifts the emphasis from a changing environment to changes in the ratio of imitators versus learners, the so-called Rogers model.

There are two important conclusions to be drawn from this discussion.

First, the distinction between imitation and learning in the B&R dual inheritance model is gradual and qualitative, depending on the relative opportunity cost of acquiring new behavioural routines and the type of neurological processes involved. In fact, this binary classification of learning channels could be replaced by a continuous variable: the relative cost of learning. That cost finds its cognitive foundations in the mode of transmission (mimetic, symbolic, embodied) and the way of processing (activation of existing bindings and categorisations; building new categorisations). Within these modes of transmission we can then look for the most economical in terms of overall cost-benefit analysis.

Second, the cost-benefit analysis approach indicates that the decision on how much an individual will learn and through which channel, is not only determined by his cognitive information processing capacity but also by the trade-off between learning costs and production benefits. That is a function of economic variables. Figures 5.1 and 5.2 express costs and benefits in terms of alternative opportunities. Learning will cease either when the cost of additional learning exceeds the benefits or when an individual's cognitive capacity is reached, whichever comes first. At first sight,

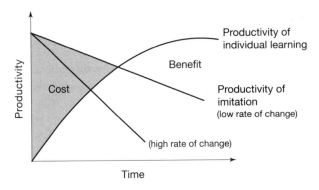

Figure 5.2 Environmental change and learning costs

there is nothing new about this conclusion: Becker's (1964) models of education and human capital formation already came to that conclusion. However, Becker's models took the economic value of learning as exogenously given. Here, knowledge is an endogenous factor in the learning model. The costs and benefits of learning are affected by how fast the environment changes, how fast learners keep track of those changes (Figure 5.2) and how much others learn (see Figure 5.3 below). The environment is partly endogenised because the knowledge held by other persons is part of the environment in which an individual operates.

The impact of communicated knowledge on overall population fitness

The B&R model compares the cost of individual learning to the cost of social learning or communicated knowledge. B&R assume that the cognitive economy achieved by communication enhances overall fitness of a population with respect to the environment. Though they offer no real proof for that assumption, they conclude that communicated 'culture' represents an evolutionary advantage. That conclusion is based on the impossibility of the contrary: if it were to constitute a disadvantage, nature would have discarded it in the course of the competitive evolutionary selection process. In their view, 'culture' must have natural origins.

At first sight, there is ample empirical evidence that this conclusion is justified. *Homo sapiens*, the 'cultural' animal *par excellence*, has proved its overwhelming adaptability and fitness in a very wide range of changing environments. However, Rogers (1988) disputes that hypothesis. He claims that, though mimetic adaptation may be faster, the long-run equilibrium fitness outcome may be exactly the same as for slower Darwinian genetic selection processes. He proves that mimetic transmission as such, through imitation or social transmission of behaviours, does not increase fitness. His proof is based on a simple model with two types of individuals, imitators and individual learners. The basic mechanism of the model is explained in Figure 5.3.

Consider a changing environment with a group of cognitive agents, with the capacity to learn individually about the environment, and define their behaviour accordingly, as well as to imitate other agents' behaviour. Learners learn about the environment and set their behaviour in function of what they learned. They adapt to the most recent information available in the environment, exploiting the resources of that environment and paying a learning cost for it. Imitators imitate the behaviour of a randomly chosen individual (not only learners but also other imitators), at no cost. Learners adapt to the state of a changing environment; imitators just copy behaviours. Rogers (1988) demonstrates that a mixed population of learners and imitators will always tend to an equilibrium composition.

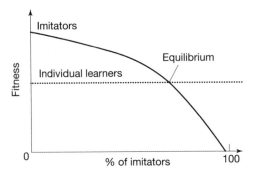

Figure 5.3 Fitness of learners and imitators
Source: Rogers (1988).

Learners' fitness does not vary with the number of imitators (the horizontal line in Figure 5.3). They always adapt to the environment, but pay a learning cost for this adaptation. Because of that cost, their fitness is below the maximum level. If the percentage of imitators is low, fitness of imitators is higher than that of learners. This is so because, even if they randomly choose an individual to copy behaviour from, they stand a high chance of copying from a learner (since there are more learners than imitators) whose behaviour is always up-to-date in a changing environment. On top of that, imitators avoid the cost of learning that drags down learners' fitness. Many people will observe this advantage, so that the number of imitators will tend to increase. On the other hand, if the percentage of imitators is high, imitators will probably imitate behaviour from those who have already imitated from somebody else. When the chain of transmission between the original learner and the average imitator becomes longer, imitators will stand a higher chance of copying a behaviour that used to be adaptive in a long-passed environment but is now no longer adaptive. Furthermore, the long chain of copying tends to induce cumulative errors in the transmission chain. Consequently, imitated behaviour is less and less adapted, the higher the percentage of imitators in the population. The decline in fitness depends on the speed of environmental change.[2] In fairly stable environments, copying an old behaviour may still be quite appropriate. In a fast changing environment, that is not the case. When imitators' fitness declines below the fitness of learners, some imitators will notice this and switch back to learning. This will keep the population in an equilibrium composition of learners and imitators. Most importantly, Rogers (1988) finds that, in equilibrium, the fitness of imitators equals the fitness of learners. Hence, cultural transmission does not increase average fitness in a population and 'culture' does not constitute an advantage.

Boyd and Richerson (1995) do not dispute this finding. On the contrary, they confirm that Rogers' (1988) findings, even though they are based on a simple model, are robust. Adding more flexible assumptions, such as moving from diachronic to synchronic variation in environmental states (changing places rather than changes in time), increasing the number or range of environmental states, or allowing selective imitation by imitators (imitation of learners only, not of other imitators), does not change the conclusions. At best, these additions shift the equilibrium to the right in Figure 5.3 (allow for more imitators); they do not increase the average fitness of a population in equilibrium. On the other hand, an increase in the speed of environmental change reduces the percentage of imitators in a population, but again does not affect the average level of fitness in a mixed population of learners and imitators: equilibrium fitness will still be fixed at the level of fitness of learners. This leads Rogers (1988) to the very important conclusion that imitation – a communication device – does not increase the equilibrium amount of knowledge in society. It does not improve the quality of adaptation in the sense of higher fitness and ability to exploit the resources and opportunities available in the environment. Cultural transmission of knowledge is a communication device, not a knowledge or fitness-enhancing device. Culture does not enhance societal fitness.

This conclusion from Rogers (1988) is diametrically opposed to B&R's (1985) conclusion. It is hard to understand why nature would have produced 'culture' if it does not constitute an evolutionary advantage. Why, then, is culture such an omnipresent feature of human societies and what, if not culture, explains the success of human societies? Ten years after their seminal book, Boyd and Richerson tried to find a way out of Rogers' 'fitness trap'. They (1995: 129) note that 'social learning would improve the average fitness of a population if it increased the fitness of learners as well as imitators', and offer two possible routes out of this trap: selective learning and cumulative learning.

In the selective learning scenario, learners experiment with individual learning but only apply the behaviour they have learned if it yields a significantly higher expected return than other behaviours available through imitation. If a learned behaviour does not yield convincingly higher returns (but this implies that it is first tested by the learner, which is costly), it is discarded in favour of an imitated behaviour. This strategy reduces error margins on learning and hence increases the average fitness of learning. As learners become more selective, the fitness of available behaviours gradually increases and so does the fitness of imitation. It makes the learners' fitness curve in Fig 5.3 slope upwards to the right. However, even a supply of improved behaviours will not protect imitators against decay in their fitness. With increasing prevalence of imitators, there are less original learners to do a comparative returns test of their own learning, so that imitators' fitness declines as the speed of environmental change and the percentage of imitators increase. Boyd and Richerson (1995) show that, in this scenario, equilibrium population fitness is higher than in a population of individual learners only (with no imitation), provided that the environment is more likely to remain unchanged than to change – that is if the probability of change is less than 50 per cent. In short, the equilibrium composition of the population between learners and imitators depends on the probability of environmental change. In fairly stable and unchanging environments, selective individual learning may turn out to be a superior strategy and increase overall population fitness. In rapidly changing environments, that is not the case.

The second route out of the fitness trap is provided by cumulative learning: learners pass behaviours on to imitators who, in turn, improve on this behaviour through learning before passing it on further. Assume that the environment can be in a continuum of different states and that the occurrence of any of these states is subject to a random probability distribution. Individuals can retain their learning and pass it on to an imitator, who then starts from a better-than-random guess as initial behaviour. The imitator can then switch to learning and improve upon the inherited behaviour. This opens up possibilities for a continuous learning process whereby learners steadily improve their fitness. Still, with increasing numbers of imitators, their fitness declines relative to improved behaviours.

B&R (1995) conclude that culture – or mimetic transmission of behaviours – constitutes an evolutionary advantage under restrictive conditions only, when it makes learning less costly and/or more accurate. This can happen when social learning allows individuals to be more selective learners, and/or when learned improvements can accumulate across generations. In other words, the three layers of cost savings in mimetic transmission (cheaper and faster selection, cognitive economy) are necessary but not sufficient conditions to turn cultural transmission of knowledge into an evolutionary advantage. Cost savings should induce increases in total knowledge to achieve this.

I find B&R's (1995) response to Rogers' (1988) critique not very convincing, for several reasons. First, it brings us back to square one in the process of trying to understand the role of knowledge in evolutionary fitness: as people learn more, they become fitter. In that view, the accumulation of knowledge as such explains the evolution of the world. That is an almost trivial conclusion and analytically not very helpful. My hypothesis is that the evolution of human societies is not only characterised by a straightforward growth of knowledge but also by changes in the way in which societies are organised to handle that knowledge, in particular changes in the distribution of knowledge in society. We have already examined how the principle of cognitive economy could explain distributed knowledge inside the individual brain, and knowledge distributed between the brain and external representations. The B&R model opens the way to extend this principle to knowledge distributed between individuals in society – that is the road I will follow in the next two chapters. Second, people do not maximise knowledge and learning; they optimise learning. For people to learn more, there must be an incentive to do so,[3] and that incentive can only come from changes in the organisation of society. Third, the model collapses when the percentage of imitators approaches 100. It is not good at handling specialisation in a population, when only one, or just a few, individual learners produce behaviours that are copied by all others. In that sense, the model is not very good at explaining modern societies where very advanced specialisation is the rule rather than the exception. Fourth and most importantly, Rogers' (1988) model and B&R's (1995) reply generate more questions than answers: Why would learners learn? What is his or her incentive to do so and why not wait for somebody else to learn and then copy their behaviour? What do imitators do with spare cognitive capacity? And so on. In the following section, I will try to answer some of these questions.

Price, substitution and quantity effects

The fundamental driving force behind the B&R model is a price effect: the relative cost of individual learning versus imitation. The introduction of a cheap communication channel, such as imitation, constitutes a price effect that, in turn, triggers a substitution effect, away from costly individual learning and towards cheaper imitation. Economists know that the price-substitution reaction chain is not complete without a third effect, the quantity or income effect. That effect is missing in the B&R model, both in the 1985 and the 1995 version. I will argue in this section that this quantity effect comes in the form of increased total knowledge in society, induced by functional specialisation that results from the substitution effect.

   Let us take a closer look at the substitution process and try to interpret this in cognitive terms. People switch from individual learning to imitation as the relative cost of imitation decreases and up to the point where that relative cost advantage is cancelled by disadvantages in terms of lower fitness of imitated behaviours. Initially learned adaptations lose their fitness as time passes and as they are transmitted through ever-longer chains of individuals. If relative cost differences increase, or if the rate of environmental change decelerates, the percentage of imitators will increase. If relative cost differences narrow, or the rate of environmental change accelerates, the percentage of imitators will decline. In the extreme case, when the environment remains constant, one individual learner is enough; all others can imitate that knowledge. In a stable environment, there is no risk of the imitated behaviour becoming outdated. For a given non-zero rate of environmental change, the optimal number of learners and imitators is a function of the cost difference between learning and imitation, or between production and consumption of knowledge. The smaller the difference, the more learners-producers. Hence the price-driven substitution effect ensures that the number of individual learners (and thus the number of imitators) is endogenously determined.

The B&R model is ultimately a model of functional specialisation but not of knowledge specialisation. It distinguishes between learning (producers of knowledge) and imitation (consumers of knowledge) as different ways of acquiring knowledge, but that does not necessarily generate knowledge specialisation or distributed knowledge in society. With functional specialisation, specialists learn particular bits of knowledge and remain specialists as long as their knowledge is not spread throughout society by imitation. Imitation by others reduces their specialisation. Indeed, knowledge has to be fully transmitted in order for others to have access to that knowledge set. That transmission restores full symmetric and equal distribution of knowledge in society. The model in Figure 5.3 showed that there is always an equilibrium between learners and imitators, so that some non-zero degree of functional specialisation will occur. But if all learned knowledge is copied by imitators, the degree of knowledge distribution and specialisation in society will be zero: all agents will know the same things.

Functional specialisation raises another question: What do imitators do with their savings in learning costs or savings in cognitive capacity? Do they just sit idle or do they use this opportunity to acquire additional knowledge? B&R (1985; 1995) and Rogers (1988) do not consider the issue of limited cognitive capacity, and consequently do not elaborate on alternative uses of spare cognitive capacity either. Their models revolve around a single knowledge set (about the environment) that produces adaptation and fitness; there are no alternative knowledge sets to be acquired. Clearly, this is not a realistic picture. Let us therefore assume that alternative knowledge sets exist (in line with our assumption in Chapter 4 that knowledge is unlimited) and that a non-zero part of spare cognitive capacity is used for additional learning. This produces a positive quantity effect on individual knowledge:[4] for a given learning or information processing capacity, individuals will acquire more knowledge because some of it was already pre-processed by the person from whom it was imitated. As such, imitated knowledge requires less use of the learner's scarce information processing capacity. The sources of this quantity effect can only be understood in a cognitive interpretation of imitation: the regularities in environmental information inflows have already been extracted by learners and turned into behavioural routines; the imitator simply observes the behaviour and copies it into his or her memory. It also produces a quantity effect at the level of society. On average, learning will become less demanding in terms of individual information processing capacity, so that, for a given capacity, more can be learned. This translates into a higher total volume of knowledge available in society.

This completes the chain of reactions, started by the price and substitution effects, with a quantity effect: increased knowledge. We can now conclude that total knowledge in society is endogenously determined and a function of the degree of (learners-imitators) specialisation that, in turn, is a function of the relative cost of individual learning versus communicated knowledge.

Incentives to learn and to trade

The quantity effect is based on the assumption that individuals do indeed invest spare cognitive capacity in additional learning. But what are the incentives for individuals to do so? Without incentives, there is no obvious reason for individuals to invest in learning; everybody might just as well sit back and wait until somebody decides to learn something, so that they can imitate it at zero opportunity cost. In that case, the price (cost) effect would be compensated exactly by a substitution effect: as communication becomes cheaper, more individuals would sit back and enjoy their leisure rather than putting effort into additional learning. The quantity effect would be zero.

In the B&R model, imitators imitate behaviour at zero cost to themselves, but also at zero revenue to the person who initially learned and incurred costs to acquire a behaviour. Once they use their behaviour in a visible way, anybody can imitate it at virtually zero cost. No rational individual would choose to be a learner if it is cheaper to wait until somebody else's behaviour can be copied. Societies operating in accordance with the modalities of the B&R model have a severe collective action problem: free riding on the benefits of others' learning efforts would be rampant.[5]

This can only be overcome if individual learning improves the fitness of learners, above the level of fitness of imitators, so that learners have an incentive to invest in learning. In Figure 5.3, this can only be the case to the right of the equilibrium, a situation where rational imitators would not venture. This led Rogers (1988) and B&R (1995) to the conclusion that 'culture' (transmission of behaviours) does not increase overall fitness of a population, contrary to B&R's (1985) conclusion. To overcome this problem, a mechanism should be found that redistributes the costs of learning from learners to imitators. For instance if the learner can charge the imitator and recuperate her costs, or even make a profit. This requires an economic exchange mechanism: the imitator (partially) compensates the learner for her opportunity costs of learning. It would also reduce the fitness of imitators, who now face a positive cost, rather than the zero cost of imitation in the B&R model. In terms of Figure 5.3, the learners' fitness line shifts upward and the imitators' downward. The equilibrium between learners and imitators (where fitness of imitators equals fitness of learners) would shift to the left, with fewer imitators and more learners because the cost differential would be reduced, for a given rate of change in the environment, and thus with a higher degree of functional specialisation and more knowledge in society. At the same time, that equilibrium would achieve higher overall fitness for both learners and imitators.

This leads us to some very important conclusions. First, whereas pure 'cultural' transmission of learning (in the B&R sense of 'imitation') does not constitute an evolutionary advantage, as proved by Rogers (1988), 'economic' transmission (i.e. transmission of knowledge combined with compensation of the learner, through trade or exchange) does. Second, because it enhances functional specialisation compared to a pure cultural transmission situation, economic exchange of knowledge increases the overall volume of knowledge available in society. Hence economic exchange is evolutionary superior to cultural exchange of knowledge.

All this rests on the assumption that, in a society where knowledge can be transmitted through imitation only,[6] that knowledge can indeed be the subject of economic exchange. The principle of cognitive economy must apply: learners incur cognitive opportunity costs in order to compress environmental information inflows and extract regularities (knowledge) from that flow. Comparative advantage between potential trading parties exists, since different learners can hold different knowledge sets. However, knowledge is a non-excludable public good: as soon as a learner applies his knowledge in behaviour, others can imitate it at zero cost. In order to turn this functional specialisation between learners and imitators into real knowledge specialisation, knowledge must be made excludable. This requires the existence of enforceable property rights. How that condition can be satisfied is the subject of Part III of this book. In imitation-based societies, individuals will not consciously invest in learning because there is no mechanism that allows them to recuperate their learning costs. Without enforceable intellectual property rights, learning will be purely random and accidental, and limited to situations where knowledge can be increased at zero opportunity cost. Consequently, the rate of knowledge accumulation will be very slow in imitation-based societies. Clearly, in modern human societies, learning is much more directed: what has caused this change?

Alternative channels of knowledge transmission

In this section I add another knowledge communication channel, symbolic communication, already referred to in Chapter 4, and examine its impact. Symbols provide a more efficient communication channel because they compress complex information into an informationally less complex (set of) symbolic signifier(s). While this narrows the communication channel itself, it still makes extensive use of scarce information processing capacity in the minds of emitter and recipient: knowledge needs to be compressed into symbols by the emitter and decompressed by the recipient.

Figure 5.4 presents a comparative flow diagram of the different cognitive steps involved in learning, transmission of knowledge and the use of

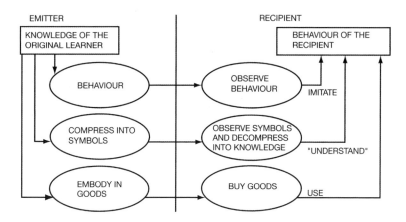

Figure 5.4 Alternative knowledge transmission channels

knowledge in behaviour, both for imitation and symbolic transmission. As explained in Chapter 4, learning requires extraction of regularities from an information flow and results in knowledge, a compressed and more complex (in the information theoretic sense) form of information storage. This first compression is the essence of knowledge accumulation. In a second stage, the bearer of that knowledge may transmit it to others, either via imitation or through symbolic communication.

Transmission through imitation involves no further compression of knowledge. The recipient simply observes the learner's behaviour and copies it. As explained before, this form of transmission is effective only if observable behaviour fully coincides with the underlying knowledge (the WYSIWYG hypothesis). Knowledge cannot be fully transmitted through imitation when the learner engages in further information processing during behaviour, because that processing is unobservable to the recipient. As such, imitation is feasible only for the transmission of relatively simple knowledge. Also, imitation requires that the learner and imitator fully share an environment in which the observed behaviour is useful. I may observe and even try to imitate tribal dancing in Papua New Guinea; it is totally dysfunctional in my European environment (unless I am a member of a tribal dancing club). The main advantage of imitation is that it gener-ates cognitive economy: the recipient saves cognitive opportunity costs related to the first stage of information compression. We explained above that this relative cost effect also generates a substitution and a quantity effect. The latter is an individual quantity effect, caused by substitution between learning and imitation. It does not cause a quantity effect at the level of society, however, because individuals simply copy knowledge that is already available in society, carried by others.

The quantity effect at the level of society depends on excludability and thus tradability of knowledge. If learners can be compensated for their learning costs, their fitness curve (Figure 5.3) will move up, so that the equilibrium number of learners in society increases, and more will be learned. Spare cognitive capacity induced by imitation will not be used exclusively for more imitation but some of it will be invested in more learning, thereby increasing total knowledge in society, up to the point where full employment of all cognitive capacities is achieved. Once that full capacity point is reached, however, imitation society is stuck and cannot further increase its total knowledge.

Symbolic transmission of knowledge involves more cognitive processing by the learner than in the case of imitation. It requires a second stage of compression of knowledge into symbolic carriers, so that an informationally more efficient signifier can replace the signified. This generates additional cognitive economy, the possibility of external storage and processing, and easier communication of informationally complex sets. It also relaxes the requirements for shared knowledge between the emitter and the recipient. While imitation requires a fully shared environment, symbolic communication requires a fully shared set of symbols only. I may not share an environment with a member of a tribe in Papua New Guinea but I may share with him an understanding of English, a symbolic language, which allows us to communicate and transmit more complex knowledge than through imitation. On the other hand, the recipient needs to unzip or decompress the received symbol set into a full knowledge set again: the signifier has to be associated again with the correct categorisations and attributes in the mind of the recipient. This decompression takes cognitive processing time and thus entails a cognitive opportunity cost, contrary to imitation where there is no decompression evolved.

Because of the compression/decompression requirement, symbolic transmission may, at first sight, appear to be less efficient than imitation. However, that conclusion is not warranted, for several reasons. First, it allows transmission of more complex knowledge sets between agents operating in very different environments, especially knowledge sets that are not fully observable to an imitator so that the WYSIWYG condition is not necessarily fully satisfied. Second, the first and second stage in compression may to a large extent coincide when the learner acquires his knowledge of the environment directly in symbolic format. In that case, symbolic compression does not constitute (much of) an additional opportunity cost. However, the final informational economy achieved is uncertain and depends on the circumstances. When I want to show somebody how to slice bread, there is no point in writing a manual and asking the other to read it (a symbolic communication device) or even in using many words to explain the process (another symbolic device); the simplest solution is to show it and for the other to imitate my behaviour. For more complex operations, such as car repair, manuals and other symbolic devices (language) may be more appropriate, however. Symbolic society can move a step further because it can go where imitation is useless: where behaviour is not identical with knowledge, or where knowledge becomes so complex that it is hard to transmit through imitation.

More importantly however, symbolic and imitation-based communication channels share a disadvantage: the set of relevant knowledge needs to be transmitted from the brain of the original learner to the brain of the recipient in order to make it useful to the latter. 'Relevant knowledge' means the knowledge that allows the recipient to undertake the necessary behavioural action to respond to a challenge or exploit an opportunity. For instance, a medical doctor may explain to a patient how to treat a disease: he needs to communicate all relevant knowledge about the treatment ('how to treat a wound') either through example and imitation or through symbolic communication via language. There is no need for the doctor to transfer his underlying knowledge about the causes and mechanisms of disease and why a particular treatment is adequate. The underlying knowledge may be important to identify the correct treatment, but not necessary in order to carry it out. The doctor has accumulated that knowledge during his own learning phase (the primary compression phase in Figure 5.4). Thus the doctor still retains a comparative advantage and specialisation in knowledge about the disease, even after he has communicated his knowledge about treatment to the patient.

Still, transmission of relevant knowledge from one brain to the other implies a reduction in specialisation every time a transfer is carried out: the original learner and recipient share that knowledge after the transfer. Consequently, knowledge specialisation is negatively affected by communication in societies that rely only on imitation or symbolic transmission to transfer knowledge. These societies benefit from savings in learning costs and cognitive economy associated with communicated knowledge as such (the savings in primary compression costs in Figure 5.4). But they benefit less from increased knowledge absorption capacity through specialisation.

If potential users of knowledge did not have to acquire the relevant knowledge in their own brains, this would constitute a saving of scarce cognitive capacity to learn and accumulate other pieces of knowledge that are not held by others. In that case, specialisation would not be negatively affected by communication of knowledge to potential users. The only way to solve this problem is to transfer knowledge in materially embodied forms that can directly produce the desired behavioural response, without that knowledge having to be absorbed by the brain of the recipient. The next chapter will show that this is what economic systems are all about: communication of embodied knowledge, through production and trade, whereby only a partial knowledge transfer is required in order to benefit from the full set of relevant knowledge. Production and trade give rise to the emergence of economic society.

6   The economy as a knowledge communication system

In the previous chapter, I introduced a new source of knowledge, next to individual learning: knowledge communicated through imitation and symbolic communication. I showed how the ability to communicate produces functional specialisation between individual learners and social communicators. The relative costs and benefits of learning versus communicated knowledge determine an equilibrium between the two. The original learner spends part of his scarce cognitive capacity on learning, extracting knowledge out of a stream of information, but the person who receives this knowledge through communication economises on the opportunity cost of that learning effort. As long as communicated knowledge is cheaper than individual learning, it induces cognitive economy in the use of the inherently limited cognitive capacity of human beings. That results in a quantity effect on knowledge: more knowledge can be acquired in a given time period and for a given processing capacity. The more society makes use of communicated knowledge, the stronger this knowledge multiplier effect will be, both at individual and societal level. But I also identified a major drawback of imitation and symbolic communication: they require the transfer of knowledge from an emitter to a recipient. Consequently, communicated knowledge reduces the asymmetric distribution of knowledge or specialisation among individuals.

The present chapter explores another knowledge communication channel that overcomes this constraint: communication of embodied knowledge. In everyday language, this channel is called production and trade, or simply an economic system: people embody their knowledge in a good or service, and trade this for other goods and services. The main advantage of transmission of materially embodied knowledge is that it does not require full acquisition of the entire knowledge set by the recipient – in contrast to imitation and symbolic knowledge communication. The learner and recipient share a cognitive interface only. This limited overlap of knowledge sets may comprise only a fraction of the entire transferred knowledge, just enough for the recipient (consumer) to understand the relevant properties of the product or service that the producer delivers to him. Because of this interface-only requirement, knowledge transmission through production and trade is a 'truncated' knowledge communication channel. This property makes production and trade a very efficient form of knowledge communication. While disembodied (symbolic) knowledge transfers induce an individual knowledge quantity effect because of savings in learning costs, transfers of embodied knowledge (through trade) induce a much stronger quantity effect at the level of society via specialisation: the volume of knowledge available in society increases with the number of individuals and their degree of specialisation. Because of this, trade-based societies have an evolutionary advantage over purely communication-based societies.

The analysis in this chapter vindicates Loasby's (1999) conjecture that economic systems are a way of organising human knowledge so that it can deal more efficiently with its inherent incompleteness. As such, economic systems are a continuation of the evolutionary drive towards ever more cognitive economy and knowledge accumulation, as a proxy for evolutionary fitness. Furthermore, I will seek to demonstrate in this chapter that, for this knowledge transfer channel to work properly, a set of 'institutions' needs to be in place to deal with the side-effects of truncated communication: transaction costs and residual uncertainty. Indeed, as Loasby pointed out, the fact that we have to live with inherently incomplete knowledge entails that we need to live with inherent uncertainty as well, not only with respect to our natural environment but also, as far as exchange is concerned, with respect to our dealings with others. The role of institutions is precisely to reduce or mitigate that uncertainty, and thereby allow us to achieve a reasonable degree of cognitive closure and certainty about the consequences of our choices. Cognitive closure carries a price, however, in the form of transaction costs. The role of these costs in specialisation is discussed in detail in this chapter, and a brief literature review on this subject is presented. A more detailed discussion of the nature and emergence of institutions is left for Part III of this book.

Production and trade as a knowledge transmission channel

As explained in Chapter 4, acquiring knowledge through learning consists of processing of raw information emitted by the material environment and detected by the sensory organs, in order to extract regularities from that information and use it for behavioural purposes (i.e. to modify the material environment). Acquiring knowledge through imitation constitutes a cognitive economy – in comparison to learning – because it shortcuts part of this process: it only requires observation (through the sensory organs) and the copying of behaviour of other individuals, who have already processed environmental information into knowledge. Acquisition of knowledge through symbolic communication still involves use of the sensory organs, but the detected symbolic information now signifies something else and needs to be decoded before it can be used for behavioural purposes.

One can imagine a more drastic way of achieving cognitive economy by shortcutting these transmission modalities altogether and delivering directly the behavioural routines to modify the material environment, or even delivering the modified material environment itself, to the 'consumer', without passing through successive phases of compression and decompression of information. Such a shortcut actually exists and we employ it on a massive scale in modern societies. It is called production and trade. In Boulding's (1966) words, behaviour means 'printing' knowledge onto a material environment, with the intention of producing a new state of that environment. When the product of that 'printing' process is a discrete good or service that can be exchanged, trade is feasible.

For instance, to produce a PC implies that people imprint their knowledge of silicon wafers, electronics, computer operating systems, management of the entire process, onto material products (metal, plastics, silicon, other components) and deliver the final product (a PC) to the consumer. The consumer has no need to acquire all that knowledge to enjoy the final product. That PC will modify the consumer's behaviour and make her respond differently to her material environment. Similarly, when something goes wrong with my PC, I can call a service technician, who will repair it. She delivers her computer knowledge directly in the form of repair behaviour. There is no need for me to imitate or acquire all that knowledge myself. Or the service technician can deliver a simple tool, for instance a virus detection and elimination software package that allows me to get rid of the problem without going through complex learning processes. All these goods and services are forms of embodied knowledge. Such transfers are more efficient than other forms of knowledge communication, such as imitation and symbolic communication, because they keep most of the transferred knowledge outside my brain and embodied in an external device, a good – or in somebody else's brain in the case of a service – thereby avoiding the opportunity costs of cognitive processing in my own brain. In case of imitated and symbolically transferred knowledge, I still have to transfer a lot of knowledge from somebody else's into my own brain, before I can use it for my own purposes.

While production and trade may seem self-evident to modern man, it is not so self-evident in nature. It requires a skill that is rare in nature: the ability to embody knowledge in a material and transferable product that can modify the material environment. Some animals have the ability to produce a very limited range of products: bees construct honeycombs, beavers build dams, birds build nests, some monkeys can use stones to crack nuts and sticks to catch ants. But the range of production skills of most of these animals is very limited. Furthermore, these products are usually not transferable. Birds do not operate real estate agencies that trade nests. Beavers do not sell dams. Monkeys that are good at finding appropriately shaped stones for cracking nuts have not been observed to trade these stones for other products.

The ability to produce a wider range of products is a key step in hominid development. Donald (1991) explains how it took more than two million years after the emergence of early hominids before the use of stone tools, weapons and other utensils became more widespread in human societies, around 30–40 thousand years ago. He associates this change with the transition from mimetic to symbolic culture and the emergence of language that enabled the construction of longer narratives, storytelling and the elaboration of causal relationships. Indeed, it would be difficult to discover what came first: symbolic communication skills or production skills. They probably evolved jointly, since symbolic communication also uses humanly produced materials as intermediaries: drawings, paintings, woodcarvings, clay tablets, etc.

Apart from the cognitive ability to embody knowledge in a material good, on the producer's side, trading knowledge also requires the ability to use that knowledge on the recipient's side. This is where a crucial cognitive characteristic of communication of embodied knowledge enters into the equation. Contrary to symbolic communication systems, there is no need for the recipient to extract all the knowledge embodied in a good in order to use that knowledge. He only needs to understand a small part of that knowledge, an interface, just large enough to enable him to understand some essential features of the good. As a result, communication of knowledge embodied in goods requires the exchange of a truncated knowledge set only: only a subset of the total embodied knowledge is sufficient to create an interface between producers and users that enables the latter to use all the knowledge incorporated in the good.

For instance, we buy and use computers without knowing the full details of microchip production and software design; we can drive a car without knowing how the engine works, and so forth. This is because goods are designed in such a way that we only need to understand a small fraction (interface) of the complete knowledge embodied in the products in order to understand their operational use. The smaller the required interface, or the more it corresponds to generally available knowledge, the easier it is to trade a good. Typically, early versions of completely 'new' products require large interfaces and substantial learning costs for the consumers. In order to drive the first cars, you had to be almost an engineer. To use the first PCs, you needed to have considerable knowledge of computer programming. Modern PC/user interfaces are often literally child's play.[1]

It is precisely this truncated communication characteristic of production and exchange (trade) of knowledge embodied in goods that makes it such an efficient channel to communicate knowledge. This cognitive characteristic has put economic systems in the forefront of cognitive evolution. It has given a cognitive-evolutionary advantage to societies that have managed to exploit these characteristics in an efficient way. Von Weizsäcker (1991) noted that there would be no point in trading goods that require complete understanding of all the incorporated knowledge in order to use them. In that case, we could as well exchange the entire knowledge set pertaining to a particular good – as is done in imitation and in symbolic transmission of knowledge – and the buyer could produce the good himself. We would all have to become doctors to benefit from the knowledge of medical sciences or engineers to build our own cars and computers. There would be no gains from trade in terms of reduced opportunity costs of scarce cognitive processing capacity, since all agents who wanted to use a particular good would have to go through the complete production learning process in order to be able to use it. There would be no specialisation any more, but only fully symmetrically distributed knowledge among all users of a particular good in society.

In order to understand the impact of truncation[2] at the level of society (and not only at the level of individuals), we need to make a distinction between the total knowledge available in society and the way in which society makes that knowledge available to individuals. In the case of imitation and symbolic transmission, knowledge available in the mind of the emitter is fully transferred to the recipient: the recipient needs to copy (through imitation) or reconstruct (through decompression) the entire knowledge set in her own mind. In the case of embodied knowledge transfers, the recipient needs a partial knowledge interface only in her mind, just enough to be able to interact with the product or service that embodies that knowledge. As such, transmission of materially embodied knowledge is the only one of these three knowledge transmission channels that generates substantial savings in the use of scarce cognitive capacity. This, in turn, facilitates the emergence of specialisation (asymmetrically distributed knowledge) in society and thereby induces a quantity effect on available knowledge in society.

The cognitive mechanics of specialisation

To see how the cognitive mechanics of truncated knowledge communication work, including the resulting specialisation and knowledge quantity effect, I develop in this section a measure of specialisation. It builds on the more rigorous description of knowledge in Chapter 4, rooted in a connectionist network approach to cognition. There, I explained how an upper limit on information processing capacity defines a choice in the composition of knowledge between two characteristics: accuracy and variety. The 'volume' of total knowledge was defined as $v(H)$, the product of variety and accuracy or $v(H) = I\,d(H)$. Volume can expand both by increasing variety (the number of subgraphs I in a knowledge graph) and by increasing accuracy (the density of links $d(H)$ between nodes in a subgraph), subject of course to the information capacity constraint. The optimal allocation between accuracy and variety is the point where total resource mobilisation for the agent is maximised, or uncertainty about his environment minimised, as shown in Figure 4.1.

We can now define $I/d(H)$ as a measure of specialisation in the knowledge of an individual agent. Agents who are specialised have a relatively low value for I and a high value for $d(H)$. Their knowledge set covers a relatively narrow domain of variety (fewer nodes) but with a highly accurate or dense network of linkages between these nodes. The reverse is true for non-specialised generalists. This definition of individual specialisation will be helpful in the next section, when we examine how an agent responds to a move from individual cognitive autarky to an environment with communication and exchange of knowledge sets between agents.

The next step is to move from the composition and characteristics of individual knowledge sets to those of knowledge in a group of agents.

Consider a group of n cognitive agents with limited information processing capacity. Without specialisation, knowledge graphs have identical contents among all agents, $\forall i,j \in [0,n]$: $H_i = H_j$ for $i \neq j$. In that case, the total knowledge set available in the group (H_T) will not exceed the knowledge of a single individual, that is $v(H_T) = v(H_i)$. This means that the intersection of all individual knowledge graphs equals their union, or $\forall i$: $\cap_i H_i = \cup_i H_i$. With specialisation, differentiation will emerge among individual knowledge graphs: knowledge will not be fully shared. As a result, the intersection will only be a subgraph of the union: $\cap_i H_i \subset \cup_i H_i$. With complete specialisation, that subgraph will be empty because no agent's knowledge would overlap with any other agent's: $\forall i,j$ with $i \neq j$: $H_i \cap H_j = \emptyset$. In that case, $v(H_T) = n\, v(H_i)$. Total knowledge in the group can thus vary between two extremes, $v(H)$ and $n\, v(H)$, depending on the degree of specialisation in a group.

Before we can proceed with the formulation of a measure of specialisation, we must clarify what it means when knowledge graphs are identical or when they have a non-empty intersection. This is done by means of the graph theory concept of *isomorphism* (Harary 1969: 10). Two knowledge graphs H and G are isomorphic, i.e. $H = G$, if there exists a one-to-one correspondence between their nodes which preserves adjacency of these nodes. Two nodes are *adjacent* if they are connected by a line. A typical property of isomorphic graphs is that they are *invariant*, or have the same values for density, variety and accuracy. From isomorphism it is but a small step to the intersection of two knowledge graphs: the intersection of H and G is the largest possible subgraph that is isomorphic in H and G. Using the concept of isomorphism to define overlapping knowledge between individuals, implicitly assumes that similar knowledge in the brains of different individuals is necessarily based on similar neuronal connection patterns. This is somewhat of a heroic assumption. In practice, neuronal connection patterns for a similar knowledge package are likely to differ between two individuals. In a theoretical setting based on artificial neuronal networks, however, that assumption is acceptable.

We can now take a closer look at the interpretation of the intersection of knowledge sets, or common knowledge held by a *group* of agents. As long as group size does not exceed 2 agents, there is no risk of confusion: the intersection is a subset that contains all neuronal connection patterns that the two have in common. When n > 2 however, neuronal patterns may be shared between two or between more agents. If we limit the inter-section to the patterns held in common between all agents in the group, the definition of common knowledge becomes very restrictive. It would actually underestimate the degree of commonality in knowledge sets: some knowledge may be held in common by some but not by all agents in a group. Is a piece of knowledge that is held in common between 10 million out of a population of 11 million people a common set or not? According to the restrictive definition it is not. Clearly, that is not a useful way to define common knowledge.

A more appropriate definition of common knowledge would make allowance for the degree of commonality of knowledge graphs. Consider the graph of all knowledge $H_T = \cup \; _iH_i$ held by a group of n agents. Assume that H_T contains m subgraphs (G_m) of knowledge, identified through a λ connectivity criterion such that $\forall i \neq j \in [0,m]: G_i \cap G_j \neq \emptyset$. Each subgraph $G_m \subset H_T$ can now be weighted by the number of agents in the group who hold this subgraph: n_m/n, where n_m is the number of agents for whom $G_m \subset H_i$ and m is the total number of subsets G_m. In the extreme case of purely individual knowledge, $n_m = 1$: only one person has it. In reality, even the most expert knowledge will be shared by at least a few individuals. Fully common knowledge would imply that $n_m = n$. The degree of commonality of knowledge held by a group of agents is the average value of that measure, taken over all subsets of knowledge in that group. Finally, to define the degree of specialisation (S), it is sufficient to take the mirror image of the degree of commonality of knowledge

$$S = 1 - [(\Sigma_{j:1 \to m} (n_m/n)] \, /m$$

S measures average knowledge specialisation in a group of agents. It has the following properties. If all knowledge is fully shared in the group, that is if $\forall j \in [0,m]: n_j/n = 1$, then S = 0. If all subgraphs of knowledge are held by one individual only, that is if $\forall j \in [0,m]: n_j/n = 1/n$, then S→1 for n→∞. How close S approaches 1 thus depends on group size.

As a last step, we can examine now the link between specialisation, the volume of knowledge v(H) and the number of agents n in a society. For a given (and hypothetical) upper limit on the volume of knowledge that can be held by an individual, v*(H), and assuming that this upper limit applies equally to all individuals in a group, the upper limit on the total volume of knowledge in that group depends on group size as well as the degree of specialisation:

$$v(H) = (1 + (n-1) \, S) \, v^*(H)$$

When all individuals are fully specialised (S=1, no isomorphic subgraphs in the group), then total group knowledge $v(H) = n\,v^*(H)$. However, since the upper limit on S itself depends on n, this extreme case can only be reached for large n. If all knowledge is isomorphic between individuals, so that S=0, then $v(H) = v^*(H)$.

Clearly, the fact that production and trade allows for the exchange of truncated knowledge sets, and thereby for the emergence of specialisation, has a strong leverage effect on total knowledge in society. Thus society as a whole gains from specialisation: it increases total knowledge and thereby enhances the survival probability for the group as a whole. This has been known in the literature for some time now as an argument in favour of specialisation. It was mentioned, for instance, by Arrow (1977)[3] and Yang and Ng (1993). Adam Smith does not mention this cognitive advantage of the division of labour among the three that he enumerates (increased 'dexterity',[4] time savings and mechanisation).

Specialisation and transaction costs

Chapter 5 and the preceding sections in the present chapter showed that specialisation can have a strong leverage effect on total knowledge available in society as a whole. That stock of knowledge can only be made available to all members of the group if a communication channel exists. As explained in Chapter 5, imitation and symbolic systems allow communication of knowledge between individuals, though they are not very efficient. For one thing, imitation and symbolic communication reduce specialisation because they transmit knowledge from the emitter to the recipient, thereby erasing any specialisation between the two (with respect to the transferred knowledge). By contrast, production (embodiment of knowledge in a good) and trade are more efficient. Economic exchange does not erase specialisation because knowledge is not transferred from the producer's to the consumer's mind: it remains embodied in a good only. Besides, specialisation is necessary in order to conclude a gainful trade between two individual agents. There has to be a comparative advantage in order to conclude a deal whereby both parties gain. If both are specialised in different skill sets, that may be a source of comparative advantage.

Adam Smith already wrote in praise of specialisation and division of labour more than two centuries ago, but he failed to see a number of problems associated with specialisation. Whatever the beneficial effect of specialisation at group level, it is not self-evident for individuals, at least not from a cognitive point of view. Specialisation implies that cognitive agents reduce the variety in their knowledge and improve accuracy in a more limited domain of variety, thereby reducing the possibility of knowledge overlaps with other agents. In Chapter 4 (Figure 4.1) we concluded, however, that given the existence of a constraint on individual cognitive capacity, the optimal composition of an individual knowledge set consisted of a combination of variety and accuracy in knowledge. Specialisation moves an individual away from this optimal composition towards a less favourable set, with reduced variety and increased accuracy. In terms of Figure 4.1, this move increases uncertainty and decreases the probability that an individual can give an appropriate behavioural response to events in an uncertain environment.

Although this is apparently a beneficial move at group level, why would an individual do such a thing and move into such an unfavourable position? What is the incentive for individuals to switch from cognitive autarky (as in Figure 4.1) to specialisation? What compensation does he get for this unfavourable move? More generally, how do specialised, knowledge-intensive and learning-oriented societies emerge from knowledge-poor societies with a low degree of specialisation? People will not continue to learn and build up specialised knowledge simply because they have the cognitive capacity to do so; they also need incentives to do so. The purpose of this section is to examine the incentives, as well as the disincentives, and link these to some conclusions regarding the equilibrium degree of specialisation.

The previous chapter concluded with the observation that, in societies that rely on imitation as a means to communicate knowledge, there are no incentives for individuals to invest in learning; free riding on knowledge acquired by others is more advantageous. As a result, imitation-based societies get stuck in a low-knowledge equilibrium where learning is accidental and random only. This argument can easily be extended to symbolic communication: there is no incentive to invest in learning either, though there is an incentive to invest in the shared symbol set that enables communication and thus access to the entire available (and symbolically codified) knowledge set. Does communication of embodied knowledge provide an incentive to invest in learning? To answer that question, we need to examine the cognitive mechanics of trade.

The equilibrium composition of knowledge (accuracy versus variety) for an individual living in cognitive autarky, as explained in Figure 4.1, is reproduced in Figure 6.1. That equilibrium composition is affected in several ways when a knowledge communication channel is brought into the picture – in this case economic exchange through production and trade of truncated knowledge sets, embodied in goods and services.

When, a single agent moves from cognitive autarky to operating in a group, total knowledge *available* to that agent increases from max H (the upper bound on individual knowledge capacity) to H_T (total group knowledge). As explained above, H_T is a function of the degree of specialisation in the group of agents (see previous section). With $S = 0$, $H_i = H_T$. With $S \rightarrow 1$, H_T increases to $(1+(n-1)S) H_i$. However, HT is not necessarily *accessible* for an individual agent because his information processing capacity is limited to max H: he can never absorb H_T in his own brain.

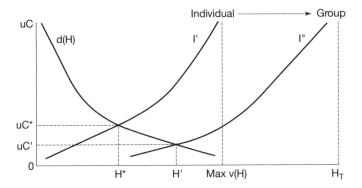

Figure 6.1 From cognitive autarky to trade: the advantages of specialisation and exchange of embodied knowledge

The only way to overcome that constraint is to make H_T available in truncated format, through exchange of embodied knowledge. On the other hand, exchange is a two-way process: the receiving party has to give something in return to make it worthwhile for the producer to part with the embodied knowledge. To make exchange worthwhile, it has to produce gains for both parties. That can only be achieved if the parties involved in the exchange have a tradable comparative advantage: the accuracy of their specialised knowledge.

From the point of view of Figure 4.1, a move towards specialisation is not advantageous. It reduces variety and increases accuracy in a knowledge set, but also increases uncertainty and thus diminishes an individual's ability to respond adequately to events in an uncertain environment. It can be made advantageous, however, if it is combined with open access to all knowledge available in the group. That compensates for the loss in individual cognitive variety and may actually reduce uncertainty. At the same time, the move towards enhanced accuracy in individual knowledge implies a strengthening of comparative advantage: one agent has 'better' (more accurate) knowledge about a limited domain than other agents. So that combines the advantages of specialisation and at the same time solves the problem of having something to trade for. This move is shown in Figure 6.1.

The individual agent reduces the variety in his own knowledge set and increases accuracy in the remaining limited variety, by concentrating his limited cognitive capacity on establishing a tradable comparative advantage. This move is made possible because he has access to total knowledge available in the group, H_T, which covers a much larger range of variety than he could possible learn on his own. Consequently, his cognitive equilibrium position moves to the right, from H^* (in autarky) to H' (in trade) and his uncertainty is reduced accordingly from uC' to uC'. This is situated below the original uncertainty level in cognitive autarky because his available knowledge set now includes both more accuracy (his own knowledge) and more variety (supplied by others). The agent is now in a better position to face events in an uncertain environment and respond appropriately to these events.

Specialisation thus represents an evolutionary advantage, for individuals as well as for society as a whole. Contrary to imitation and symbolic knowledge communication, trade provides an incentive to specialise and acquire more specialised knowledge through learning. Trade makes an agent better off in terms of his capacity to respond to the challenges and opportunities of his environment. However, it makes him better off if and only if the increase in uncertainty due to his specialisation is more than compensated by the decrease in uncertainty resulting from his access to a wider variety. This condition is not necessarily satisfied. The degree of specialisation in a group may be insufficient to trigger a significant southeastward move of the group's H^{var} curve, insufficient to compensate the increase in uncertainty induced by the change in composition of individual knowledge (more accuracy, less variety).

Individuals cannot pursue extreme specialisation, though. They cannot maximise accuracy in a single subset of knowledge at the expense of variety in all other knowledge. They need to have an acceptable degree of overlapping knowledge sets with other agents, in order to keep communication channels open. Truncated knowledge exchange can only work in the presence of an appropriate interface that enables communication between agents with different knowledge sets. The larger the required common interface, the more it reduces the extent of specialised (accurate) individual knowledge. The common interface takes up scarce information processing capacity but has no tradable value, since it is common and shared between all individuals in society; there is no comparative advantage in that interface. It prevents the specialisation index S from moving to the maximum value of 1.

Common knowledge could be considered as a necessary and unavoidable cognitive opportunity cost that is required to enable trade. New Institutional Economists, such as Coase (1937), Williamson (1985) and North (1990) have another name for this shared knowledge interface: transaction costs. Transaction costs are the opportunity costs of searching for the knowledge set that you need to complete an exchange, the learning costs to acquire a sufficient degree of understanding of the goods you intend to buy, the opportunity costs of negotiating the terms of exchange and monitoring the implementation of the exchange after the deal has been concluded. These are all opportunity costs related to the establishment of a common interface of knowledge between trading parties.[5]

The size of the common knowledge interface thus holds the key to the degree of specialisation and to the gains from trade in general. The next question to be answered is how much scarce information capacity an individual agent will devote to this common interface, or to de-specialisation. How much of this scarce cognitive capacity is he going to spend on transaction costs to realise an exchange of embodied knowledge?

Secondary uncertainty, transaction costs and institutions

In order to answer this question, we first need to understand how trade in truncated knowledge sets introduces a new source of uncertainty, or secondary uncertainty[6] (Beck 1986). While knowledge was meant precisely to reduce uncertainties related to events in the material environment, the exchange of truncated knowledge introduces a new source of uncertainty, on top of the first: uncertainty created by the exchange of knowledge itself. Because the buyer has partial knowledge only of the goods and services involved in the transaction, he never knows exactly what he buys. A transaction involves the transfer of some *known* technical qualities and quantities – known to both parties through their common knowledge interface – as well as some *unknown* residual uncertainties, only some of which may be foreseen in the transaction agreement (for instance, through a guarantee). In fact, the buyer is unlikely to want to know the exact contents, since that would involve a substantial investment of his scarce information processing time in learning about the details of the production process. The opportunity cost of this investment is called (realised) transaction costs:[7] the cognitive cost of establishing a common knowledge interface with the producer or seller. Because of scarce cognitive capacity, that would also reduce his ability to build up his own specialised knowledge. Achieving full knowledge of the traded good would completely erode the comparative advantage of the seller, and there would no longer be any point in doing the transaction: the buyer might as well produce the good or service himself.[8] Consequently, agents face a trade-off between the proportion of their scarce information processing capacity that they invest in the common knowledge interface (or realised *ex-ante* transaction costs) and the residual (secondary) uncertainty they are willing to accept in a transaction (or unrealised but potential *ex-post* transaction costs).

This trade-off is presented in Figure 6.2. The shape of the trade-off is hyperbolic as it tends towards infinity for both variables in the extreme positions: zero uncertainty comes at an infinitely high transaction cost while zero transaction costs result in complete uncertainty. The hyperbolic shape suggests diminishing returns, with $duC/dTRSC < 0$ and $d^2uC/d^2TRSC < 0$. The level of the trade-off curve is determined by the institutional environment within which the exchange takes place. An improvement in institutions is defined as a change in the contractual architecture of an exchange that reduces uC for a given level of TRSC or, alternatively, reduces TRSC for a given level of uC.

A definition and detailed discussion of institutions is left for Chapter 8.

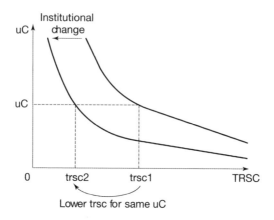

Figure 6.2 The trade-off between residual uncertainty and transaction costs

It suffices here to give a functional explanation of what institutions do. Institutions are humanly designed constraints on human behaviour (North 1990). They do not refer to natural or physical constraints on human behaviour, but to constraints that humans impose on themselves and on each other, through custom, contract or coercion. Institutions reduce the range of behavioural options for an individual. They determine what individuals are allowed and not allowed to do, the limits to their rights and the extent of their obligations. They impose constraints on behaviour and thereby provide a (partial) solution to the cognitive problem of uncertainty (Loasby 1999). For instance, institutions regulate the issue of warranty: if a good does not live up to the announced technical standards or does not operate as intended, the customer may return it to the producer or vendor. Also, if it should break down within the warranty period, the producer pays for the repairs. As such, institutions regulate the allocation of costs and benefits that may occur as a result of secondary uncertainty, events that occur *ex-post* of the transaction. This way, they mitigate that uncertainty.

In the absence of institutions, it would be difficult to engage two specialised agents in a mutual exchange of their goods.[9] Secondary uncertainty about the nature of these goods and the *ex-post* behaviour of the trading partners might be so high that it exceeds the extent of primary uncertainty reduction that these goods are supposed to achieve. Only for the simplest goods and services that can be fully inspected and understood by the buyer at low transaction costs, and without *ex-post* uncertainties, would exchange be feasible. Institutional innovation consists of finding a new institutional architecture that reduces *ex-post* residual or secondary uncertainty, for the same level of *ex-ante* transaction costs (or alternatively: achieves the same level of *ex-post* residual uncertainty for a lower level of *ex-ante* transaction costs).

Institutions are thus another expression of the principle of cognitive economy. They allow agents to save on their scarce cognitive capacity and avoid investing it in transaction costs, by mitigating and regulating certain sources and types of uncertainty in a collective manner.

We can now combine Figures 6.1 and 6.2 in a single diagram, Figure 6.3. Since the common knowledge interface never resolves all residual uncertainty, truncated exchange adds a new layer of uncertainty, over and above the primary uncertainty contained in total knowledge available in the group. This transaction cost – residual uncertainty trade-off (from Figure 6.2) – is added on top of the group's I" curve, which now climbs much more steeply (the bold TRSC curve in Figure 6.3). Secondary uncertainty increases hyperbolically for an individual agent: if she invests all her cognitive capacity in building up her own comparative advantage (increased accuracy of her own knowledge), there is no capacity left to invest in a common knowledge interface. Consequently, secondary or residual uncertainty in her transactions with other agents will come close to infinity: she has no way of knowing what other agents are selling to her. On the other hand, if she invests a substantial share in transaction costs, secondary uncertainty will considerably decrease, at the cost of lower accuracy in her own knowledge and thus increased primary uncertainty. Secondary uncertainty sharply increases the gradient of the upward sloping part of the total uncertainty curve.

This changes the knowledge optimisation problem for cognitive agents living in cognitive exchange with others, compared to cognitive autarky. Assume that institutional technology (the level and shape of the institutional trade-off in Figure 6.2) and the degree of specialisation (as well as

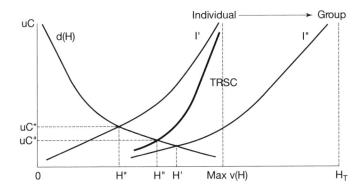

Figure 6.3 Adding transaction costs to the move from autarky to trade

total knowledge in society) are exogenously given. Assume also that the knowledge contribution of a single individual is marginal in society; an individual is unlikely to significantly add to total knowledge and specialisation on her own. Consequently, in a large specialised society, total knowledge available to an individual is constant and not significantly affected by change in her own knowledge set. Her choice problem then becomes a classic case of minimisation of uncertainty, generated by the accuracy of her own knowledge set (primary uncertainty) and by trading of truncated knowledge sets with others (secondary uncertainty), subject to her own cognitive capacity constraint.

Her equilibrium cognitive capacity allocation (H'' in Figure 6.3) will be reached when the marginal decrease in primary uncertainty from an additional allocation of cognitive capacity to her own comparative advantage (accuracy in her own knowledge) is be compensated by the marginal increase in secondary uncertainty generated by drawing that additional allocation of cognitive capacity away from an investment in transaction costs. In other words, in equilibrium the marginal benefit of a re-allocation of a slice of scarce individual cognitive capacity leaves fitness unchanged.

At this equilibrium point, we must have $uC'' < uC^*$. If not, there would be no point in trading and the agent would be better off staying in cognitive autarky. This condition is not necessarily satisfied. The institutional setting that determines the trade-off between residual (secondary) uncertainty and transaction costs may be such that trade generates much more secondary uncertainty, for instance through contractual uncertainties, than it reduces primary uncertainty (through an increased supply of variety in knowledge). Such a situation would of course prevent people from specialising and trading. Transaction costs and the slope of the institutional trade-off in Figure 6.2 determine a ceiling on specialisation and tradable comparative advantages. They reduce – and ultimately eliminate – the incentive to learn more accurate knowledge.

Figure 6.3 determines a number of key characteristics of an economic system. It sets the proportion of total cognitive capacity spent on transacting with others (the common knowledge interface) and, as a corollary, on individual comparative advantage. In societies with poor quality institutions – the institutional technology trade-off in Figure 6.2 is situated far to the northwest – individuals need to invest a substantial part of their cognitive resources in communication to reduce secondary uncertainty to acceptable levels, leaving relatively little room for investment in specialisation. Consequently, total knowledge will be lower and opportunities for exchange will be diminished. The level of transaction costs or the size of the common knowledge interface determines the degree of specialisation, and thus the total amount of knowledge available, in the group. This also sets the volume of trade. In short, the quality of institutions determines the degree of specialisation and the size of the economy.

Transaction costs reconsidered

It is generally recognised that the concept of transaction costs finds its origin in Coase's well known 1937 article on 'The nature of the firm', though that article does not use the term 'transaction costs' as such. Coase tried to answer the question why firms exist, why all production is not handled by one single company or, alternatively, by individuals exchanging their individual outputs through the market. His answer was that firms will vary in size until 'at the margin, the cost of organising within the firm will be equal to the cost...involved in leaving the transaction to be organised by the price mechanism'. This resulted in the idea that organising a transaction is costly, and that there may be alternative ways of doing so, within or without a company, or with specific types of contractual arrangement. But what exactly are the costs of carrying out a transaction? Despite the rapid rise of modern New Institutional Economics in the 1980s and 1990s, a school of economic thought that is almost entirely built around transaction costs, the concept itself remains notoriously vague and undefined. We all seem to have an intuitive understanding of transaction costs – which probably explains why the term gained currency fairly easily. However, every author on the subject has their own definition – or rather, description. The vagueness surrounding transaction costs has facilitated criticism and remains a liability on the balance sheet of institutional economics, which culminated in the North-Williamson controversy on the measurability of transaction costs.

North and Wallis (1986) take the description of transaction costs employed by Coase (1937) literally and define them as the effectively *realised* opportunity costs of organising a transaction: the costs of searching for a trading partner, finding the right information, measuring quantities and qualities of the traded goods and services, negotiating a contract, and enforcement of that contract. Transaction costs occur mainly *ex-ante* of a transaction. They distinguish these transaction costs from transformation costs, which are the opportunity costs of inputs used for production only. Together, transformation and transaction costs constitute the total costs of a good. Transaction costs are thus treated as any other costs. The only distinction resides in the functional role of the incurred costs.

One can easily see how this classification system is somewhat arbitrary and quickly runs into problems. What to do, for instance, with the cost of the designer who shapes cars according to the latest fashion? Does she produce a good or simply facilitate an exchange? Adding fashionable attributes to a car is both part of transaction costs (it reduces search costs for fashion-minded customers) and transformation costs (attributes have an opportunity cost). In a way, every production aspect that contains a signal-function towards the customer reduces transaction costs but also affects transformation costs. The distinction is perhaps clarified by linking transaction costs to the division of labour. In that case, transaction costs are all costs that would not arise if an agent sold his production to himself. Cheung (1970) has formulated this more eloquently: transaction costs are everything beyond the Robinson Crusoe economy – everything beyond autarky. Consider teaching, the pure transfer of knowledge: since there is no point in teaching things to yourself, teaching would be considered a transaction cost. More generally, any activity that consists of pure transfer of knowledge between persons is considered as transaction costs under this definition. As a corollary, all activities that consist of embodying knowledge into a material product, without the aim of transferring this knowledge to another person's mind, would be classified as generating transformation costs only. Eight years after their path-breaking publication 'Measuring the transaction sector in the American economy (1870–1979)' (North and Wallis 1986), North and Wallis (1994) seem to have come a long way towards agreeing that the distinction between these transformation and transaction costs is somewhat artificial. At least, they agree that both categories are not totally independent of each other.

The main achievement of North and Wallis (1986) is that they were among the first to attempt to give empirical content to the concept of transaction costs. They demonstrated how, in the course of long-run economic development, transaction costs increase more than proportionally to the size of an economy. However, they have no real explanations for this phenomenon. Have improvements in transaction technology (institutions) contributed to a fall in transaction costs and shifted the supply curve, thereby increasing demand for transaction services? Or have advances in the division of labour and further specialisation increased the derived demand for transaction services? The model developed in this chapter clearly points in the direction of specialisation or the division of labour as the main driving force behind increased transaction costs, for a given institutional architecture. Improved institutions may reduce that cost again, for a given degree of specialisation.

Williamson (1975; 1985) does not take Coase too literally but tries to interpret and give more analytical content to both the concept of 'transactions' and the associated cost of doing transactions. But Williamson is not satisfied with an intuitive understanding, and digs deeper into the reasons for this costliness. He follows in Herbert Simon's footsteps and adopts bounded rationality or imperfect and asymmetric information. This distinguishes his approach from North, who tries to keep his analysis as much as possible within the confines of the neo-classical paradigm of perfect information, at least until North (1990). Furthermore, Williamson adds the assumption of 'self-interest seeking with a guile'. While bounded rationality and opportunism are necessary conditions for uncertainty in transactions, they are not sufficient conditions in Williamson's view. In case of low asset specificity – the degree of non-separability between the seller and the buyer of an asset – parties to an agreement can always look for alternative trading parties. Only when assets are highly specific to a particular transaction and leave few or no alternative transaction options, could they entail high opportunity costs in case of default. Asset specificity is thus added as a sufficient condition for uncertainty to occur.

Uncertainty can be overcome through contractual arrangements or governance structures that include commitment devices to contract execution, which are costly to negotiate *ex-ante* and to enforce *ex-post* of contract signature. Uncertainty is thus considered to be the real reason why parties in an exchange invest in finding suitable partners and products, spend time on metering qualities and quantities, negotiate a contract and invest in enforcement devices. In sum, this is the reason for incurring *realised* transaction costs so as to avoid potentially larger but hopefully *unrealised* transaction costs during contract execution. Williamson (1985) then shows how various organisational or governance arrangements for production processes entail various degrees of efficiency in the underlying commitment devices for the execution of agreements, and thereby different levels of efficiency of production. Hierarchy is, according to his theory, the most efficient organisational arrangement when asset specificity, bounded rationality and opportunism are present. However, it requires costly contracting with *ex-ante* (search and negotiation) and *ex-post* (enforcement) transaction costs. Coase's (1937) remarkable insight was precisely that it may not pay to extend hierarchical (contractual) arrangements beyond a certain limit, because the transaction costs of doing so exceed the transaction cost of going through a non-hierarchical (market) arrangement. This explains why Williamson does not consider transaction costs to be directly measurable. One may be in a position to measure the *ex-ante* part of transaction costs, but it is usually not possible to measure the *ex-post* part because it remains un-realised. Besides, both parts are interdependent: a well designed contract will reduce *ex-post* costs.

In fact, the trade-off between *ex-ante* realised transaction costs and *ex-post* potential uncertainty was already explained by Demsetz (1968), who defined transaction costs as the cost of exchanging ownership titles. He presents an empirical study of transaction costs at the New York Stock Exchange, where they consist of two components: brokerage fees and ask-bid spreads. The spread measures the price of waiting in a transaction. The larger the spread and the higher the volume of transactions per time unit, the lower the waiting time. The lower the waiting time, the lower the risks or uncertainty in a volatile market. This is one of the first studies that shows a systematic trade-off between realised transaction costs – the spread – that trading parties are willing to incur, and unrealised transaction costs – changes in uncertainty.

Figure 6.2 pictures the trade-off between *ex-ante* realised transaction costs and *ex-post* potential costs or uncertainty. Since economic transactions involve an exchange of truncated knowledge in a distributed knowledge setting, they generate cognitive economy for the parties involved (no need to transfer the full knowledge content of a good). The extent of partial overlap in knowledge sets represents the realised transaction cost: information search, monitoring, measurement, etc. The trade-off between *ex-ante* and *ex-post* transaction costs is conditional for a given institutional architecture. This way, the transaction cost concept becomes more firmly embedded in the cognitive nature of transactions themselves.

As such, the cognitive approach to transactions in this chapter provides a unifying framework for the different hypotheses that underlie North's and Williamson's approaches to transaction costs. Residual or secondary 'tail-end' uncertainty in a transaction can be equated to Williamson's interpretation of transaction costs: the unmeasurable costs of post-contractual implementation arrangements. We may be able to measure some of these post-contractual costs in the event that they occur; we will never be able to measure those that might have occurred but did not. Demsetz (1967) and Grosmann and Hart (1986) have shown that this residual or tail-end uncertainty of contracts gives rise to the emergence of property rights: the costs and benefits that result from unspecified residual uncertainties are always allocated to the owner of the good. For this reason, I define institutions as property rights arrangements, or arrangements concerning residual uncertainty in an exchange (see Chapter 8). Similarly, North defines institutional arrangements as agreements on appropriation and allocation of cost and benefits resulting from an exchange, in the form of contracts, laws and regulations (North 1990: 33). An institutional innovation re-arranges the allocation of residual uncertainty among trading parties, and thereby changes the allocation of realised transaction costs or the common knowledge interface required for the exchange. That way, changes in institutions change the level and slope of the trade-off in Figure 6.2.

As such, the cognitive approach to transaction costs presented here may bridge the divide in the New Institutional Economics literature between the Coase-North branch, which revolves around realised *ex-ante* transaction costs for a common interface (North 1990), and the Williamson (1985) branch that focuses on unrealised transaction costs due to imperfect governance structures or property rights allocations that leave some residual *ex-post* uncertainty. The literature has so far failed to mint these two sides into a single coin. The present approach endogenises transaction costs and institutions in an economic system, as a function of the degree of specialisation.

Conclusions

In Adam Smith's view, and in that of most of the classical school, the degree of specialisation or division of labour is determined by the extent of the market. In the cognitive model presented in this chapter, however, it is endogenously determined by transaction costs. The larger the share of his limited cognitive capacity that a person invests in common knowledge, the less he can invest in his own specialised knowledge, and thus the lower the degree of specialisation in society.

At this stage, there are only two variables that remain exogenous to this cognitive economic model: limited individual information processing capacity and institutions. Specialisation, tradable comparative advantages, transaction costs, the extent of the market, etc., are all endogenously determined. In Part III, I will try to endogenise institutions as well.

The cognitive economic model presented here remains rather static, however. We can explain the emergence of specialisation and trade, but not much is happening in that model once a society has settled into a cognitive equilibrium. It can continue to operate in reproductive mode, churning out the same goods and services endlessly. That sounds very much like the neo-classical general equilibrium model – and contrary to the intentions expressed in Part I of this research. So before we move on to institutions, we need to examine how the cognitive mechanics of economic development can be used to generate a more dynamic picture of the economy, with continuous learning, innovation and growth. That is the subject of the next chapter.

7 Economies of scope

In Part I of this research I started with a number of purely economic questions and investigated the state of the art in economic growth and development theory. I concluded that modern economics was in a rather sorry state, not being able to shed much light on the stylised empirical facts of growth. The explanatory value of the neo-classical Solow (1957) growth model, that has dominated macro-economic growth theory for the past half-century, is rather poor. That model accounts for embodied forms of knowledge only – capital and labour – but not the source of these embodiments, knowledge. As a result, the Solow model has a hard time tracking the role of knowledge accumulation, or innovation, in economic growth. More recent models that explicitly account for unembodied knowledge as an explanatory variable, such as the Augmented Solow and Endogenous Growth models, perform better in empirical terms. However, they quickly run into incompatibilities with the neo-classical competitive markets paradigm, because of their insistence on increasing returns, caused by the non-rivalry and partial excludability properties of knowledge. We traced all these problems back to the history of economic thought, and found out how economics had lost track of the role of knowledge, and especially distributed knowledge. While Adam Smith (1776) gave a pivotal role to the division of labour when he kick-started the modern economics literature, that concept disappeared rapidly in the wake of neo-classical thinking.

In Part II, I restarted the investigations into the nature of economic development with a clean slate. The only credible clue at hand was the idea that knowledge played a pivotal role in economic development; how and why was not clear. I first proposed an operational definition of knowledge, and then investigated the properties that could be derived from that definition. Taking into account the inherently limited cognitive processing capacity of the human brain, the search for cognitive economy turned out to be an all-pervading issue. The introduction of communication channels between individuals opened up possibilities for substantial cognitive economy, because it permitted agents to copy knowledge from others without having to process it themselves. While imitation and symbolic communication provided important shortcuts in learning processes, a major step forward was taken with the emergence of exchange of knowledge embodied in goods and services. Contrary to imitation and symbolic communication, exchange of embodied knowledge requires exchange of truncated knowledge sets only. This creates the possibility for knowledge specialisation between individuals in a group.

Chapters 5 and 6 demonstrated that, whereas specialisation actually constitutes a disadvantage in societies without trade because it increases individual uncertainty, it turns out to be a strong advantage when trade is possible. Specialisation allows societies to absorb far more knowledge, and creates an incentive for individuals to invest in learning and knowledge accumulation. It reinforces their comparative advantage in markets and facilitates their access to knowledge available in society. Specialisation actually reduces uncertainty and improves the fitness of individuals as well as societies. Societies based on imitation and symbolic communication offer weak incentives only for learning. Consequently, knowledge accumulation is slow, based on random learning and learning-by-doing only. In this way, the emergence of economic exchange turned out to be an extension of cognitive evolution in nature in general and the search for cognitive economy in particular.

Though we started from cognitive and evolutionary concepts and models, without any apparent link to economic concepts, Part II has gradually taken us back to the basics of economics: production and trade. In this last chapter of Part II, I intend to close the circle and connect the cognitive mechanisms of the preceding chapters to the economic growth theory issues discussed in Part I. It would be preposterous to claim that a single new model could replace existing theories of economic growth. Modern growth theory includes a very large set of relevant factors, with complex interrelationships. The purpose of this research, and especially Part II, is to demonstrate that the introduction of some cognitive mechanisms, in particular distributed knowledge or specialisation, in economic growth theory could complement the views offered by neo-classical and endogenous growth theories, and provide some explanations for hitherto unexplained but observed stylised facts of growth.

A major difference between the cognitive approach and these established theories of economic growth emerged in the preceding chapter. The concept of knowledge and its applications in economics is too complex to capture in a one-dimensional variable, a variable that can only go up or down. Knowledge has other characteristics that are important, such as accuracy, variety, and its distribution across a group. Augmented Solow models treat knowledge as another form of capital, that can be accumulated and reduced. Endogenous growth theory drew attention to additional characteristics such as non-excludability and non-rivalry. These characteristics sparked a debate on convergence and increasing returns to scale. Still, these debates remained confined to a one-dimensional interpretation of knowledge. This allowed Stern (1991) to ask whether there is any difference between the human capital approach of the 1960s and 1970s and the Endogenous Growth approach.

The introduction of additional cognitive characteristics of knowledge in the preceding chapters raises a whole series of new issues. It forces us to rethink the link between learning, knowledge accumulation and economic growth. Is knowledge subject to increasing or decreasing returns? What is the direction of additional learning: does it increase accuracy, or variety, or both? How does it affect specialisation and, most importantly, how does it affect growth? The present chapter explores these issues and aims to come up with a more dynamic model of the link between knowledge, specialisation and economic growth.

The model developed in the preceding chapters is rather static. For an exogenously given institutional architecture, the trade-off between transaction costs and residual uncertainty is fixed, and so is the degree of specialisation, total knowledge in society and the number of gainful trading opportunities. In short, economic development remains stuck in an equilibrium situation where economic activity will continue but in purely reproductive mode. Agents continue to exchange the same goods and services at the same prices and in the same quantities. It looks as if this cognitive model has brought us back full circle to the world of neo-classical general equilibrium, where innovation is eliminated and all economic activity runs in a purely reproductive mode. In its present state, it is not able to explain economic growth and continuous development. Clearly, the real world is more dynamic than that. Knowledge grows, there is continuous technological innovation and there is economic growth, including the occasional economic decline. How can we improve the cognitive approach of the preceding chapters to take into account these real-world dynamics?

The model presented at the end of Chapter 6 was based on total knowledge absorption capacity over an entire lifetime, and excluded the factors that motivate learning within that lifetime. Specialisation was defined as an average degree of specialisation of society, not in function of the composition of individual knowledge sets. Obviously, this is a rather static and not very realistic picture that needs correction. Learning is a dynamic process within a lifetime. It affects an individual's degree of specialisation during their life and with respect to other individuals in society. In this chapter, I first propose a series of mechanisms that can explain variations in the degree of specialisation of individuals. Next, I examine how this could affect the overall degree of specialisation in society and, most importantly, the rate of economic growth. This will help to lift the cognitive economic model of Chapter 6 out of its equilibrium trap, and explain the cognitive mechanisms that provide an impetus for continuous economic growth and development.

I discuss five cognitive mechanisms that affect specialisation. All but the first of these mechanisms revolve around the principle of increasing returns to knowledge – which will actually be referred to as 'economies of scope'. As such, they provide an escape route from the entropy-increasing convexity requirements of the neo-classical general equilibrium model. The first three mechanisms affect individual specialisation, the last two connect individual with overall specialisation and create a link to economic growth.

One could of course argue that economic growth is driven by institutional change, the variable that we have kept exogenous and fixed so far. A lot of empirical research in that direction was carried out in the 1990s and most of these studies do indeed confirm that institutional reform is conducive to economic development. However, I would like to explore first the dynamics of the cognitive model without institutional change. The factors that affect economic growth through institutional change, and the endogenisation of institutional change into this cognitive approach, are left for Part III of this book.

Schumpeterian competition

The earliest economic models of learning and human capital accumulation can be traced back to Becker (1964). According to Becker, the decision to invest in learning is similar to any other investment decision. A cost-benefit calculation can be used to determine the optimal amount of learning. When the marginal cost (the cost of learning, the opportunity cost of time spent on learning instead of working) equals the marginal benefit (additional income gained from additional learning), the volume of knowledge acquired has reached an equilibrium position and learning stops. Going through school and university offers good pay-offs in terms of increased personal income in most modern societies. However, studying for a law degree and then deciding on an additional engineering degree may not be a good investment. It entails additional costs (for instance, engineering school costs, lost income as a lawyer during the time spent at engineering school) and uncertain additional benefits (for instance, do engineers earn more than lawyers?). The main conclusion from Becker's model is that formal learning ultimately stops when it reaches an equilibrium situation. People may continue to learn by doing while working, but will not invest deliberately in learning beyond that point.

However, in reality, there are mechanisms at work that erode the value of individual knowledge. The neo-Schumpeterian models of technological innovation, referred to in Chapter 2, extensively investigate the mechanisms of knowledge competition. In the neo-Schumpeterian view, an entrepreneur invests in innovation to gain a comparative advantage over his competitors that puts him in a monopolistic position in the market. The advantage is gradually eroded by innovations in his competitor's products, so that the market eventually returns to pure price competition when competitors have caught up again. However, continuous innovation will prevent the occurrence of such an equilibrium; it will shift comparative advantages and monopolistic competition between competitors; it will not eliminate monopolistic competition. Contrary to neo-classical economists, neo-Schumpeterians consider monopolistic competition, based on advantages in knowledge produced by innovation, to be the standard form of the market, rather than pure price competition without monopolies.

Competition thus constitutes an incentive to invest in continuous learning and knowledge accumulation to maintain and improve the terms of trade with the rest of society. If learning should stop (as the equilibrium suggests), comparative advantage will quickly be eroded by other agents who are catching up with specialised knowledge. Consequently, learning will not stop, contrary to the predictions of the Becker model.

Knowledge competition can be brought into the model by returning to the underlying Boyd and Richerson (1985) evolutionary biology model of cultural transmission and its interpretation by Rogers (1988). In these evolutionary biology models, cognitive agents play against a given environment, 'nature'. They acquire knowledge for behavioural purposes, but the use of that knowledge does not alter the environment. 'Nature' is exogenous to the model. In an economic environment however, agents play against each other's competitive position. A move by one player may alter the environment for all other players. The 'environment' here consists of the knowledge, production processes, marketing and innovation strategies, of other economic agents. It is not exogenously given but endogenously determined in the model. The stronger the competition, the stronger the incentive to invest in enhancing one's comparative advantage and bringing about changes in behaviour. This accelerates change in the economic environment.

Rogers' 1988 model (see Chapter 5) explicitly revolves around a changing environment. If the environment did not change, imitators could once-and-for-all copy a behaviour that would remain valid forever; there would be no decline in the fitness of imitators. The faster the environment changes, the sooner knowledge becomes obsolete, however, and the lower the fitness of imitators. Speeding up environmental change results in a shift in the equilibrium composition of the population (see Figure 5.2): it will result in more individual producers of knowledge (learners) and less imitators. With faster environmental change, learned and imitated behaviours quickly become out of date, so that imitation becomes less appropriate and more agents switch back to individual learning of behavioural responses to cope with the changing environment. With more learners, the rate of knowledge accumulation accelerates. In a neo-Schumpeterian world, where learning by others constitutes the environment, this accelerates the rate of environmental change for others and thereby provokes a self-accelerating effect. Consequently, endogenisation of the environment as a function of learning by others will increase total investment in learning.

In most present-day economic growth theories, that would be the end of the story: investment in learning increases and thus the rate of growth of the production factor 'knowledge' accelerates. Augmented Solow models would simply translate this into increased economic growth. Endogenous growth models would add that some of this knowledge might spill over to other agents and economies and thus result in convergence in growth rates. Neo-Schumpeterians might point out that more learning does not necessarily result in more knowledge since there is also 'destruction' of knowledge: knowledge that becomes obsolete or loses its economic value. However, in the cognitive approach proposed in the preceding chapters, this is just the start of another series of questions. The first question is: which direction does additional learning take? Does it increase accuracy or variety of knowledge, or both? To answer that question, we need to bring in the concept of economies of scope.

Economies of scope

Rosen (1983) introduces the concept of economies of scope, as a special version of economies of scale. His paper is among the very few in the modern economics literature that attempt to explain incentives for learning and specialisation in terms of increasing returns to learning. His model can be summarised as follows. Workers try to maximise income (Y) or the difference between the value of output (w) produced by applying their skills (k) over a time interval (t) and the cost of learning these skills (C(k)), subject to a time constraint:

$$\max Y = \max [(\Sigma_i w_i k_i t_i - C(\Sigma_i k_i))]$$

subject to: $0 < \Sigma_i t_i < 1$ and $(\forall w_i, k_i > 0$

If several skills are available for learning, should workers invest in a mix of these skills or chose a corner solution with a single skill? Rosen shows that, if the cost function of learning these skills is separable, that is if C(k1, k2) = C(k1) + C(k2), then costs are minimised and income is maximised by investing in one skill only (specialisation). If the cost functions are not separable, that is if C(k1, k2) < C(k1) + C(k2), i.e. if it is cheaper to learn both skills jointly rather than separately, then workers should learn the entire package and earn income from several skills. Specialisation is thus shown to be economically advantageous under conditions of separable learning costs only. With non-separable learning costs, workers will tend to acquire a larger set of skills. Rosen calls this 'economies of scope', a special version of economies of scale: with non-separability, there is scope to learn more skills at a lower cost. While economies of scale are the result of fixed costs that can be spread out over a larger number of outputs, economies of scope are the result of fixed learning costs for one skill, that can also serve as a learning input into other skills, with non-separable knowledge sets. Economies of scope are economies of scale in learning and knowledge production.[1]

A concrete example may help to clarify this concept. Consider learning languages. Learning French and German can be done separately as well as jointly; that will not significantly affect the learning effort or cost. They are separable. By contrast, consider learning the grammar and vocabulary of a language separately. Because C(voc, gram) < C(voc) + C(gram), it would take considerably less effort to learn them jointly rather than separately. Once you start learning grammar, there is scope for learning vocabulary at a considerably reduced cost.

Another example: consider a medical doctor. Acquiring the skills of a general practitioner paves the way for further learning to become a surgeon. Clearly, C(GP, surgery) < C(GP) + C(surgery). It is much more likely that a general practitioner will enhance his comparative advantage and income by moving towards surgery, rather than that he will study additionally to become a lawyer or an engineer, because C(GP, lawyer) = C(GP) + C(lawyer) while C(GP, surgery) < C(GP) + C(surgery).

Rosen's model formulation has several drawbacks. First, it separates learning from producing, as the time constraint does not apply to learning. Learning-by-doing (on-the-job learning) is thus excluded from the model. Second, the formulation focuses on one time period only and does not allow for a time-ordering of learning and doing: learning might as well come after doing, and learning a specific skill does not generate opportunity costs of time that exclude learning a second skill in the next period. Third, this formulation does not take into account the extent of the market for the outputs of a particular skill. A fourth and major drawback of the Rosen (1983) model in the above formulation is that it does not allow us to distinguish between two crucial properties of knowledge, accuracy and variety, and the role of these two properties in creating economies of scope. In fact, Rosen lacked the concepts to provide a cognitive explanation for separability of learning costs and economies of scope. He simply assumed the existence of different types of cost functions without providing a cognitive rationale for these differences. He did not distinguish between variety and accuracy of knowledge. The cognitive analysis of learning and knowledge processes in Chapters 4 and 5 now allows us to make that distinction and give cognitive meaning to non-separability. In line with the graph theory interpretation of knowledge sets, economies of scope can be interpreted as increasing the density of pair-wise links or bindings within an existing set of neuronal nodes, by increasing the number of bindings within the set. As such, economies of scope build on existing knowledge sets. They exploit the non-separability of existing and new knowledge.

This leads us to the important conclusion that non-separability, and the resulting tendency towards specialisation, is a consequence of the structure of knowledge and its distributed network organisation in the brain.

Rosen's (1983) demonstration of the advantages of specialisation in a single set of non-separable tasks reflects Adam Smith's intuition that there is no need to pursue two different jobs if one gives you greater satisfaction and recognition than the other. This so-called 'fourth argument' in favour of specialisation (Rosenberg 1976) was presented only in Smith's *Lectures on rhetoric and belles lettres* (1762–3) and not in *The Wealth of Nations*. Clearly, it does not pay to invest in learning to become both a plumber and a car mechanic because one can only practise one of these jobs at the same time. Doubling the learning effort will not double income – unless of course the extent of the market comes into play. We had already come to the same conclusion in the previous section, based on Becker's (1964) model of learning. Rosen's formulation, however, permits us to make the connection with a cognitive interpretation of learning and arrive at a more general conclusion regarding the direction of learning.

The way in which the human brain processes and stores knowledge thus induces a trend towards specialisation. This does of course exclude the fact that people have a range of interests and feel attracted towards acquiring knowledge in a variety of domains, sometimes even domains that are remote from their everyday occupation and professional knowledge. People may actually deliberately seek to acquire a variety of knowledge. Rosen's conclusion is valid only for rational cost-minimising or profit-maximising behaviour. Much human and cognitive behaviour in everyday life is driven by other considerations, of course.

All that answers the first question on the direction of learning. But it immediately raises a new question: if the direction of learning has a tendency towards further specialisation, how does this affect the distribution of knowledge in society, the cognitive equilibrium between specialisation and common knowledge and the institutionally determined trade-off between transaction costs and residual uncertainty, defined in Chapter 6? In other words, can specialisation continue without limits? That is the subject of the next two sections.

The extent of the market

So far, Rosen's arguments have been looked at from the cost side of learning only; but his maximisation function contains a benefits side too: wages. All the above is true *ceteris paribus* only, as long as we do not consider variations in income or in the benefits side of learning. In reality, benefits do vary, of course, with the quality and content of knowledge. Adam Smith (1776) already noted the importance of the benefits side of learning in his famous statement that specialisation (or division of labour) is limited by the extent of the market: if market size for a particular set of specialised skills is too small, income will decrease and there is no point in investing in those skills.[2] If the benefits of increasing variety are higher than the benefits of increasing accuracy, then people will choose non-specialisation and more general knowledge. For instance, an international traveller will prefer to expand the number of languages she covers, so that her satisfaction from wider travel increases. A professor of languages, by contrast, may prefer to deepen her knowledge of a single language, so as to strengthen her competitiveness in the market for language teaching. Another example: when the size of the market for plumbing jobs is limited so that there is spare time left to practise car repair and earn additional income, then people will invest learning costs in the separable skills sets of plumbing and car repair, despite the fact that it would be cheaper to invest in only one skill.

The conclusion that can be drawn from Adam Smith's line of reasoning is that specialisation will not continue indefinitely. Smith takes market size as an exogenous variable, not affected by changes in specialisation or the division of labour. Rather, the degree of division of labour adapts to the prevailing market size for products. The point that I want to raise here is that Smith overlooked the fact that market size *is* actually affected by the degree of specialisation, so that it becomes endogenous to an explanatory model for the division of labour. The impact of a single plumber deciding to become a car mechanic too is very likely to be marginal and negligible (unless the population of skilled workers is very small). But changes in the degree of division of labour in society usually ripple across the entire population, under the influence of technical, economic and institutional changes. In that case, the reverse of Smith's original statement is also true: the extent of the market is limited by the division of labour.

To illustrate my argument, consider the following example. Two persons produce two goods, one unit of each, and consume both units. There is no market for these goods; both persons live in autarky and consume their own production. They are not specialised in any of these goods. Now consider full specialisation among these two persons: each person produces two units of only one good. He consumes one unit and sells the other. Each person is fully specialised and the size of his market has increased to two units of his product (though the total number of units produced of each good in society has not changed). This could be interpreted as an economy-of-scale argument in favour of specialisation. Market size increases from one to two units, for a given fixed cost to learn how to produce the good. If the investment in learning is the only production cost, then the marginal cost of the second unit produced is zero and the average production cost for the two units is halved. The example can be generalised to the n-persons case. If they are not specialised, n persons produce one unit of n different goods, for their own consumption, at a learning cost of n times $c(n)$. If fully specialised, they produce n units of a single good, at a learning cost of $1 \times c(n)$, or n times lower than in case of non-specialisation.

Specialisation thus increases the size of the market and allows us to reverse Adam Smith's famous dictum. Not only is the division of labour limited by the extent of the market, but the reverse is equally true: the extent of the market is limited by the division of labour. Nevertheless, despite this market-expanding effect of specialisation, there remains a limit to the degree of specialisation; it cannot go on indefinitely.

Complementarity of knowledge sets

Market size is not the only limit on specialisation, however. There are other cognitive factors that prevent specialisation from increasing indefinitely. The cognitive interpretation of separable learning cost functions, as presented above, provides an explanation for Rosen's (1983) 'economies of scope' *within* an existing knowledge set, for a single individual. However, we can also interpret economies of scope *across* knowledge sets held by different individuals. That has been overlooked in the economics literature, probably because it is hard to interpret without the cognitive background presented above. It concerns the complementarity or matching of knowledge sets between specialised individuals.

The ideas behind economies of scope across individuals have slowly emerged from the Endogenous Growth Theory literature and the concepts of non-rivalry and partial excludability of knowledge that are nested in that literature. Both these characteristics give rise to increasing returns to knowledge. As explained in Chapter 1, this puts knowledge at odds with the decreasing returns assumption that underpins the neo-classical general equilibrium paradigm. Easterly (2001) presents a very pointed summary of the key issue that goes back to the debate between Romer (1994) and Mankiw *et al.* (1992). Mankiw's economic growth model was based on the typical neo-classical assumption that production factors, like labour, move from situations where they are abundant to situations where they are scarce, for the simple reason that production factors are likely to receive a higher remuneration when they are scarce, a supply and demand argument. Romer (1994) pointed out the incoherence between this theoretical assumption and the empirical observation that labour actually moves from countries with scarce knowledge (usually the low-income developing countries) to countries with more abundant knowledge (the most advanced countries). Migration to a country where knowledge is more abundant actually increases personal income for the migrant. Easterly gives another example about professionally specialised people who tend to cluster together, not only in richer countries but also in high-income and high-cost urban areas within countries, because that is where they find complementary specialised knowledge sets to work with and maximise the return on their own knowledge. They do not move to rural areas where specialised knowledge is scarce.

That incoherence between the predictions of the neo-classical model and the empirically observed facts can only be explained by assuming some source of economies of scale that make knowledge more productive when it is abundantly available. As explained in Chapter 1, neo-classical growth models do not allow for economies of scale in production; so this

tipped most mainstream economists overboard in the search for an explanation. Endogenous growth models can assume increasing returns to
knowledge, based on the macro-properties of non-excludability and non-
rivalry of knowledge, but that boils down to an economies-of-scale-in-production
argument: the more often knowledge is copied, the lower the average
production cost. It is not clear how that applies in the case of migrants
moving their skills to another knowledge environment. Somehow, an
explanation had to be found that yields increasing returns independently
of economies of scale. The combination of Rosen's economies of scope
with the cognitive model developed in the preceding chapters is a more
appropriate construction for doing just that.

If we dig somewhat deeper into Easterly's examples, however, they look
more like examples of increasing returns to complementary inputs into a
joint production function, rather than increasing returns to scale. There
are two possible interpretations here, both related to the idea that
specialist production has the characteristics of a joint production function.

The first interpretation looks at joint production from the angle of a
team of *complementary* specialists, each in their narrowly defined disci-
pline, that need to collaborate to produce a joint product or output. Joint
production may require a substantial number of different skills (variety) to
be available within the team. But the lower the variety in individual
knowledge of a team member, the higher their accuracy (for a given
volume of knowledge) and thus their productivity and quality of output.
Also, the lower the individual degree of variety, the more experts are
needed to fill up the entire span of variety required to produce a particular
output. Ever increasing specialisation means slicing up a production
process in ever thinner slices of higher-quality intermediate outputs. This is
very much in line with Adam Smith's original pin factory example.
Another interpretation of specialist production also starts from joint
production, but among specialists with *identical* knowledge in the same
domain. To produce a large software package, for instance, a group of
experts in one particular programming language may need to collaborate.
They all share the same expertise and their joint input is required because
of the sheer size of the task. Working together not only speeds up the
production process but also allows for joint problem solving.

Joint production in teams requires communication *between* individual
knowledge sets. As explained in Chapter 6, this involves setting aside part
of an individual's scarce information processing capacity to act as a
common knowledge interface. The size of that interface is determined by
the trade-off between transaction costs and residual uncertainty (or
between *ex-ante* and *ex-post* transaction costs). The smaller the required
interface the better. That objective can be achieved by putting together in a
team individuals with closely related knowledge sets. If the knowledge sets
are identical, then no specific interface is required any longer. If they hold
different knowledge sets but with a common base, little interfacing will be

required. For instance, computer programmers who share the same programming language but specialise in building different parts of a software package will have a fairly easy time communicating. If their knowledge sets are very different and have little overlap, common knowledge interfacing may become a time-consuming job, for instance in the case of an accountant and a programmer trying to develop an accounting software package.

The cost of communication will depend on the degree of overlap between their knowledge sets, and the level of accuracy at which this overlap is situated. For example, individuals who share only a common knowledge of the English language but not specific technical vocabulary, will need to spend more time and cognitive resources on conveying accurate and unambiguous messages. Individuals who share a more accurate technical knowledge interface will be able to convey messages more efficiently. For instance, as with a programmer and an accountant who share some knowledge of their respective specialisations. In modern parlance this is called 'networking': specialists build their own communication networks with slightly overlapping but still limited knowledge interfaces. Each of them on their own is unable to fit into society's needs, but together they can deliver a product that does. The advantages of these network 'subcultures' is that members can operate at much lower transaction costs than they would need in interactions with the rest of society.

So far, we have focused on the individual aspects of complementarity in knowledge sets, in production teams. Let us now look at the wider societal aspects of complementarity.

Specialists do not only team up to produce outputs; they also live together in societies of very diverse individuals, both as producers and as consumers. How can specialised computer programmers sell their software packages to a wide market of non-specialised consumers who have no inkling of the programming technicalities that go into that software package? The programmers will need to build a common knowledge interface into their package, in order to make it accessible to non-specialists. In cases where technical knowledge is not embodied in a material product, a team of specialists may need to hire an individual to act as a go-between with non-specialist outsiders. The common knowledge interface then becomes a fixed cost that can be shared between many experts, again reducing costs. This demonstrates how specialisation in non-tradable common knowledge can actually constitute a source of a tradable comparative advantage. Though that common knowledge has no direct tradable advantage, it helps others to save their opportunity costs. At first sight, this looks like an exception to the rule that gainful trade has to be based on comparative advantages. A closer look reveals, however, that the rule still holds: not having any comparative advantage (holding a common knowledge interface) is also a comparative advantage, compared to those who do (specialists).

Teaming up with other specialists with identical or complementary knowledge sets is economically and cognitively advantageous, because it minimises scarce cognitive capacity that needs to be invested in knowledge interfacing. This is a source of economies of scope that results in increasing returns to cognitive clustering or professional 'ghetto' formation among highly specialised individuals. In fact, Easterly's example of complementary knowledge sets could be rephrased in terms of economies of scope *across* individual knowledge sets (and not economies of scope *within* an individual's own knowledge set). Both types of economies of scope occur for the same reasons. Just as an individual can realise cognitive economies of scope by further specialisation within a given range of variety, so can collaborating individuals achieve these economies of scope if their knowledge sets fall within the same domain of specialisation and comparable levels of accuracy. Highly specialised (high accuracy, limited variety) knowledge sets need to be combined with each other. Combining them with less specialised sets or individuals with non-overlapping knowledge reduces the efficiency of communication.

For instance, there is no point in a highly specialised HIV researcher moving to a developing country, with a high prevalence of HIV but only general AIDS researchers. His skills are of little use there and he will have to de-specialise (reduce accuracy and widen variety) before his knowledge can be fitted in the general pool of knowledge in that society. His productivity is likely to decline because he will find it hard to team up with equally skilled researchers in slightly different but complementary domains. Though there is a lot of demand for his highly specialised skills, and they would be very useful in solving the HIV problems in that country, his specialised knowledge is likely to remain unproductive. His comparative advantage would fetch a higher price on labour markets where complementary specialised skills would be available too. In the absence of the latter, his skills are useless.

We can now develop a measure of the uniqueness or fit of an individual's specialised knowledge into his society's total knowledge set. Specialisation (S) was defined in Chapter 6 as a measure of how common a specific subset of knowledge is within a group of individuals. What we need here is a measure of an individual's degree of specialisation compared to group knowledge, or a measure of how un-common his knowledge is compared to that available in the group. To do so, we need to measure the difference between the composition of an individual knowledge set and 'average' knowledge in society. If a knowledge subset G_m, subset of H_T, is rare in society, so that the number of individuals n_m holding G_m is low, or the ratio n_m/n (where n is the total number of individuals in society) is low, then G_m is a highly specialised piece of knowledge held by that individual. On the other hand, if the number of individuals holding G_m is high, then it has little value as specialised knowledge. The degree of individual specialisation is thus, in a sense, the inverse of the degree of commonality of his knowledge. The ratio n/n_m measures the degree of un-commonality of knowledge. By summing this up over all subsets of knowledge held by an individual, and dividing that sum by the total number of subsets m, we obtain the average degree of specialisation of an individual in a group:

$$Si = [(\Sigma_j:_1 \rightarrow m (1 - n_m/n)]/m$$

where m is the total number of knowledge subsets held by individual i. The lower limit on S_i is 0 (when all subsets held by the individual are also known to everybody else) and the upper limit can approach 1 (when n_m is low and assuming that n is high). Note that S_i can be manipulated by varying the size of the group and especially by limiting the group to individuals who hold fairly similar knowledge sets.

The need for complementary skills may explain why so many developing countries have an oversupply of over-skilled secondary school and university graduates who can find no proper job in society, a phenomenon studied by Pritchett (1996). Pritchett's controversial paper 'Where has all the education gone?' observed the discrepancy between the microeconomic and the macro-economic impact of education. Despite the fact that educated labour is usually scarce in developing countries, the macroeconomic returns to education in terms of increased growth rates often remain low. In other words, investing in individual specialisation through further education has little effect in a developing country economy. This constitutes a disincentive for further learning. Complementary knowledge may provide an answer to that puzzle. If we insert an individual with a considerably higher degree of individual knowledge specialisation into a low-specialised developing country economy, finding complementary (or identical) knowledge sets to collaborate with for the production of joint outputs may become problematic. Instead, specialised individuals are often forced to de-specialise and take charge of a range of production tasks that are outside their own domain of specialisation, in order to make up for lack of closely connecting complementary (or identical) specialisation among their collaborators. This inflates their common knowledge interfacing requirements with collaborators and consequently reduces their comparative advantage, productivity and revenue. The skills of highly educated individuals are too narrowly defined and accurate for a society that operates at a much lower degree of specialisation.

Note that neither the neo-classical Solow growth theory nor the Endogenous Growth model has an explanation for this phenomenon. The neo-classical growth model has no way of handling increasing returns. The Endogenous Growth model would assume that knowledge from a highly specialised individual would eventually spill over into the rest of society, through non-excludability of knowledge, resulting in some sort of convergence of skills within society. It does not consider the transaction costs and inefficiencies that result from such discrepancies in specialisation, and would simply add in the knowledge of the specialist to the general pool of knowledge in society, independently of its complementarity. Krugman's (1994) increasing returns within geographical growth clusters come perhaps closest to the concept of economies of scope, though without the underlying cognitive explanations for this phenomenon. These can only be found in a cognitive approach that distinguishes between accuracy and variety of knowledge. Complementarity of specialised knowledge sets, like economies of scope, is a consequence of the distributed structure of knowledge in our brain, and the way in which knowledge is assembled from fragmented neuronal networks.

We can conclude from this discussion on complementarity that the degree of specialisation in society is constrained by a variety of factors, from Adam Smith's extent of the market (for a specialised skill) to the way in which society organises production in teams and allows specialised teams to cluster, providing them with common appropriate interfaces where need be. Complementarity is clearly a crucial factor in explaining the role of knowledge in economic growth and development. It is not only the volume of knowledge and the degree of specialisation in that knowledge set, but also the degree of complementarity between specialised knowledge sets, that determines the returns to knowledge and thus its contribution to economic growth.

We started this chapter with the observation that learning is unlikely to stop, even though society may reach a cognitive equilibrium situation (see Chapter 6) that determines the degree of specialisation, or the ratio between common and specialised knowledge. Schumpeterian competition will force individuals to continue learning, as part of their existing knowledge may lose its economic value. Economies of scope will drive them into ever further specialisation. That may put pressure on the cognitive equilibrium to diminish the part of scarce cognitive capacity taken up by common knowledge and thereby allow more room for specialisation. The average degree of specialisation may not be a good indicator to go by in this case, as complementarities between knowledge sets may vary. The formation of sub-groups of professional specialists may be a way out. It allows further specialisation within the sub-group and, provided they equip their products and services with appropriate common knowledge interfaces, it may facilitate exchange with the rest of society without putting too much pressure on the cognitive equilibrium situation. Still, room for manoeuvre via changes in organisational arrangements is likely to diminish in the course of time. At that point, changes in the institutional architecture of society will have to create more space for further specialisation and economic growth.

Fisher's Theorem

Economies of scope explain how further learning has a tendency to produce increasing specialisation and accuracy in knowledge, rather than increasing variety in knowledge. This is one direction of causality that links learning to specialisation. But what about the reverse direction of causality? Does the degree of specialisation affect the rate of learning? In this section, I examine the causal link between the two, using an old theorem from evolutionary biology, Fisher's Theorem.

Fisher's (1930) *The Genetic Theory of Natural Selection* constitutes a milestone in the synthesis between Mendel's genetic theory of inheritance of traits and Darwin's theory of natural selection. Fisher starts from the observation that, in order for differential natural selection to take place, there must first be a cause that creates differentiation within a species. Blending of traits through mating cannot be such a source because it would quickly erode all differentiation. A genetic theory of inheritance, however, allows for differentiation to take place without blending, and for traits to be transferred across generations without necessarily becoming apparent in each generation. Fisher calls this 'particulate inheritance', 'particles' of traits that are transmitted through genes. He demonstrates how particulate inheritance provides a more likely basis for differentiation than blending, because it is far less demanding in terms of differentiation factors. He then sets out to prove his 'Fundamental Theorem of Natural Selection'. This theorem states that the rate of increase in fitness of any organism at any time is equal to its genetic variance in fitness at that time. In other words, the higher its genetic variance, the higher the growth rate of fitness.

In Chapter 1, we equated fitness with knowledge and defined it as the ability to respond appropriately to changes in the environment. Genetic adaptation was explained as a form of knowledge of the environment, acquired through mutation (or differentiation) and selection, that is translated into behavioural traits. Cognitively acquired knowledge is also a form of behavioural adaptation to an environment. It is acquired through different means: learning and storage in the brain rather than random genetic mutation and natural selection. Also, it is stored in a different format: knowledge, and its various forms of representation and embodiment, rather than genes. If this extension of the fitness concept to all forms of knowledge is correct, then Fisher's Theorem should be applicable to knowledge in general. Translated into cognitive terms, the theorem would read as follows: the rate of increase in knowledge of any organism at any time is equal to the variance in its knowledge at that time. Variance in knowledge can be measured by the average degree of specialisation in a population. Consequently, the cognitive version of Fisher's Theorem would predict that higher degrees of specialisation result in higher rates of growth of knowledge. For a given limited individual information processing capacity, and a given number of individuals in society, the use of that capacity for learning purposes will result in more additional knowledge, the higher the degree of specialisation.

The validity of this conclusion can easily be demonstrated by means of the equation that linked specialisation and total knowledge, proposed in Chapter 6 and repeated below:

$$H_T = (1 + (n - 1) S) H_i$$

where H_i is individual knowledge, S the average degree of specialisation and H_T total knowledge in society. If we keep n and S constant, the rate of growth of knowledge in society, dH_T/dt, is the product of the individual rate of knowledge growth dH_i/dt and a constant ≥ 1. For S close to zero, the constant will be close to 1. For $S > 0$ however, the rate of growth in total knowledge will accelerate, the higher the degree of specialisation. For S approaching 1, the constant will approach n – the number of individuals in society. For large societies, one can immediately see the enormous leverage effect of specialisation on growth of total knowledge. Knowledge growth is thus bound to accelerate with increasing specialisation.

However the question remains whether accelerated growth of knowledge will also accelerate economic growth. Maddison (2001) observes a slow but steady rise in the rate of economic growth between 1000 and 1820 AD, from 0.05 per cent per year to 1.33 per cent. However, evidence over a much shorter time period (Jones 1995) shows that increased investment in knowledge in the developed economies (measured by R&D as a percentage of GDP) is not correlated with increases in GDP growth or productivity growth. This finding somewhat undermines the rationale behind Endogenous Growth Theory. Another problem with Endogenous Growth models is created by scale effects to knowledge since they cause exploding growth rates. Jones (1999) and Li (2000) present ways of building stabilisers into these models. From a Neo-Schumpeterian point of view there is no immediate reason why growth in knowledge should be correlated with economic growth. Increased R&D may increase monopolistic profit margins in successful companies, but erode profits of others. The structure of competition in markets thus puts a "cushion" between knowledge and GDP growth.

Conclusions

A first purpose of this chapter was to connect the cognitive approach to economic exchange, presented in Chapter 6, with some of these stylised facts, in particular increasing returns to knowledge that extant growth theories have such a hard time dealing with. Modern economic growth theory is in disarray, with many competing models vying for attention and providing partial but incomplete explanations for the stylised empirical facts of growth. It would be presumptuous to propose a completely new model of economic growth to replace all these partial attempts. However, this chapter has demonstrated how accumulation of knowledge entails a variety of mechanisms based on increasing returns, be it as pure economies of scale (extent of the market) or in the form of economies of scope – a special version of economies of scale. This has several implications for our understanding of growth theory.

First, these mechanisms present an innovative view, since they go beyond the traditional view of returns to scale in knowledge as a consequence of non-rivalry and partial excludability – arguments that were frequently used in the debate between the neo-classical and the Endogenous Growth schools.

Second, they have shed new light on phenomena such as clustering of specialists and increasing returns to abundant rather than scarce knowledge. Whereas the Endogenous Growth school is still split between decreasing returns (the convergence school) and increasing returns (non-convergence), the cognitive approach proposed here clearly points towards increasing returns. However, the reason for doing so is not derived from non-rivalry and partial excludability characteristics of knowledge, as the Endogenous Growth school does, but from the underlying cognitive characteristics of learning and knowledge storage in the human brain.

Third, the cognitive mechanisms discussed in this chapter demonstrate the importance of specialisation in explaining economic development, a variable that has been neglected ever since Adam Smith first mentioned it (see Chapter 3). This yields a different picture of economic growth, compared to the neo-classical and Endogenous Growth models. It is not just investment in embodied (capital goods) and disembodied knowledge (human capital) that drive growth, but also changes in the distribution of knowledge across society that are at the roots of long-term economic development.

Another purpose of this chapter was to take the issues of knowledge, learning and specialisation out of the straightjacket of a single overall measure of specialisation and the lifetime learning equilibrium model presented in Chapter 6. We have examined three mechanisms that influence individual learning and specialisation: Schumpeterian competition, economies of scope, and complementarity between individual knowledge sets. Moreover, we looked at two mechanisms that link individual specialisation to the overall degree of specialisation in society, and further to economic growth: economies of scale in the extent of the market, and Fisher's Theorem. These mechanisms have generated a more dynamic picture of learning and specialisation, with some insights into cognitive mechanisms that may drive economic growth and that are not accounted for in existing neo-classical Solow nor Endogenous Growth models.

The five mechanisms examined in this chapter all point in the same direction, namely a tendency towards increasing specialisation, not only among individuals but also at the level of society. This inevitably puts pressure on the equilibrium degree of specialisation and will upset the transaction costs – residual uncertainty equilibrium. Some of that pressure can be relieved through different organisational arrangements in society, as suggested in the second part of the section on complementarity knowledge. Specialists can team up in groups, or professional organisations in society, with a designated communication interface to make their knowledge accessible for, and exchangeable with, the rest of society. But that offers only temporary respite from increased pressure towards further specialisation, beyond the equilibrium allowed by the institutional architecture of society. Consequently, in the longer run, institutional change that reduces residual uncertainty for a given level of transaction costs (or common knowledge) will be inevitable. How institutions change as a result of specialisation pressure is examined in Part III of this book. In Part III, the remaining exogenous variable, institutions, will be endogenised in this model, and the consequences for cognitive economic development will be explored.

Part III

The cognitive mechanics of institutional change

It may be worthwhile at this stage to pause for a moment and take stock of where we stand in the arguments that have been developed so far.

In Part II, I proposed a theory of knowledge, derived from the concept of bounded rationality and based on the identification of regularities in an apparently chaotic environment. These regularities permit individuals to better respond to threats and opportunities. Knowledge accumulation is a recurrent feature throughout evolution but humans are, up to this stage, the evolutionary champions of knowledge accumulation. They are able to make extensive use of symbolic media and have the ability to embody their knowledge in produced goods that can be exchanged. I showed that transmission of knowledge in embodied forms (economic exchange) is evolutionarily superior to symbolically mediated exchange. More importantly, it results in the emergence of distributed knowledge and specialisation in society, a phenomenon that is typical of human societies.

Specialisation and trade, in turn, induce residual uncertainty and transaction costs in the exchange of goods. Residual uncertainty can be partially overcome if scarce cognitive capacity is spent on transaction costs – the acquisition of common knowledge that does not have exchange value. In Chapter 6 we found that this trade-off between ex-ante *transaction cost and* ex-post *uncertainty is determined by the state of institutions, and that it determines the degree of division of labour and thus knowledge accumulation and exchange potential (or potential economic development) in society. Transaction costs are a function of the degree of specialisation in society. Rather than locking society into an inescapable equilibrium situation, I suggested that the transaction costs/residual uncertainty trade-off could shift as a result of institutional change. However, I kept institutions exogenous and did not really define what they are or where they come from. I only showed their functional role in the exchange of embodied knowledge between specialised individuals: the state of institutions affects the level of specialisation, knowledge accumulation and thus the level of economic development. Chapter 7 constructed a wider view of economic growth and development around these cognitive foundations of specialisation and exchange.*

The approach in Part II was basically institutions-neutral. Like the neo-classical economic paradigm it takes institutions as exogenously given, though unlike the neo-classical economic model it assigns an explicit role to institutions. It is time now to get rid of that neutrality and consider the active role of institutions in economic development. That is the subject of Part III.

Keeping institutions exogenous is an unsatisfactory situation, which must be remedied by explaining (a) what institutions are, (b) where they come from, and (c) how they relate to the division of labour. Question (a) is tackled in Chapter 8. It explores various definitions of institutions and ends up with a cognitive definition – behavioural regularities – which has a striking resemblance to the definition of knowledge. Clearly, institutions and knowledge are two sides of the same cognition coin. This suggests that knowledge, institutions and economic exchange all have the same cognitive origins.

Question (b) is explored in Chapter 9. First, I argue that the voluntary cooperation approach (Prisoners' Dilemma games), very popular over the last 10–15 years, does not produce a satisfactory explanation for the emergence and evolution of institutions. In search of more satisfactory answers, the research then takes a long detour through the literature on anonymous trade. This may look like an unnecessary digression, but it will soon become obvious that there is a link between the division of labour, a key concept in this book, and anonymous trade. Rather than interpreting this concept in a geographic sense (long-distance trade), I opt for a more general cognitive interpretation (trade between specialised individuals who have little knowledge of each other's knowledge). I show that division of labour (or specialisation) requires anonymous trade and, borrowing from Barzel's work, demonstrate why this can only emerge in the presence of some kind of centrally enforced institution. This conclusion introduces an additional variable (compared to the model in Chapter 6) to the link between institutions, division of labour and trade: 'enforcement'. It points in the direction of force, conflict or (in a very broad interpretation) enforcement technology, which is functionally (though not conceptually) different from production technology. Taken together, there is a triangular relationship between division of labour, institutions and enforcement technology, that needs to be explained. In other words: I need to explain why increasingly decentralised knowledge (increasing division of labour, or specialisation) goes hand-in-hand with increasingly centralised enforcement of property rights on that knowledge.

That relationship is explained in the model presented in Chapter 10. I start from the simplest case: a society with no division of labour and a fully shared conflict or enforcement technology. I demonstrate how this gives rise to sharing norms and why this is economically inefficient. The combination of division of labour and a monopoly on enforcement technology is, from an economic point of view, the most efficient and generates a set of private (decentralised) property rights institutions. The model explains the endogenous emergence and evolution of property rights, based on this combination of conflict and organisation theory with the division of labour model developed in Chapter 4. This model hinges on the trade-off between the centralising force of decisive conflict technology and the decentralising force of distributed knowledge. This leads to the conclusion that institutions are endogenous to the cognitive state of societies: they depend on the degree of division of labour and on the state of military technology. This completes the circle: whereas Chapter 6 assumed exogenous institutions, Chapter 10 endogenises institutions into a more comprehensive cognitive approach to economic and institutional development.

The reader may notice that Parts I, II and III each have a distinct flavour. Part I criticised the neo-classical economic paradigm and especially neo-classical growth theory for its inability to handle (distributed) knowledge. Part II focused on cognition, information theory and communication of knowledge, though it ended up by making a link again to economic growth and development concepts. In Part III we change the subject again and dive into institutions, borrowing a lot from New Institutional Economics. However, the reasons for switching to this subject are not only related to the need to endogenise institutions into this cognitive approach to economics developed in Part II. Institutions in themselves are cognitive constructions. They represent regularities in behaviour, just like other types of knowledge. They emerge in response to the need to deal with asymmetric distribution of knowledge in society. As such, institutions are the flip side of the economic coin. While the traditional (neo-classical) view of economics focuses on exchange of things we know (the perfect information hypothesis), trade between specialised individuals inevitably entails an exchange of things we don't know much about. If we knew a lot about the things we exchange, there would be no specialisation any more. Institutions are there to help us manage (not solve) the consequence of this ignorance in a more efficient way. In Part III, I will demonstrate how trade and institutions are two inseparable sides of the same economic coin and how they are both generated by distributed cognition, or specialisation or division of labour. The switch to institutions in Part III is thus not a complete change of subject. Rather, we take a look at the same cognitive subject again (trade), but from another cognitive angle (institutions). An additional complication in Part III is that most economic institutions require enforcement, especially those that are related to anonymous trade between individuals who do not have strong social ties with each other. That requires a distinction between voluntary and involuntary exchange of goods. The first is the domain of economics in the traditional narrow sense ('markets') while the second belongs to the domain of institutions (constraints on freedom), and inevitably raises the question of enforcement technology, or the use of knowledge to enforce contracts and institutions. That is a domain covered by conflict theory.

The cognitive approach advocated in this research provides an integrated model for understanding the implications of trading knowledge (economics) and for handling ignorance (institutions). Institutions are therefore endogenous to the level of cognitive and economic development of societies. This vindicates Loasby's (1999) conjecture that the study of economic processes necessarily requires the study of institutions, since economic processes are based on incomplete knowledge that generates uncertainty, and institutions are there to mitigate and reduce that uncertainty. Economic processes and institutions are ways of organising our ignorance in a more efficient way, driven by the principle of cognitive economy.

8   The role of institutions

What are institutions?

A long time ago, Kuhn (1962) pointed out that the absence of well defined concepts and a profusion of alternative and often incompatible definitions is the typical situation of a young and immature science. When scientific disciplines grow older and become better established, they tend to converge around a single paradigm and a widely accepted set of more coherent definitions. That is probably what accounts for the strength of neo-classical economics. The Arrow-Debreu model provides that paradigmatic and rigorously defined foundation stone for modern mainstream economics. As a corollary, it is also what accounts for the weakness of present-day neo-institutional economics. There is no single foundational paradigm, and not even a single set of definitions of basic concepts. The vagueness of institutional economics concepts may be due to the fact that it is a young domain of social science research. However, three decades after it was born in the 1970s, the time may have come to bring some order to that definitional chaos. Greif (2000) notes that understanding the common aspects of various definitions and developing a unifying concept of institutions may be the key to advancing institutional analysis. In this chapter, I explore the possibilities of establishing such a unifying concept on the basis of the cognitive theory that I developed in earlier chapters.

Modern or neo-institutional economics is a tree with many branches and twigs. The terminology 'institutional economics' covers a wide range of schools of thought and methods. It includes several varieties of transaction cost economics, from Coase (1937; 1960) to North (1990) and Williamson (1985), as well as various branches of organisation theory, including agency theory (Jensen and Meckling 1976), property rights (Grossman and Hart 1986) and incomplete contracts theory (Tirole 1999), and its analysis of organisational design (Holmstrom and Milgrom 1991; Aghion and Tirole 1997). All these schools of institutional economic thought have a common characteristic: they examine how informational problems affect performance, though from different angles. That is precisely what distinguishes neo-classical from neo-institutional economics. While the former generally assumes that (near-) perfect information is available in transactions at (near-) zero costs, the latter assumes positive information costs. Transaction cost economics looks at the cost of the information required to conclude a contract or exchange (North 1990) and the potential costs of post-contractual uncertainty or absence of information (Williamson 1985). Incomplete contracts theory is based on quite similar principles, but focuses on the incentives embedded in a contract and the likely behavioural outcomes that they produce under imperfect information (Tirole 1999). Property rights theory examines how different allocations of this residual contractual uncertainty create different incentive structures. Modern organisation theory combines these different techniques to study incentives, delegation of tasks and exchange of knowledge in large organisations and hierarchies.

This variety of interpretations of neo-institutional economics has produced an equally varied range of definitions of the basic concept of institutions. Let us turn to a few well known authors and handbooks of institutional economics to see how they approach institutions. Eggertsson (1990) does not explicitly define institutions. Instead, he jumps straight into a discussion of transaction costs, property rights, contracts and organisational forms. After all, that is where institutional economics originated historically. Coase's (1937) foundation stones are built on transaction costs and organisational arrangements. Pejovich (1998: 5) also considers that New Institutional Economics is basically about property rights and that 'institutions' is simply another word for property rights allocations. The latter are a problematic issue because of transaction costs, the real costs of information, measurement and enforcement of property rights. He then defines institutions as the legal, administrative and customary arrangements for repeated human interactions (23). Their major function is to make human behaviour more predictable. Furubotn and Richter (1997: 6) are more precise, and define institutions as 'the set of formal and informal rules, including their enforcement arrangements'. In fact, this definition dates back to Schmoller, an early-twentieth-century member of the German branch of the old institutional school. They also cite Ostrom (1991), who defines institutions as 'the set of working rules' that 'contain prescriptions that forbid, permit or require some action or outcome'. It is easy to see how these definitions facilitate the inclusion of beliefs and behavioural norms. North (1990: 3) is the first to make a clear distinction between institutions and organisations. Institutions are the humanly devised constraints that shape human interaction; they constitute behavioural incentives. Organisations are the groups of individuals that follow a particular set of constraints or rules. North's emphasis on 'constraints' also suggests a property rights interpretation, although he presents a separate definition for property rights as the rights of individuals to appropriate their own labour, goods and services (1990: 33). These rights are a function of, but not necessarily identical with, the institutional framework, in North's view.

Greif (2000: 7) concludes that all these definitions share a basic concern with the factors that generate a *regularity in behaviour* by coordination, enabling and constraining. This brings us back to the concept of 'regularities'. In Chapter 4 I concluded that learning consists of the identification of regularities in information emitted by the environment. I labelled these regularities as 'knowledge'. They enable agents with cognitive capability to make future events more predictable and guide behavioural responses to these events. This leaves us with an ambiguity between behavioural regularities that result from knowledge about the environment and behavioural regularities that are imposed through human interaction. The former enable a reduction in primary uncertainty, the latter in secondary uncertainty.

In line with March and Simon's (1952) research on the origin and role of behavioural routines, Mantzavinos (2001: 87) also distinguishes between regularities that guide interactions between individuals and those that bring cognitive 'relief' because they simplify decision-making and replace a range of decision options by predetermined routines. Knowledge about the natural environment falls into the former category, while knowledge about the social environment falls into the latter. Because of limited cognitive processing capacity, both types of regularities generate cognitive economy: they save scarce information processing capacity for important decisions while putting routine decisions into the background, following well established behavioural procedures.

In terms of the cognitive mechanisms explained in Chapter 4, such cognitive economy can be achieved through categorisation of behavioural patterns: the various behaviours and attributes of a particular behavioural routine are stored in a single category (set of bindings in the brain). When activated by an information signal, that category produces the entire set of behaviours, without having to (re-)establish the necessary set of bindings through learning and information processing. Note that the principle of cognitive economy surfaces again here; we have already encountered it in Part II. Institutions in human societies can thus be considered as another extension of the evolutionary drive in nature for further cognitive economy.

Mantzavinos classifies both types of regularities as institutions. That does not solve the ambiguity: both are humanly devised regularities that guide behaviour and may guide social interaction as well. Though some of these regularities might be externally generated in social contexts and put constraints on behaviour, others might well be generated internally through learning processes and thus form part of the set of regularities that we defined as knowledge. A possible way out of this ambiguity is to consider pure knowledge-based behavioural regularities as a range of *potential* behavioural options, while social-interaction-based regularities allocate costs and benefits to these behavioural options (caused by the responses of others to these behaviours) and thereby narrow that range to

an *economically feasible* set. For many daily problems, we can theoretically conceive of a range of behavioural response options. To alleviate
hunger, we can think of hunting animals in the forest, stealing food from
the corner shop, or work, earn money and pay for food at the shop. We
usually settle for the last option because all other options are likely to
trigger costly reactions from other persons who intend to defend their
rights over these resources. These reactions change the costs and benefits
pattern from its 'natural' state. Behavioural options that fall outside the
economically feasible set generate more costs than benefits, so that individuals avoid choosing these options. It is the combination of both types of
regularities (the set of possible behavioural actions and the corresponding
set of social reactions) that enables human societies to operate and
develop.

Institutions could thus be considered as humanly devised responses to
actions, with a view to re-allocating the costs and benefits of behaviour,
and producing outcomes that differ from the primary or natural outcome
(in the absence of social responses). Institutions thus re-shape incentives
for human behaviour and interaction by changing the costs and benefits
attached to various behavioural options. This interpretation of the concept
of institutions establishes a firm connection, if not equivalence, between
institutions and property rights. Pejovich (1998), for instance, defines
property rights as 'the norms of behaviour that individuals must observe in
interaction with others or bear the cost of violation. They define the relationship among individuals with respect to scarce goods'. Moreover, and
perhaps more importantly, this interpretation links the study of institutions
and property rights to the study of the ability of persons to impose costs
on each other's behaviour. Institutions and property rights are based on
coercion. The study of institutions becomes the study of power relationships between persons.

This brings us to the domain of politics, the study of how these power
relationships work and produce institutions. Bertrand Russell defined the
realm of politics as the ability to coerce, bargain and persuade. The ability
to persuade depends largely on the capacity to manipulate inherently
imperfect information, such as beliefs or other types of information
shortcut that help people to reach cognitive closure and come to a decision,
despite incomplete information (Choi 1993). Bargaining is an essential part
of the neo-classical competitive market paradigm. Neo-classical models
describe how persons can improve their resource situation through voluntary (un-coerced) bargaining within the confines of an initial set of
property rights that have been allocated to them. It implicitly assumes that
such an initial set of rights (or institutions) exists, but does not explain
how it emerged or how it is enforced. Since we explicitly want to study the
factors that explain the emergence of these property rights institutions, we
need to drop this assumption and step outside the neo-classical paradigm.
Institutional economics makes explicit what remained implicit in neo-clas-

sical economics. That move can be illustrated with a quote from Edgeworth (1881, quoted in Garfinkel and Skaperdas 2000a: 5)

> The first principle of economics is that every agent is actuated only by self-interest. The workings of this principle may be viewed under two aspects, according as the agent acts without or with the consent of others affected by his actions. In wide senses, the first species of action may be called war; the second, contracts.

Edgeworth, and most of the marginalist and neo-classical economists that came after him, limited their studies to the category of exchanges within a contractually defined framework. War, or in less dramatic terms, conflict over the allocation of property rights (institutions), is assumed to be exogenous and settled prior to exchange. If we want to study the emergence and evolution of institutions, we need to trace our steps in economics back to the time before Edgeworth made his crucial decision: conflict has to be endogenised again in the economic model. Bertrand Russell's third component of politics is the real subject of our investigations here: coercion or involuntary exchange through conflict. We need to explore how conflict technology affects the costs associated with various behavioural options – in short, how it affects institutional or property rights constraints on behaviour.

In a way, recent developments in economic theory have contributed to turning the history of economic thought back full circle to Edgeworth's starting point. In modern contract theory, the borderline between contract and conflict has become more permeable. With incomplete contracts, that borderline is endogenously determined as a function of transaction costs. This point deserves a short digression into contract theory.

Contract theory explains how the inherent incompleteness of contracts affects the allocation of costs and benefits and exposes the inherent uncertainty in property rights. It is often assumed that all contracts are inherently incomplete: no property right or behavioural regularity can be described in such detail that it foresees and clarifies all possible *ex-post* or future events and cases. A complete contract would be of infinite length and infinitely costly. In fact, it is very easy to write a complete contract of finite length at finite transaction costs. A complete contract could even be very short and cheap. It would simply specify that, whatever happens, all costs and benefits that occur after the exchange is carried out accrue to the buyer. This is not a hypothetical case; we do occasionally enter into such deals in daily life. For example, we buy cheap goods at flea markets or ice cream from roadside vendors without much possibility of recourse to corrective actions should the deal turn out to be a big mistake. We do take such risks for small transactions because the cost of verifying the deal would often exceed the value of the traded goods. But for more expensive or risky deals, we would not accept such an implicit or explicit contract that transfers all residual risks to us, as buyers. So complete contracts are not impossible but unlikely. They are rarely accepted because they are too risky. Contract theory also explains the existence of lawyers and judges: since no contract can be complete, interpretation will be required in many cases. Filling in the inherent gaps in contracts is the role of lawyers and judges.

Contract theory may either be interpreted as complementary or as contradictory to property rights theory (Tirole 1999). It is complementary to the extent that it explains the need for *ex-ante* defined property rights (laws and general rules) to fill up the gaps in a bilateral contract. Legal property rights allocate all residual *ex-post* costs and benefits to the owner of a good, except those costs and benefits that are explicitly allocated to another party. Property rights can thus be defined as residual rights or residual claims, the right to claim the benefits but also the obligation to bear the costs that were not allocated *ex-ante* of the transaction. On the other hand, contract theory may be contradictory to property rights theory in its explanation of the origin of the disputed claims. The neo-classical branch of property rights theory (Grossman and Hart 1986) is based on the assumption that complete information can be achieved, at a positive but not infinitely high cost. Contracting parties voluntarily limit the level of detail in a contract in order to save on transaction costs. Contract theory (Laffont and Tirole 1993) starts from a different assumption : even if the contracting parties wanted to write a complete contract, they would not be in a position to do so because of inherently incomplete information. In both cases, contracts necessarily generate secondary uncertainty or residual unresolved claims. Both contract and property rights theory agree that general property rights laws can allocate these claims to 'owners', though even that may require additional third-party interpretative efforts through judges and lawyers. This equates contract theory with agency theory (Jensen and Meckling 1976), another branch of institutional economics, and explains the need for third-party intervention.

In line with the theory of knowledge that I developed earlier on in this book, I concur with Eggertsson (1990), Pejovich (1998) and Furubotn and Richter (1997) and many other authors on this subject, that institutional economics, the study of humanly devised constraints on behaviour, is basically about property rights. Furthermore, the inherently incomplete contracts interpretation of property rights theory is compatible with the existence of transaction costs, residual uncertainty and the need for third-party judgement to come to a closure on uncertain deals. Investment in *ex-ante* transaction costs improves the specifications and reduces uncertainty but cannot achieve completeness. I consider that general laws, social and moral norms, normative beliefs and taboos, private contracts, etc. are all specific types of institutions. They differ in the sources and types of behavioural costs that they impose and how they allocate costs.

The advantage of this approach is that it provides for a logical continuum between the theory of cognition and knowledge accumulation that I developed in Chapters 2 and 3, the cognitive model of economic production and exchange developed in Chapter 4, and the model of endogenous institutions that I will present in Chapter 10. These are not separate and unconnected domains of social and economic science, but rather intimately interwoven domains that cannot be separated. The advantage of the cognitive interpretation that I stick to in this research is that it allows us to integrate all these concepts in a single model.

Before I turn to the next section, a short note on semantics. Though I equate institutions with property rights in an incomplete contracts setting, I stick to the term institutions, simply to reduce semantic confusion and transaction costs for the reader. Occasionally, the terms 'behavioural constraints', 'rules of behaviour', 'incomplete contracts' and 'property rights' may slip in again, hopefully to clarify rather than to blur the picture. Only time will tell whether this semantic choice is an auspicious one.

The how and why of institutions

In the previous section, I defined institutions as property rights and equated that with humanly devised and imposed costs that alter the economically feasible range of behavioural options. That defines the subject area, but does not explain yet why institutions exist and how they operate. That is the subject of this section.

As the emphasis on 'interaction' in North's (1990) definition of institutions indicates, institutions are devices that regulate human interaction, reduce uncertainty and avoid free riding and conflict. By restricting the behavioural range of one person, they avoid costs and create benefits for others. If a person wants to use his full range of behavioural options to obtain food, for instance, he has the choice of growing his own food, hunting, or simply taking food from another person. Growing his own food, he may occupy land that was already used by somebody else. Hunting and simply taking food may deplete the food stock of others too. Institutions are all about the regulations of these potential externalities (Papandreou 1994), the spillover of costs and benefits from the behavioural choices of one agent to the resource situation and behavioural options of others. By imposing costs on particular behavioural options, institutions reduce the range of economically feasible options for one person and thereby enhance the economically feasible range for others.

There are several ways in which institutions can emerge. Barzel (2001) classifies institutions according to the source of costs that are imposed on deviant behaviour. His classification is not original or unique; many other authors have come up with similar classifications. But it is useful to illustrate the various mechanisms that can impose costs on social interactions.

Barzel distinguishes between conventions, social norms and third-party enforced institutions. In the latter category he makes a further distinction between non-violent and violent enforcement. I discuss the first two categories in this section; the latter category will be the subject of the remainder of this chapter.

At the most immediate and personal level, there are *conventions*: behavioural constraints that are basically self-enforcing and generate immediate costs if not complied with. For example, a number of traffic rules are of that nature. If you fail to drive on the correct side of the road or stop before a traffic light, chances are very real that you will run into an accident – a costly sanction for non-compliance that you impose upon yourself. Languages also belong in the category of conventions. If you fail to speak a language that your interlocutors understand, you will not be able to convey your message and incur costs, or forgo benefits, as a result of that. Note that there is no need for a third-party judge or an active enforcement authority. The defector automatically incurs non-compliance costs but nobody else incurs costs to impose costs on the defector – though some may incur costs because of his defection: the traffic accidents that he causes or the linguistic misunderstandings that result in lost opportunities. Trespassers of conventions may generate negative externalities for others; more importantly, they trigger severe negative 'internalities' for themselves.

At a somewhat less immediate and personal level, we find *social norms*. These are behavioural constraints that are collectively enforced through negative feedback from other group members. It requires other agents to take action to impose costs on defectors. Action is triggered when an agent imposes costs or reduces the benefits of other members – in short, when behavioural externalities occur. Externalities are a well known concept in economics. They create discrepancies between the private and social costs of individual behavioural choices. As such, they are the scourge of neo-classical economics because they induce market failures: market prices and individual choices no longer reflect the true (marginal) costs and benefits of an exchange. As a result, outcomes of market processes become sub-optimal, below the welfare optimum that could be achieved without these externalities. Neo-classical economics strives to minimise externalities in order to reach its cherished Pareto optimal welfare outcome.

There is a large class of externalities that is associated with pure public goods (Samuelson 1954; Olson 1965), and most attention in neo-classical economics has been focused on those. Pure public goods are non-excludable, or non-divisible, and non-rival goods. Non-excludability means that once they are produced, everybody can benefit from them or it is at least costly to exclude somebody from enjoying the benefits. Non-rivalry refers to the fact that one person's use and benefits from a public good do not in any way affect or diminish another's use and benefits from that same public good. (Non-) rivalry is a 'natural' property of non-material goods, such as knowledge; (non-) excludability is a regulatory characteristic and depends on the existence and cost of systems that can exclude or detect use of specific goods and services. See Chapter 2 for a more detailed discussion of these characteristics of goods. Typical pure public goods are national defence, legal and security systems, clean air and environmental controls. Motorways used to be considered as public goods but nowadays electronic systems exist that are perfectly able to track individual use of motorways, and even neighbourhood streets, so that this public infrastructure could in fact be turned into a purely private good; technological advances have turned it into a (potentially) excludable good. Most of these public goods are likely to be produced by formal government systems, though some may be informally produced, for instance social norms or spontaneous local collective action to solve environmental problems.

However, externalities are not restricted to public goods alone. Many, if not most, pure private goods – excludable and rival goods – also exhibit externalities. Externalities abound; they are everywhere. When somebody builds a house, he creates positive and negative externalities for his neighbours. When you drive a car, you create externalities for other road users. When you wear a new dress, you create externalities for passers-by. Individuals are rarely in a situation whereby their decisions do not have any impact on others. The role of institutions is to rein in at least some of these externalities and keep them within limits.

Neo-classical economics has a hard time dealing with externalities. Some economists thought that externalities are rather exceptional situations that do not really invalidate the neo-classical way of thinking and that could be solved by appropriate and exogenously determined ad-hoc institutions. Pigou was among the first economists to propose a more systematic solution to this problem. He suggested that all discrepancies between private and social costs could be eliminated through taxes and subsidies, costs and benefits imposed by governments. In other words, it was the government's role to eliminate them. Coase's (1960) article on 'social costs' was an innovative response to Pigou's government-led approach. Coase argued that many of these discrepancies could be eliminated through private negotiations, without government interference and constrained only by the level of transaction costs. Demsetz (1986) describes in great detail how this led to the birth of a disagreement that was characterised by ideological dividing lines rather than academic debate. The libertarians hijacked Coase while Pigou ended up in the Keynesian government intervention camp. Several years later, Olson (1965) looked at the problem in his 'Logic of collective action'. He proposed another solution to free riding in pure public goods, whereby the production of a private and a public good were linked to each other so that free riders on the public good would be denied access to the private good too. Admittedly, this may work in a very limited number of cases only. Olson was pessimistic about markets being able to solve externalities and free riding, and argued in favour of government intervention and coercion, or formal institutions. That message stood somewhat at odds with the neo-classical free market idea. It triggered a frantic search for institution-generating mechanisms that were not based on coercion or government intervention.

A first class of solutions for the problems of cooperation among individuals came with game theoretic approaches to cooperation in a non-cooperative setting, i.e. settings where free riding is likely. This was pioneered originally in social anthropology by Ullmann-Margalit (1977), who demonstrated how Prisoners' Dilemma game situations could result in the emergence of socially constrained or normative behaviour. Axelrod (1984) imported these ideas into economics and was among the first to stage an experimental test of Ullmann-Margalit's theory. His work gave birth to today's booming business of experimental economics.

The classic Prisoners' Dilemma (PD) game is derived from the typical choice situation of two prisoners who are guilty of collaboration in a crime (Table 8.1). Confession may result in a reduced prison sentence, while denial may either result in a release (if no witnesses can be found) or a long prison sentence (if the other prisoner witnesses against him). If both prisoners deny, however, they may both be released for lack of evidence; that would clearly be the most beneficial situation. To achieve this most favourable outcome, the prisoners need to cooperate and agree to tell the same story. The problem with individual players in a voluntary cooperation game is that they do not have information on the other players' intentions, strategies and perceptions of uncertainty. If the prisoners are separated from each other and cannot communicate, they need to take a decision under uncertainty regarding the other's stance. In real life situations, prisoners usually get only one chance to decide their stance: there is only a single round of the game. The rational stance in single-round PD games is a Nash equilibrium (the northwest quadrant in Table 8.1), with no cooperation between the prisoners: they both confess and get a reduced prison sentence. Confession reduces risk (variation in outcomes), in return for a low but certain advantage: a one-year reduction in the prison sentence.

Axelrod's (1984) contribution to the analysis of PD-game situations was that he empirically demonstrated the gains from repeated rounds of play. Repeated play generates a track record of players' behaviour and constitutes an indirect source of information that reduces uncertainties regarding others' behaviour. Repeated rounds of play enable them to move towards a more optimal strategy and Pareto equilibrium (the southeast quadrant in Table 8.1). How fast players reach a Pareto equilibrium is a function of the width of the communication channel. More direct forms of communication between the prisoners would shorten the number of rounds required to achieve a stable equilibrium strategy.

Axelrod also demonstrated that behavioural rules that emerge from repeated play are not credible, and remain ineffective if not backed up by commitment devices that ensure that the rule is followed. Whatever information you have on a player's past track record does not ensure that he

Table 8.1

	Prisoner A confesses	Prisoner A denies
Prisoner B confesses	A's sentence: 3 years B's sentence: 3 years	A's sentence: 4 years B's sentence: 1 year
Prisoner B denies	A's sentence: 1 year B's sentence: 4 years	A's sentence: released B's sentence: released

will stick to the same behaviour in future rounds of the game. Axelrod (1984) demonstrated that a tit-for-tat strategy constitutes such a commitment device. If a player trespasses the rule in any round of the game, the other players treat him likewise in the next round. Tit-for-tat strategies thus reinforce the credibility of behavioural rules that benefit all players. Credibility is enhanced by the imposition of costs for trespassing the rule. If players do not restrict their range of behavioural options to the more cooperative behaviours, they will have to bear the costs of their choice.

Skaperdas (1991; 1992; 1995) further develops the idea of commitment devices, though in a somewhat different setting, where players are not forced anymore to make an exclusive choice for a single strategy: confess or deny. He uses similar static balance-of-power or deterrent games to demonstrate the emergence of collective rules of behaviour. Consider a group of agents who try to maximise consumption subject to a finite resource constraint. As *isolated* individuals, they would simply invest all their resources in the production of consumer goods. As *interacting* individuals, and in the absence of enforceable property rights, they have to invest in credible deterrent devices – arms – to protect their goods against theft. Investments in arms are not directly productive and divert resources from production. Furthermore, the outcome of a fight over property rights is uncertain, unless one of the parties has a clearly overwhelming fighting power. Table 8.2 presents a Skaperdas-type game that is somewhat different from the traditional Axelrod PD game. While the PD game allows players to play pure strategies only ('cooperate' or 'defect'; there are no intermediate options), the game in Table 8.2 allows for mixed strategies. This version will be useful to guide us through a number of issues.

Clearly, the solution whereby both players decided to invest all their resources in arms results in starvation: there is no food for consumption. It is risky for an individual to choose the arms option because it implies death, as much as choosing the food production option may result in starvation because the other party may run away with all your food. In short, corner solutions – investing all resources either in consumer goods or in arms – are high-risk strategies. The Nash equilibrium strategy that

Table 8.2

	If Player A chooses arms	If Player A chooses production
If Player B chooses arms	A: 0 B: 0	A: 0 B: 10
If Player B chooses production	A: 10 B: 0	A: 10 B: 10

minimises risk is no longer to be found in the northwest quadrant but somewhere in between the northwest and southeast. The Pareto-optimal southeast quadrant may also be out of reach of the players because it is too risky and unstable. In order to minimise risk, agents should choose a mixed strategy, based on an appropriate balance between production and theft, depending on their perceptions of risks attached to each of these strategies. How that appropriate balance can be determined, will be worked out in Chapter 9. However, because of the dead-weight investment in arms and inherent uncertainty of the outcome of fights, it is usually preferable to negotiate a settlement rather than to fight. Negotiation may permit a switch of investments away from the unsatisfying all-arms equilibrium (the northwest quadrant in Table 8.2) to the most optimal all-food equilibrium (the southeast quadrant), thereby increasing total production and food consumption. That move can only be made when the inherent risks of the all-food equilibrium are able to be eliminated. Note that, unlike the Axelrod-type PD games, reducing risks in a Skaperdas game is not just a question of increasing information and observation of others' behaviour. Rather, it is a question of commitment devices that reduce uncertainty about the behavioural responses of others and force others to walk in line with the agreed behaviour. Note that the Skaperdas game has moved us away from simple voluntary cooperation to cooperation with commitment devices: coercion (the opposite of voluntary cooperation) becomes an important element in the establishment of institutions.

Fifteen years after Axelrod's first laboratory experiments with PD games, there is a voluminous literature on this and similar types of game. A summary by Hoffman *et al.* (1998) concludes that a move from Nash towards Pareto equilibrium, or voluntary cooperation and private provision of public rules of behaviour, is indeed likely with increasing information intensity and repetition of the game. While these experiments show that more public goods are produced than predicted by the neo-classical competitive markets paradigm (the Nash equilibrium), they also show that a Pareto-optimal equilibrium is usually not reached because of remaining uncertainties.

Does the voluntary cooperation PD approach really explain the emergence of institutions, or the emergence of humanly imposed constraints on behaviour? For modern law and economics textbook authors, this Prisoners' Dilemma game has become the creation(ist) myth of legal systems (for instance, Cooter and Ulen 2000). They illustrate how humanity can work its way out of a Hobbesian world and into the bountiful world of modern democracies. Economists' fascination with game theory over the last two decades, combined with the relatively low cost of running empirical tests of these models in a laboratory setting, have contributed to the popularity of this approach. Part of the excitement was due to the fact that they were the first type of models and experiments to support the thesis that voluntary production of public goods, or public institutions, was indeed feasible for a group of self-interested agents. They demonstrated that methodological individualism did not stand in the way of the emergence of social behaviour, and were perceived as strengthening the position of the neo-classical competitive markets paradigm. Prisoners' Dilemma experiments offered a way out of Olson's (1965) predicament, without the use of force or the need for state intervention. It blew new life into the Coase theorem and provided moral and political support for voluntary market-based approaches to institutional reform. It may even have given new hope to libertarians and anarchists. Ellickson's (1991) *Order without law* demonstrated how informal institutions may supersede formal law because the retaliatory costs that can be imposed through social pressures may exceed the costs imposed by law and courts.

A critique of the voluntary cooperation approach

However, there are many critiques of the voluntary cooperation approach to the emergence of institutions. There are many situations where voluntary cooperation will not work, or circumstances in which it works inefficiently. I regroup these critiques under four labels: finitely repeated interaction, transaction costs, information asymmetry and power asymmetry.

Finitely repeated games

It has been observed in the game theory literature that, in games with a finite number of repeats, the players' strategy collapses to the strategy for a single round game. In the last round of the game, a player has no incentive any more to live up to expectations, because there will be no subsequent round in which the other player can retaliate. Consequently, defection is rational in the last round. Rational players will, however, anticipate defection in the last round and therefore defect in the second-last round, to pre-empt actions of the other player. By extension, this regressive logic breaks down the entire game right from the start. Cooperation is unlikely to occur.

This is not the case for infinitely repeated games or games with a finite but uncertain number of repeated rounds. It is of course debatable to what extent specific types of social interaction fall into the first or the second category. Typically, repeated types of exchange within even loosely knit communities are subject to an undetermined number of repeats. You never know when will be the last time you will shop at the local grocery store, go for a haircut or fill up the car at the local petrol station. Even if the consumer is an infrequent client, word-of-mouth ensures the traders' compliance with fairness norms and his reluctance to cheat on clients. The situation differs in, say, seasonal tourist resorts. The local restaurant or souvenir boutique is unlikely to see its clients again and the tendency to overcharge and cheat on customers is stronger. Clients are unlikely to be in a position to pass on their experience to other tourists; there is hardly any social interaction between them. Tourist guidebooks may help tourists to overcome this informational disadvantage, at the cost of purchasing the guide. Local tourist guides, however, are an unreliable source of information; their interaction with the locals is infinitely repeated while their interaction with tourists is normally limited to a single round.

Transaction cost inefficiency

PD games demonstrate how self-interested persons can produce non-excludable public goods, such as security or general laws, provided there are repeated rounds of interaction and players can build up a credible track record of adherence to mutually beneficial norms of behaviour. However, these public goods are not produced without costs.

First, they require repeated play and cumulative investments in transaction costs to emit behavioural signals to other players and to observe their responses. This sequence of games enables the players to derive a behavioural rule that reduces uncertainty and allows them to move away from Nash towards a Pareto equilibrium. In fact, in most laboratory games, these transaction costs are not accounted for or deducted from the players' gains, thereby giving the false impression that transactions and information are cost-free.

Second, the repeated play of PD games requires investments in retaliatory measures against free riders. Retaliation is costly, both for the retaliating party and the party that is retaliated against. In terms of Figure 6.2, the target of the retaliation loses all his production (if he was caught off-guard and without his own defence in place) or at least part of it (if he expected the retaliation and invested in arms too). The retaliating party has to divert some resources away from production into arms, thereby losing benefits. It can, at best, hope to recover these sunk costs in arms by stealing production from the targeted party.

As such, voluntary cooperation games are all about trading off *ex-ante* transaction costs against reduced *ex-post* uncertainty. The more confidence-building information is emitted and received during successive rounds of the game, the less likely is free riding – but it can never be excluded and should be guarded against. The voluntary route to cooperation describes a move along the trade-off curve between transaction costs and residual uncertainty (Figure 6.2), not a shift in the curve itself. It does not represent a change in the institutional landscape; only a shift towards higher transaction costs with an unchanged institutional setting. Voluntary cooperation is a possible but not very efficient route. Higher transaction costs reduce specialisation because part of an agent's limited cognitive capacity needs to be allocated to non-tradable common knowledge: the knowledge of others' behavioural track record. Reduced specialisation has a negative impact on the potential for economic exchange and development. Costs may also increase significantly if retaliation is required. An efficient solution would reduce residual uncertainty without increasing transaction costs. That requires a structural shift in the institutional landscape.

Furthermore, transaction costs increase with the number of players in the game. The repeated PD-game approach may be suitable for small and closely knit communities with little division of labour who can spend a lot of time socialising, talking and observing others' behaviour. This helps to integrate the community and keep it tightly knit, with strict enforcement of informal institutions or social constraints on behaviour. It diminishes the opportunities for free-riding, but also involves substantial opportunity costs: a lot of time is invested in the transaction costs of social interaction, including observation and retaliation. For larger communities, however, the PD-game approach may become excessively costly, precisely because of these transaction costs.

Greif's (2000) discussion of the historical decline of the community responsibility system in thirteenth-century Europe provides a good illustration of the transaction cost disadvantages of informal and socially controlled exchange through repeated interaction in closely knit communities. *Ex-post* moral hazard in the execution of trade contracts between cites was avoided through a retaliation system. This consisted of impounding the goods of other traders from the same city in case one trader reneged on his contract. The threat of retaliation provided strong incentives for traders to stick to the terms agreed in the contract. However, with growing city size, number of traders and trade deals, cities became more anonymous places where social control diminished. Less credible characters were able to slip onto the stage and externalise retaliation costs to the wider community. The risk of being caught up in retaliatory actions increased. On top of that, the unwinding of retaliatory actions was a costly affair. It involved substantial time losses for all traders involved and often required a lot of bargaining between many parties. In the end, the community responsibility system and its retaliatory action scheme had to be abandoned and replaced by enforcement systems that were not based on social control.

Milgrom *et al.* (1990) explain how the law merchant managed to overcome some of these transaction costs and thereby provided a more cost-efficient alternative to the community responsibility system. Rather than forcing all traders to check one another's reputations and impose costs collectively, it provided for an independent judge to keep records of those transactions where a dispute had arisen. While that judge had no power to enforce his judgement, reputation effects alone were usually sufficient to induce traders to accept the judgement and pay whatever dues they owed. The law merchant did away with the necessity of repeated interactions between any pair of traders. It made reputations portable across the community of traders and thereby overcame the problem of asymmetrically distributed information. However, it still required repeated interaction within a limited group. Indeed, the system was limited to a single market place where a single law merchant could keep track of all trade disputes.

Greif (1989) describes a somewhat similar reputation-based system of overseas trade among Magribi Jewish traders. They formed coalitions and relied on agency services by other members of the coalition to handle their commercial interests in other trading posts and cities. Reputation was of the utmost importance in this system. It worked more efficiently than formal legal procedures, but required great social investments in reputation. Still, such non-anonymous reputation-based mechanisms had a hard time overcoming asymmetric information induced by more complex goods and larger groups of traders.

Information and situational asymmetry

The underlying (and often implicit) assumption in most voluntary cooperation game experiments is that the information on other players' behaviour is a public good: all players have equal access to it at zero opportunity cost. With specialisation (see Chapter 4), that condition breaks down. All players aim to specialise and restrict the range of variety in their own knowledge set. They try to minimise the amount of common knowledge between them because it is non-tradable. Knowledge has a positive opportunity cost in such a setting. Players would want to maximise their tradable comparative advantage by maximising the asymmetry in the distribution of knowledge between them. Maximisation of individual specialised knowledge and minimisation of common knowledge necessarily results in partial knowledge only of the goods that are being traded (see Chapter 4). This gives rise to another type of uncertainty: secondary uncertainty with respect to the contents and qualities of these goods. Consequently, the cognitive conditions for the emergence of Pareto-efficient institutions in a voluntary setting (publicly shared information or knowledge) are thus contradictory to the cognitive conditions for the emergence of Pareto-optimal economic exchange (asymmetrically distributed knowledge, maximum specialisation). One cannot have it both ways in a voluntary cooperation setting. The fundamental task of institutional change is to produce institutions that reduce the tension between these contradictory cognitive requirements. The law merchant was a step in the right direction because it exploits economies of scale through centralisation of information. I will demonstrate in the next chapter why non-voluntary enforcement of institutions is a more efficient solution to this dilemma.

The informational asymmetry requirements of specialisation are further aggravated by situational asymmetry, caused by non-reversible roles. Axelrod's (1984) tit-for-tat commitment device assumes that players' roles are completely interchangeable; they have equal capacities to impose costs and benefits on each other. With division of labour, or specialisation, that is not the case. Players hold specialised knowledge and positions in society and are not interchangeable. For example, when a customer goes to a computer shop, he has little knowledge of the technical qualities of the computer he buys. The seller is likely to have more knowledge. Tit-for-tat does not work as a commitment device in that case. The buyer is unlikely to be confronted with the seller in a future situation whereby roles are reversed, so that he can repay the seller for any costs that were imposed on him.

Power asymmetry

Most voluntary cooperation game experiments rely on an equal distribution of power among players: no player can force another into a particular choice of behaviour. In reality, that is often not the case. One player may have an overwhelming power and force others into submission. In terms of the PD game in Table 8.2, player A's overwhelming investment in violence may put player B into slavery. This way, A can force B to produce food and expropriate all surpluses. B has no incentive to produce food but coercion makes him do so. The game ends up in the southwest quadrant, away from Nash equilibrium but also far away from a Pareto equilibrium. Player A's virtual monopoly on violence or coercion powers causes this result. Power relations between the players are a very important aspect of cooperation games. I defer a detailed discussion of this subject to Chapter 10. That chapter examines the impact of conflict technology on cooperation outcomes. I will argue there that the type and distribution of conflict technology among the players determines the outcome of cooperation games, much more so than information.

In conclusion, game theory approaches that demonstrate the emergence of voluntary cooperation in a non-cooperative setting are but a very partial and not so cost-effective solution to the externalities problem and the question of the emergence of institutions and property rights. They can be effective only in relatively small communities with a low degree of specialisation, where power is equally distributed and information on all relevant players and products is shared between players and available at low *ex-ante* transaction costs and *ex-post* retaliation costs. These conditions are unlikely to be realised with growing specialisation when trade requires large numbers of players, information asymmetry and low transaction costs. The voluntary cooperation approach in reputation or trust-based systems, like the ones operated by the Magribi traders or the medieval community responsibility system, represent movement along the institutional trade-off curve (see Figure 6.2), not a shift in the curve itself. There is no institutional innovation that reduces *ex-ante* transaction costs for the same level of *ex-post* uncertainty. A central law merchant can exploit economies of scale in information gathering and imposition of fines, and thereby enable a shift in that trade-off curve. As such, the possibilities for structural institutional change are very limited under voluntary cooperation.

9 The state's monopoly on violence

Specialisation and anonymous trade

In the previous chapter I examined various definitions of institutions as well as explanations of the role and sources of emergence of institutions in society. It was concluded that the spontaneous emergence of voluntary institutions, with decentralised retaliation as a commitment device, was not a very efficient and credible explanation for the emergence and evolution of institutions in the context of specialisation and trade. A more credible explanation should be able to overcome a series of criticisms of the voluntary cooperation approach. It should

(a) reduce transaction costs for a given level of uncertainty;
(b) be workable in large communities and avoid the high transaction costs of frequent interaction;
(c) it should work under information asymmetry where knowledge is not a common good; and
(d) it should allow players to move closer to a Pareto equilibrium even in the presence of strong power asymmetries.

The first three conditions are usually associated with the concept of 'anonymous' trade: the ability to conclude a trade deal with low *ex-post* uncertainty within a single round of exchange between parties that have no prior knowledge of each other and have only a minimal degree of common or overlapping knowledge. The last condition refers to the emergence of a monopoly on violence (usually vested in the state), the ultimate form of power asymmetry. With asymmetry in power, we move from voluntary to involuntary exchange, the borderline that Edgeworth identified between contractual market exchange and institutions. In fact, anonymous trade and a monopoly on violence are closely related issues, because the combination of the two enables societies to overcome the contradictory information or knowledge requirements of Pareto-optimal trade (information asymmetry) and Pareto-optimal institutions (shared information). I will demonstrate in this chapter that the link between the two is forged through specialisation.

In most of the literature, anonymous trade is associated with long-distance trade, or with the absence of direct communication between the trading parties. Long-distance trade extends the size of the market and fuels economies of scale, thereby enabling further specialisation. This geographical distance argument is basically an economies-of-scale argument, and could be associated with Smith's statement that 'the division of labour is limited by the extent of the market'.

I would like to generalise this argument here, using the concept of cognitive distance between the trading parties rather than geographical distance only. With increasing specialisation, trading partners have less overlapping knowledge sets. Indeed, their aim is to minimise knowledge overlaps because they are costly and non-tradable. Anonymous trade is a condition that allows potential trading partners to exchange goods and services without much common knowledge, either of each other's behaviour or of the goods they trade. As such, anonymous trade is not only important to bridge geographical distance, but also to bridge cognitive distance without incurring high transaction costs. There is no need to get involved in analysing each other's track record in previous exchanges. The parties simply don't know each other and – most importantly – do not care about knowing each other. The cognitive resources that they save by avoiding socialisation can be more beneficially invested in accumulating more private knowledge to strengthen one's own comparative (and tradable) advantage. Anonymous trade allows trading partners to overcome the transactions cost, large community size and information asymmetry problems identified in the previous chapter. 'Socialised' non-anonymous trade, generated under repeated PD-game conditions, does neither of these.

The cognitive interpretation generalises and expands the concept of anonymous trade and brings it more in line with the characteristics of modern market economies, based on specialisation, in at least two ways:

First, anonymous trade conditions are not only necessary to enable trade between parties who do not know each other because of geographical and social distance; they also facilitate trade between parties who do know each other because of proximity but don't want to let their business come between their social relations. For instance, if you buy your portable computer from a friend's store in your neighbourhood, you do not expect that friend to be responsible for any failings you may detect in that machine or any *ex-post* problems that may arise with its use. A warranty arrangement and a contract between the producer and the storekeeper will take care of these problems. It relieves your friend of a lot of potential social pressure and enables him to keep a normal social life while selling complex technology, much of which he probably does not even understand himself. Anonymous trade conditions reduce tension in communities. Imagine selling computer software under the medieval community responsibility system, described by Greif (2000). Citizens from Redmond would be *persona non grata* in most of the world. Now they can travel in peace, despite the sometimes-nasty behaviour of my Microsoft Windows computer operating system.

Second, Williamson's (1985) view that *ex-post* uncertainty necessarily requires the presence of 'opportunism with a guile' is not necessarily true any longer. *Ex-post* costs may arise even without opportunism and without guile, simply because of lack of overlapping knowledge sets between two trading parties. The computer storekeeper who bought the computer from a producer and sells it to you is unlikely to have any idea about the hidden bugs and problems in the machine or software. Still, you will not hold it against him personally if a bug shows up; contractual arrangements will take care of that. In Williamson's interpretation, any problematic exchange has a moral dimension to it: somebody wanted to exploit a hidden opportunity. With the cognitive interpretation of specialisation, that is no longer necessarily the case.

The necessary conditions for anonymous trade

The move away from exchange in tightly knit social groups and towards more anonymous exchange is usually associated with the emergence of third-party enforcement. Third-party enforcement implies that a single agent has been given the authority to verify non-compliance with the relevant set of rules and, if necessary, to impose a cost on the defector. The need for a third-party judge can be explained in the context of cognitive specialisation:

First, because most contracts are necessarily incomplete, verification, interpretation and judgemental decisions are unavoidable, especially with increasing specialisation and incomplete knowledge of the goods that are being traded. Contracts cannot foresee all possible occurrences of events, and somebody needs to decide what to do in the case of an unforeseen event. Also, because of inherent incomplete information, the interpretation of events is often ambiguous. A neutral third party can break that deadlock. Third-party judges can help to resolve the problems associated with informational and situational asymmetry.

Second, it reduces transaction costs (including enforcement costs), even for very large groups, as the costs of verification, judgement and enforcement of rules are born by a single agent, not by the entire community. This may induce economies of scale, at least if the sanction does not consist of some form of social exclusion, in which case other players may incur enforcement costs as well, as in the PD game. There is no need for the group to shun exchanges with a deviant individual – as required by the tit-for-tat rule in the PD game – and thereby spread retaliation costs throughout the community.

Whether third-party monitored exchanges are also good at handling power asymmetry and finite (or even single-round) games, depends on the type of enforcement. Barzel (2000) distinguishes between non-violent and violent third-party enforcers.

Non-violent enforcers are third parties with the authority to interpret agreements and decide on possible penalties in case of non-compliance. These penalties can take all kinds of forms, from financial fines to social exclusion costs. All types of private organisations, from households to tennis clubs, religious, professional and social associations, to commercial companies, are examples of non-violent enforcement authorities. Membership of these organisations gives access to economic benefits and social circles that facilitate cooperation and exchange, subject to compliance with a set of implicit or explicit behavioural rules. The hierarchical leaders and governing boards in the organisation have the right to interpret compliance and impose sanctions. Ultimately, their enforcement capacity rests on social and economic exclusion. However, exclusions may not only entail costs for the excluded but also for other members of the group, as this deprives them from business opportunities with the excluded. Non-violent enforcers are necessarily non-governmental organisations that have no direct access to the state's monopoly on violence to enforce compliance. Law may regulate some of their activities, however.

Violators will take these social costs seriously if and only if they perceive the social organisation that imposes these costs as beneficial for them; if not, they will evade the costs by quitting the organisation. This has two implications. First, it puts a cap on the cost that can be imposed on free riders. Organisations can never impose a cost that is higher than the perceived benefits of membership. Second and related, to impose costs requires continued membership and interaction within an organisation; it cannot impose costs on non-members. This exposes the limits to non-violent third-party enforcement: it still requires some form of social interaction. The main benefits of third-party enforcement, compared to community-enforced social norms, reside in cost savings in monitoring and enforcement costs.

Milgrom *et al.*'s (1990) analysis of the law merchant provides an example of a non-violent third-party enforcement institution. A trader could file an *ex-post* complaint against another who breached a contract, provided he had made *ex-ante* enquiries about the past conduct of his trading partner. Although the system is not based on repeated direct interaction between the same traders and thus facilitates single-round trades, it is still based on (admittedly weak) interaction within the group of registered traders. It economises on transaction costs and exploits economies of scale: a trader can now check records filed by other traders in order to assess a potential trading partner's track record. It reduces residual uncertainty for a given amount of transaction costs because the probability of a contested exchange is reduced. As such, it represents a shift in the institutional trade-off curve.

Coase's (1937) seminal finding was that voluntary commercial organisations – firms – exist because they reduce transaction costs for a given level of residual uncertainty, although Coase did not use this terminology at the time. Members of such an organisation voluntarily stick to behavioural constraints that limit their range of options and rein in free riding because they get a reward for doing so: a salary, bonuses, stock options, etc. Enforcement is ensured through the hierarchical organisation of the firm: bosses can impose sanctions on their subordinates. This finding can be generalised to any form of voluntary organisation. Voluntary association and acceptance of constraints on behaviour makes exchange more efficient because it reduces transaction costs. It represents an institutional change or outward shift in the trade-off curve between transaction costs and residual uncertainty.

Violent enforcement has a major advantage over non-violent enforcement. It does not require repeated interaction among the parties. Unlike non-violent third-party enforcement, violent enforcement can be imposed on a single interaction – the same interaction that gave rise to non-compliance – even with an individual agent who is not a member of any community. Violent enforcement can overcome the constraints of finitely repeated or even single-round games. In line with several other authors on the subject, from North (1981; 1990) to Bates (2001), Barzel (2001) claims that the potential for violent third-party enforcement is a necessary condition for the emergence of impersonal trade and, in general, compliance with most of the institutions that we observe in daily life. This has become a standard assumption in the literature. Why this is so, and what the conditions are for a successful transition from voluntary to enforced institutions, is not explained.

Another implicit underlying assumption in most of the literature is that violent enforcement is, by definition, the exclusive domain of the state. North (1990) defines the state as an organisation with a monopoly on violence within a geographically defined domain where it has the ability to raise taxes.[1] But the effectiveness of a central monopoly on violence is variable. It is determined by the state of the art in violence production technology. Some arms technologies may actually result in decentralisation of violence. This would make institutions less effective because parties may be in a position to resist the costs that are being imposed on them. Furthermore, in the case where a monopoly on violence does indeed exist, a new problem occurs. The party that has the power to impose costs may as well use this power for its own advancement, not in function of agreed contracts and rules. While third-party enforcement reduces transaction costs, it may worsen the problem of power asymmetry in the distribution of benefits.

Clearly, the cognitive conditions for the emergence of specialisation and trade (anonymous trade with specialised individual knowledge) are in contradiction with those required for the spontaneous emergence of institutions (shared knowledge). Looking for economies of scale through pooling of knowledge, for instance under the law merchant system, may go some way towards reducing this contradiction but still does not facilitate fully anonymous trade outside established communities. Only third-party non-voluntary enforcement offers a way out of the cognitive dilemma between trade and institutions. Two conclusions can be drawn from this. First, institutional and economic development are intimately connected and that link is ensured by their common roots in asymmetrically distributed knowledge. Second, inside institutional development, we need to explore the mechanisms that contribute to the emergence of non-voluntary (enforced) institutions rather than voluntary institutions.

The relevant social science literature in a nutshell

Before we dig deeper into the cognitive mechanisms that link institutional and economic development (in Chapter 10) I first examine, in the remainder of this chapter, what the social science literature in general has to say on the possibility of a causal relationship between the economic realm and political and property rights institutions, as well as some empirical evidence in support of mutual causality between institutions and economic development. I then explore some existing institutional economics models that seek to explain the link between the two. They can be divided into two categories. The 'top-down' or 'predatory' models perceive states as imposing themselves because of their monopoly on violence. The key issue here is how that monopoly can be regulated so as to avoid predatory taxation and exploitation of the ruled. The ruler's time preference plays a key regulatory role in most of these models. The 'bottom-up' or 'contractual' models perceive states as 'enthroned' or 'invited' by citizens who voluntarily relinquish their right to the personal use of violence and centralise it in the hands of a ruler, with constitutional constraints attached to it. I then present a critique of both types of models that focuses on their rather naive treatment of violence, conflict and military technology. That provides a starting point for an alternative approach – in the next chapter – based on the twin regulatory powers, conflict technology and distributed knowledge.

The direction of causality between the economic and political realm of society is not a new question. Karl Marx was among the first social scientists to explore this link. He concluded that the underlying economic structures and relationships in society determine the political structure. Max Weber turned the relationship upside down and argued that ideologies and politics had a determining influence on economic development. It is now widely accepted in modern social science that economic and political systems mutually influence each other and that one cannot be explained without the other.

There are by now a vast number of *empirical* studies on this subject. They go back to Lipset's (1959) path-breaking study that presented empirical evidence that higher levels of income and economic development foster democracy. Lipset's study is firmly rooted in modernisation theory, the view that democratic political institutions are endogenous to economic development. However, soon other studies attempted to demonstrate that authoritarian regimes were more conducive to economic development (Huntington and Dominguez 1975). The underlying view there is that authoritarian regimes promote long-run investment rather than short-run consumption and redistribution. Authoritarian rulers are less constrained in their decision-making by the demands of consumers. These studies err by perceiving investment decisions as a matter of the state. Individual consumers will invest in long-term projects provided they have the necessary incentives and security to do so. Przeworski and Limongi (1993) survey a series of studies that find contradictory and non-conclusive evidence regarding the relationship between political regimes and economic performance. Barro (1997) presents equally strong evidence for both directions of causality: political regimes determine economic outcomes, but the reverse is also true in his empirical analysis. Burkhart and Lewis-Beck (1994) follow a more traditional Marxist line of thinking and apply sophisticated econometric analysis to support the view that the economy determines the state of political regimes, subject to a country's degree of marginalisation in the global political system. Przeworski *et al.* (2000) take another look at the whole issue. They find that democracy is generally correlated with higher levels of economic development and that it is far more frequent and stable at higher income levels, though it does occur at lower income levels too, albeit in an unstable form. Poor countries are rarely, if ever, democratic; if they happen to become democratic, it is usually short-lived. Middle-income countries (the $4,000–8,000 per capita range) appear to be political regime transition zones, with considerable turbulence. Contrary to Lipset and the modernisation theory approach, however, they find that economic development is not necessarily a cause of transition from authoritarian to democratic regimes. Democracies emerge at all income levels but are much more likely to survive in high-income countries. Still, they admit having no real explanation for this finding. They also conclude that modernisation theory, despite having revealed the obvious empirical link between economic and political development, has no explanatory value.

Przeworski and Limongi (1993) and Barro (1997) lament the absence of *theoretical* models to explain economic and institutional variables (political and property rights regimes) as endogenous outcomes in a single model. Przeworski and Limongi (1993) remark that the main methodological problem in all these empirical studies is a missing exogenous variable. If both political regimes and economic development are endogenous, there must be at least one exogenous variable that determines the state of the entire system; if not, the model is undetermined. It is only with the rise of New Institutional Economics in the 1990s that the focus of attention shifted from political regimes themselves to the products of political regimes: property rights. Property rights are a good candidate for the job of exogenous variable that underlies both political and economic development. First, the idea that well defined, stable and enforceable private property rights are a prerequisite for economic development gained ground. The World Bank (1997) devoted an entire World Development Report to that question and demonstrated the close correlation between 'good' property rights regimes and economic growth. Second, 'good' private property rights regimes can be established by democratic as well as by autocratic political regimes. Both Singapore's mildly autocratic regime and Chile's violent dictatorship produced strong private property rights legislation that stimulated investment and growth. However, the incentive to be a dictator diminishes as private property rights strengthen. The dictator reduces his own opportunities to appropriate surplus income and thereby puts a constraint on his revenue-maximising behaviour. Ultimately, when residual claim rights (property rights) are fully assigned to private individuals and enforced by law, the autocrat's margin for discretionary behaviour is reduced to zero and he becomes a civil servant without residual claim rights (or powers to claim residual rights). There is no point in being a dictator in that situation.

One of the important messages from modern property rights theory and New Institutional Economics is that the key variable to be observed and explained is not political regimes but rather their product, property rights regimes, and the evolution in property rights regimes from centralised appropriation by an autocratic ruler to decentralised allocation of residual claim rights to private individuals. Rather than trying to explain how political and economic development mutually influence each other – a question that leaves experts in the field, such as Przeworski *et al.* (2000), puzzled – we can work our way around this problem, in two steps. First we should provide an explanation for the link between property rights and economic development; and then, in a second stage, link political regimes with property rights. The cognitive approach to economic development, presented in Chapter 6, already offers strong clues as to how the mechanism for the first step may work. Property rights, or claims to the costs and benefits of residual uncertainties, are closely linked to the distribution of knowledge (or division of labour) and to transaction costs (the costs of obtaining information and processing it into a contract). For a given division of labour and set of property rights, the higher the transaction costs, the lower the residual uncertainty in an exchange. This locks the economy in an equilibrium situation. Improvements in property rights institutions can lift the economy to a higher equilibrium, with a deepening division of labour and more trade. Further privatisation of property rights to residual claims thus holds the key to a deepening division of labour and economic development in general.

There are very few models in the contemporary (institutional) economics and political science literature that explore the link between, on the one hand, the division of labour, and on the other hand, economic and institutional development. At first sight this is somewhat surprising, since that link is an old subject in the social sciences. Karl Marx's work and the entire Marxist social science tradition is characterised by an integrated view of political and economic systems, with the division of labour as a central concept (see Levi 1988: 185–98 for a more detailed discussion). However, as explained in Chapter 3, when Marx turned the division of labour into a contentious issue, economists were glad to pass on that hot potato to sociologists to deal with. Durkheim (1893) made an attempt to take the discussion on the division of labour away from the political arena where Marx had put it. He provided an explanation for the causal link between the division of labour and legal systems, based on the transition from mechanical to organic solidarity. But that model never got much mileage outside sociology, partially because economic science had by then completely dispensed with the need for explanations in terms of division of labour and had to wait for Hayek (1949) to raise the issue again.

There have been some attempts to introduce the subject of division of labour among legal scholars. Max Weber (1924) analysed the evolution of law in response to changes in the division of labour. Another legal scholar, Hoebel (1964) attempted to link the division of labour and evolution in formal institutions. He classified the evolution of legal systems in terms of increasing complexity in society, and explained how differentiation in societies increases the chances of conflict and demand for legal power. But the subject never seems to have taken hold of the minds of modern legal scholars. Even those who specialise in law and economics hardly mention the subject in their popular handbooks (Cooter and Ulen 2000).

Still, many prominent modern political science and institutional economics studies make explicit reference to the role of the division of labour in shaping formal institutions, including property rights and political systems. However, they stop short of providing an explicit causal mechanism, and usually simply conclude that a deepening division of labour requires more collective action. For example, Levi (1988: 1) states at the start of her introductory chapter, 'as specialisation and division of labour increase, there is a greater demand on the state to provide collective goods where once there were solely private goods or no goods at all'. However, the remainder of her book does not further explain the mechanics or investigate the validity of that opening statement. Barzel (1997; 2000; 2001) also repeatedly refers to the importance of the division of labour in shaping formal political and property rights institutions, but does not work out a concrete causal mechanism. In his study on slavery, Barzel (1977) comes very close to such a mechanism when he explains that slave owners could reduce the cost of monitoring the increasing diversity in activities of slaves (read: division of labour) by delegating residual claims or ownership rights to them. Barzel's theories of the evolution of the state are based on purely political mechanisms, however, and no longer link that evolution to the division of labour. Similarly, North (1981; 1990) repeatedly refers to the importance of the division of labour in shaping the institutions in societies, but does not develop an explicit model to explain that link.

In the early New Institutional Economics literature, North and Thomas (1973) still follow a neo-classical line of reasoning and explain institutional change as a result of changes in relative prices. The concept of division of labour was not involved in this. North and Thomas was a trailblazer study, however, if only because it made explicit the implicit institutional assumptions that underpin neo-classical economics reasoning; they put the institutional issue back on the table. Since then, the economics landscape has considerably changed and the study of institutions and organisations has become a respectable and booming area in economics. In further developments, North (1981) added transaction costs as an explanatory variable for the link between institutional and economic systems. North and Wallis (1986) provided empirical evidence for this hypothesis. North (1990) proposes a more comprehensive institutional approach to explain economic performance, including a theory of political institutions, based on transaction costs. The importance of the division of labour is mentioned several times in that book, but not worked out in detail. Dixit (1996) also applies transaction cost approaches to explain institutions and policy-making.

But neo-institutional economics somehow remained a bit stuck in transaction cost approaches to explain political institutions. Levi (1988), for example, presents a 'predatory' theory of the state. She considers the state as a revenue-maximising organisation, sometimes run by a single dictator but often by an oligarchy of rulers or even a democratically elected group of representatives. Whatever the type of ruler, they aim to maximise the state's revenue in Levi's view. In line with North (1981: 23) she contends that states 'act like discriminating monopolists, separating each group of constituents and devising property rights for each so as to maximise state revenue'. The state faces a number of constraints in selecting the objects and activities that it wants to tax, most importantly transaction costs and the rulers' own time preference or discount rate. These constraints determine the choice of revenue or tax system. Transaction costs are the costs of monitoring, implementing and enforcing policies. Rulers' own discount rates express their concern for the future, as compared to the present. Levi's work is an incomplete theory of the state; it focuses on the revenue-raising aspects only, and does not cover property rights (re)allocation or the management of productive activities.

The transaction costs approach to institutions and politics takes only one aspect of economic systems into account, namely the cost of doing transactions, as a determining variable of political and institutional decision-making. It does not really explain institutional change and stops short of a fully fledged feedback loop between economics and politics. Much of the transaction cost approach to politics is based on the assumption that political rulers do not work for the greater benefit of humankind and do not aim to maximise a hypothetical welfare function – an assumption that often underlies neo-classical economic models of policy-making. Instead, rulers are considered to behave like ordinary human beings, maximising their own personal revenue. Rulers who have obtained a monopoly on violence within a geographically defined domain will use this coercive power to tax their subjects in such a way as to maximise their personal revenue. While that may be a realistic assumption to explain much of politicians' behaviour, both in democracies and in autocratic regimes, it is not sufficiently powerful to explain the transition from autocratic to democratic regimes, or from centralised to decentralised appropriation of residual claim rights, whether or not under the influence of structural changes in the economy.

McGuire and Olson (1996) make the first genuine attempt in the modern economics literature to explain the transition in residual claim rights in an integrated model of economic and political development. They compare the economic performance of three different types of political ruler: a roving bandit, an autocrat and a democrat. Rulers have two choice variables: the amount of surplus that they expropriate and how much of that they re-invest in the production of public goods in order to increase economic output. Olson's concept of 'encompassing interest' ensures that rulers do not take whatever they can but leave at least some part of the surplus in the hands of those who produced it, as an incentive to enhance production. In Olson's view, it is in the autocratic ruler's own interest not to exhaust his residual claim rights (or powers). Consider a roving bandit who seizes a territory. He can fully expropriate the inhabitants. However, his return on his territorial asset would increase if he organises a basic property rights system that protects his subjects from expropriation, thereby providing them an incentive to produce, which is in his own interest. The extent of encompassing interest changes, however, with the duration or insecurity of tenure: less secure and shorter tenure reduces the encompassing interest and increases extortion. As a benchmark in efficient government, McGuire and Olson choose the 'consensual society', where all decisions are taken by consensus and the marginal tax rate for each individual is exactly equal to his marginal benefit from the public good that is produced with this tax revenue. As a result, the marginal social and marginal private benefits and costs are equal. There is full private appropriation and privatisation of all costs and benefits. It represents the perfect private property rights system. Since no real society is expected to be consensual, majority rule under a democratic system is the nearest approximation to a consensual society. The elected majority will, however, limit expropriation and redistribution to itself and invest part of its tax revenue in the production of public goods for society at large. Because the majority is part of the citizenry that also earns market income, it has a more encompassing interest than an autocratic ruler and will thus redistribute less to itself than would an autocrat. Majority rule ensures a re-allocation of private property rights to individuals, away from the autocrat. The dead-weight loss from expropriation through taxes will be limited. Consequently, the majority's direct income from tax revenue is lower than the ruler's income, but still higher than under consensual rule.

McGuire and Olson's model is a meta-static theory of the evolution of the state. The discrete institutional steps from centralised autocratic appro-priation to decentralised private appropriation are still exogenously fixed and not generated within the model. Monopoly on violence plays no func-tional role in this model, or only indirectly and implicitly through the production of public goods that require enforcement to avoid free riding. Why and how public goods increase production efficiency is not explained. There is no underlying theory of property rights to support this mecha-nism, and no link to the division of labour. The model could be considered as a meta-static explanation of the evolution of the state to the extent that it shows how residual income or residual claims, accruing to a single auto-cratic ruler or a ruling class, diminish with the extent of democracy or consensus. Under autocracy, the ruler appropriates the surplus and is the sole residual claimant. He has a private property right on all residual (surplus) income, enforced by means of his monopoly on violence. Under total consensus, all citizens are residual claimants on property rights on income. The ruler is no more than a salaried civil servant who is paid his opportunity cost of time for the work of managing the country. In fact, in most modern democracies, rulers are civil servants, though they may still appropriate some residual claims in other ways, for their political parties. For instance, through redistribution of jobs, property rights and tax revenue.

Barzel's theory of the state

This brings us to the seminal work of Yoram Barzel that deserves a detailed discussion here, for two reasons. First, it is a good summary of the state of the art in institutional economists' thinking about the emergence and control of the state's monopoly on violence, including the ambiguities and unresolved issues regarding the evolution of residual claim rights. Second, it prepares a lot of groundwork for the division-of-labour-based model of endogenous political and property rights institutions that I will present in the next chapter. Barzel's work, like North's, alternates between the top-down and bottom-up approach to the regulation of a government's monopoly on violence. As pointed out before, both approaches lack an exogenous variable that stabilises the system and determines both economic and institutional variables.

Barzel (2000) starts by pointing out the lack of true endogenous institu-tional dynamics in McGuire and Olson. His paper on 'Property rights and the evolution of the state' (Barzel 2000) aims to present a more dynamic model with endogenous evolution of formal institutions. In fact, he could have easily built such a model on the foundations laid in his much older theory of slavery (Barzel 1977). In that paper, he argued that slave owners have an incentive not to appropriate their slaves' entire production, but leave at least part of it for the slave to appropriate. This will provide slaves with a residual claim over production, thereby giving them an incentive to work harder and produce as much as possible. Barzel also argues that with increasingly complex production technologies, slave owners will find it harder to control and monitor their slaves' efforts. Rather than investing an ever-increasing part of surplus production in control, owners will be better off if they pass on residual claims to their slaves. To the extent that slaves become residual claimants to their production, they have an incentive to work harder. In that case, slave owners only need to control total output, not input (effort) and output.

What then prevents dictators, or for that matter, slave owners, from giving at least limited freedom to their subjects? Barzel (1977) argues that fear of rebellion prevents them from letting too much resources slip into the hands of their subjects. The more surplus they extract, the higher the chances for successful rebellion. Once rulers feel more secure, they will tend to give more rights to subjects because it benefits the ruler too. This is equivalent to the ruler's time preference model, used by North (1981) and Levi (1988). It is a top-down approach to property rights: the ruler gives whatever rights he deems in his own interest. The exogenous variable is the ruler's security of tenure.

Somewhat surprisingly, Barzel (2001) diverts from that most logical and straightforward route. In his *A Theory of the State* (2001) he moves towards a 'bottom-up' model and claims that citizens will 'invite' a violent third-party enforcer into their community once they have created a collective action mechanism that prevents the enforcer from becoming a dictator. Societies basically have two options to reward their third-party rule enforcers. Either a third-party enforcer can claim whatever costs or benefits he derives from carrying out his duties: he is the residual claimant and 'owns' the protection system. Or he gets a fixed salary only. In that case, all residual costs and benefits under the scheme go to the citizens. They are the residual claimants and thus 'own' the protection system. At first sight, it looks as if the first option gives stronger incentives to the protector, at least if he decides to deliver his services. He might also renege on his contract when things get too hot under his feet. Barzel admits that, unless a dictator endorses it, erecting collective action mechanisms under dictatorship is very difficult (2001: 124).

Thus, in Barzel (1977; 2000) internal and external security threats are the exogenous variable that drives control of the ruler's monopoly on violence. By contrast, in Barzel (2001) regulation of the ruler's monopoly seems to be driven by citizens' ability to organise collective action among themselves and the perceived security threat to citizens from 'inviting' a ruler to rule over them. This pendulum movement between bottom-up and top-down regulatory mechanisms characterises Barzel's work on the emergence of the state. That same ambiguity concerning the factors that regulate the use of the ruler's monopoly on violence already pervaded his seminal *An Economic Theory of Property Rights* (Barzel 1997 [1977]). In Chapter 6 of the second edition he argues in favour of the hypothesis that citizens 'invite' violent third-party enforcers once they get their collective act together; in Chapter 7 of the same book he endorses the view that slave owners will only delegate rights to their subjects if they feel secure.

There are of course instances in history when citizens have 'invited' a plenipotentiary ruler to take over their country. Belgium invited a foreign king to rule when it became independent in 1830, but not before a democratic constitution had been worked out. The Iranian people 'invited' Ayatollah Khomeini to rule the country after the Shah fled, long before an appropriate constitution had been worked out. No wonder, then, that collective action mechanisms seem to have worked better in the first case than in the second. But rulers may of course violate the constitution. After all, they have a monopoly on violence that enables them to do so. The only self-interest mechanism that would prevent them from doing so is Barzel's slavery theory: giving rights to subjects reduces control costs and stimulates subjects' efforts to produce.

Barzel's theory of the state is not a dynamic theory. It offers little insight into how dictatorships might turn into democracies, other than the vague notion that rulers might feel more secure and, almost out of gratitude for letting them feel safe, give more rights to their subjects. When and under what conditions these 'feelings' occur, is not explored. In short, there is no clearly defined exogenous variable that drives the evolution of the state system. As a result, the probability of failing democracies is high and the probability of reversing a dictatorship into a democracy is low. Consequently, Barzel's theory would predict the number of dictatorships to increase over time – which is inconsistent with the historical record.

A critique of models with exogenous monopolies on violence

Top-down models take the ruler's monopoly on violence as given and then try to find mechanisms that limit the extent to which he can exploit this monopoly to maximise his own revenue. They focus on the trade-off between the ruler's short-term and long-term interests, and consider the ruler's time preference to be the dominant factor that determines any restraint on the use of his monopoly position (North 1981; 1990; Barzel 1997; 2000; 2001; McGuire and Olson 1996), possibly combined with transaction costs (Levi 1988; North 1981). Barzel reformulates this in terms of the ruler's feeling of security, while Olson prefers the terminology of 'encompassing interest'.

If the time preference argument were correct, then the most prosperous states would be kingdoms, because monarchs have a dynastic long-term interest in the state of their economy. Empirical evidence seems to contradict this. Many prosperous modern states moved away from monarchies to elected governments and presidents with relatively short time horizons, a few years at most. Consequently, it is unlikely that the time preference argument can explain much about the state of political institutions, property rights or economic performance. Poggi (1978) provides another piece of empirical evidence that contradicts the time preference theory. Empirical evidence from late medieval Europe shows that rulers, in times when their position was threatened by invasions, became more cooperative and were willing to give more liberties to their citizens, in return for taxes and levies that helped to finance wars. Clearly, rulers felt they could not fight on two fronts at the same time: the threat of external invasion triggered more internal liberties.

'Bottom-up' models of the development of the state also start from an exogenously given ruler who is 'invited' by a community to become their ruler. The community voluntarily gives him a monopoly on violence. Most 'bottom-up' models are implicitly or explicitly based on the work of North and Weingast (1989), who examine constitutional reforms in seventeenth-century England at the time of the Glorious Revolution. They show how citizens were able to organise collective action and force the king into retreat, granting them constitutional rights, including the right to depose the king. Similarly, the Magna Carta period could be cited as a historical example of citizens' ability to wrest more rights from their rulers. Weingast (1997) casts these historical findings in a game-theory format, showing how rulers can be locked into commitments if citizens can solve their internal collective action problems. Barzel (2000) also refers to these historical examples in support of his bottom-up approach.

Bottom-up models do not explain how the ruler obtains his comparative advantage in violence, nor why he should refrain from trespassing the constitutional limits on the use of this monopoly, once he has been given this monopoly. The historical examples of delegation of power to a central ruler suggest some sort of balance of power between ruler and ruled, as both possess arms. Once all arms end up in the hands of the ruler, this balance would be disturbed. Note that North (1990) did not defend the example of England's seventeenth-century bottom-up revolution as a universal model; he considered it to be merely an example and cautioned that no one at this stage in our knowledge knows how to create a state with coercive force and the ability to monitor property rights and enforce contracts (North 1990: 59). It looks as if North's caution is still valid today.

Surprisingly, all the authors discussed so far seem to neglect the role of violence production or military technology in their models. This is all the more surprising because enforcement mechanisms are at the centre of these models. The historical events in England that are used in support of these models, such as the Magna Carta in the thirteenth century and the Glorious Revolution of the seventeenth century, are struggles between kings and nobles, both armed and equipped with coercive power. These were no struggles between armed dictators with a monopoly on violence and unarmed defenceless citizens. Naturally, a more decentralised distribution of military capabilities led to situations whereby a balance of power between two armed forces was reflected in the outcome. What these historical examples fail to explain is how unarmed citizens can wrestle rights from armed rulers.

Barzel (2000) cites Umbeck (1981), who shows how an equal distribution of violence technology among gold miners in the California gold rush led to collective action and the emergence of property rights. However, there is no third-party enforcement of these rights and miners had to fend for themselves. From such beginnings, one might conceive the gradual 'bottom-up' emergence of third-party enforcement, because it is economically more efficient for all parties concerned. However, if violence technology is unequally distributed (Skaperdas 1991; 1992), dictatorships are likely to emerge from the start. So Barzel's implicit assumption seems to be that violence technology is equally distributed. But that makes the 'invitation' to a third party with a comparative advantage in violence all the more puzzling: where would that comparative advantage come from?

In conclusion, neither time preference models of monopolistic rulers nor bottom-up models of 'invited' monopolists seem to be able to solve the basic question about the factors that affect the balance of power between an armed ruler and unarmed citizens: what makes a monopolist on violence, who can easily claim all residual rights on surpluses for himself, voluntarily relinquish these rights and allocate private property rights to individual citizens? This suggests that violence technology should be brought more explicitly into the picture, in order to account for the emergence and evolution of a monopoly on violence.

Endogenising violence

Bates' (2001) *Prosperity and Violence* offers an historical account of the role and organisation of violence, or conflict technology, in the emergence and evolution of the state. His proposals are somewhat similar to Barzel's model, although he gives a more explicit role to conflict technology within the state. He starts from a simple agrarian society, without a central state. Property rights are not formalised. At best, they are socially recognised, through repeated interaction of the kind discussed above under the game-theory approach to voluntary cooperation. Occasionally, disputes will arise over issues that are not covered by the 'social contract'. While violence is a last resort in the defence of individual or kinship clan rights, a credible commitment to violence, often based on the importance of honour, may act as a credible deterrent to prevent trespassing on rights. The honour mechanism ensures that the party whose rights are violated is committed to their violent defence (Berger 1970). Rules of behaviour and property rights that emerged through repeated social interaction may thus be subject to violent enforcement. The more credible the clan's deterrent, the more likely the respect for these rights. Security and enforcement is privately supplied and costly. The cost of supplying security can be reduced if economies of scale can be tapped. That implies moving towards a central monopoly on violence, taking the right to violence away from individuals.

Bates suggests several mechanisms that may have led to such an outcome. First, competition and specialisation among kinship groups may have produced one group with a comparative advantage in violence, establishing a lineage of rulers which is able to expropriate other groups (taxation) to finance their fighting efforts. However, seduction may have been more efficient than expropriation: selling protection services in return for voluntary taxes saves on tax collection costs. Physical seizure of assets yields few rewards, except in the short run. Negotiation and diplomacy may be a more efficient tool. Second, cities may buy liberties from rulers, construct walls and pool military resources. Guilds within the cities provided non-violent enforcement of constraints on behaviour, with the ultimate threat consisting of expulsion from the guild, and possibly from the city – compare this with Barzel's non-violent enforcement. Finally, the ruled may invite rulers to rule over them, combined with private disarmament, and provided they set up credible ruling mechanisms that prevent dictatorships. These rulers might then delegate the right to judge, backed up by their ultimate monopoly on violence, to independent judges. Centralised violence attracted a lot of rural retainers to the urban courts, and thereby reinforced the power of central governments. These three mechanisms made populations move away from private to publicly organised violence and enforcement of rules of behaviour, thereby saving on transaction costs and at the same time reducing uncertainty. Bates does not really discuss the issue of how to avoid the misuse of a centralised and monopolised right to violence.

Bates *et al.* (2001) have cast Bates' (2001) narrative account of the emergence of the state into a game-theory model. Citizens have a choice in the allocation of their scarce time between production, military activity and leisure. They derive income from production and from raiding others. In a repeated game setting and in the absence of strong discounting of future revenue, an equilibrium whereby all resources are allocated to production could emerge, but is unstable. It will only hold as long as no one invests in military activity and raiding. A more likely and stable equilibrium would imply positive investments in military activity, to protect production and deter potential predators. It entails a positive but low level of production of consumables, as predicted by the Skaperdas model (see Chapter 10). To move to a higher level of production and economic welfare, citizens may 'invite' a specialist in violence, who sells 'protection' services in return for payment of taxes by the protected. That would allow citizens to demilitarise and reallocate at least part of their scarce resources to production. However, the specialist may also prey on his protégés and loot their production. Whether he will do so depends on a cost-benefit analysis between, on the one hand, the cost of raiding and the probability of a successful raid and, on the other hand, the benefits from raiding. If his expected net benefit does not exceed his tax revenue, he will refrain from raiding. In the model, the probability of a successful raid is exogenously determined, and not a function of military balances and investments.

The Bates *et al.* model is somewhat of a hybrid of bottom-up and top-down models of the emergence of the state. It combines characteristics of both types: citizens 'invite' a specialist in violence but that specialist also holds the citizens in his grip. The key innovation of their model is that it moves away from the traditional Prisoners' Dilemma approach, with voluntary cooperation, and explicitly introduces conflict technology and involuntary cooperation as factors in institution building. The violence specialist's incentive to refrain from raiding is that he derives alternative revenues from taxation. Alternatively, he might confiscate the means of production (enslave the citizens) and expropriate all surpluses, not only the taxed part of the surplus. So the cost-benefit analysis could be simplified to a comparison between the specialist's revenue under decentralised production (taxation of part of the surplus) and his revenue under centralised and confiscated production (expropriation of the full surplus, minus the expected cost of raiding).

Before I move on to the next chapter, I need to mention another author who endogenises not only conflict technology but also information technology as a determining factor in the emergence and evolution of states. In *The Word and the Sword*, Dudley (1991) argues that 'informational and military scale economies are the glue that holds society together. A revolution in any of these technologies will alter the optimal boundaries and levels of government intervention of the typical state' (1). His reasoning goes as follows. Communities are groups of individuals who acquire, store and exchange information; they are information networks. Access to a wider range of information constitutes an incentive for membership of a community. A 'state' is an organisational arrangement of such a community, within which a set of rules applies. Dudley distinguishes between the external margin of the state, the territorial boundaries to be defended against potential intruders, and the internal margin, the boundary between private and public allocation or the state's power to tax individual wealth. Changes on the external margin depend on comparative advantages in military or conflict technology. Economies of scale in military technology will result in integration of larger territories into a single 'state' unit.[2] Changes in the internal margin depend on technology for storing, reproducing and transmitting information, in short on information technology. Better information technology will allow larger communities to communicate more effectively, and thus generate more benefits through economies of scale from cooperation. This will allow rulers to increase their tax revenue. Thus tax receipts will depend on information processing capacity. These receipts, in turn, will finance more investment in military technology and generate economies of scale in that domain. In short, 'states' emerge and evolve at the interface between bureaucrats and warriors.

Dudley presents his arguments in a historic setting, exploring eight examples of innovations in information and conflict technology that have, in his view, shaped the course of history of empires. Like Bates (2001), he does not make much of an attempt to present an abstract model as such. I will present a similar dual-technology model in the next chapter, combining it with the evolution of the division of labour (or distributed knowledge).

10 Endogenous institutions

> Ultimately, all ownership rights are based on the abilities of individuals, or groups of individuals, to forcefully maintain exclusivity. Force underlies all allocative systems....No wealth maximizer would accept less wealth than he could have through the use of his personal force, the agreed upon contract must initially endow each individual with the same amount of wealth as that which they could have through violence.
>
> (Umbeck (1981: 39–40))

Introduction

The previous two chapters looked at the definition of institutions and how they emerge and evolve in society. We examined models of spontaneous bottom-up emergence of institutions as well as models with top-down institutions, enforced by a centralised state with a monopoly on violence that is used in a predatory or a contractual manner, including Barzel's attempts to combine them in a single model. While there are valuable elements in all these models, none of them integrates the essential cognitive features that we identified at the end of Chapter 9, namely:

- the trade-off between the need for distributed knowledge or specialisation, as a condition for the emergence of gainful trade, and shared knowledge as a condition for the spontaneous emergence of institutions
- the regime switch between decentralised (but economically less efficient) enforcement of institutions under conditions of shared knowledge, and (economically more efficient) centrally enforced institutions.

In fact, institutions were kept exogenous to the cognitive economic model in Part II that dealt with distributed knowledge only. Chapter 8 explained how economic exchange and institutions are two sides of the same distributed knowledge coin. Consequently, we need to endogenise institutions into this model and demonstrate the co-evolution of distributed knowledge, institutions and economic development in society.

Any attempt to endogenise institutions in an overall model of cognitive (and economic) development implicitly or explicitly assumes that institutions do not fall out of the sky; nor are they 'invented' by social and political geniuses. They are the endogenous product of social systems, outcomes of social interactions. The federalists did not 'invent' the American constitution; they were just well tuned to the ideas and needs of their time. Neither did Napoleon invent the Napoleonic Code, nor Hammurabi his famous codex. These institutions were the product of their times and circumstances. How that production process works has been the subject of innumerable theories in the social sciences, far too many to even attempt to summarise here. One way of classifying these theories is to split them into the following two categories: theories that rely on voluntary cooperation between citizens and theories that rely on force or non-voluntary enforcement of behavioural rules. In the first category, each citizen is a voluntary rule-follower as well as a voluntary enforcer. The second category usually assumes the existence of a single centralised enforcer, endowed with a monopoly on violence or a dominant enforcement technology. Centralised enforcement is the domain of the state; states produce formal institutions. A further distinction can be made between centralised enforcers who are not constrained in the pursuit of their own interests (predatory states) (North 1981; Levi 1988; Barzel 1997; 2000) and those who are constrained by a contract with citizens (contractual states) (Barzel 2001; Weingast 1997; North and Weingast 1989). All these theories were discussed extensively in the previous chapter.

There is, so far, no seamless integration of all these theories in a single approach. In particular, the conditions for regime switches between voluntary and involuntary institutions and, within the latter category, between predatory and contractual states, are ill defined. Furthermore, many of these models produce institutional outcomes that are unrelated to events in other domains of social interaction, including economic development. Predatory state models, for instance, often rely on the ruler's time preference and security as a determining factor for the rights that he is willing to grant his subjects. Contractual state models often disregard the role of conflict technology in reaching an agreement. Voluntary cooperation models neglect transaction costs, the deadweight cost of enforcement and the disincentive of sharing norms. The conditions that govern the evolution of sharing norms, a particular set of informal institutions prevalent in many less developed societies, are still unclear (Platteau 2000).

In this chapter, I present an approach to the emergence and evolution of institutions that aims to overcome some of these shortcomings. I integrate voluntary and involuntary cooperation, including predatory and contractual regimes, in a single framework and determine the conditions for regime switches between the two. That framework includes a detailed transmission mechanism between economic and institutional development, and distinguishes between property rights and political institutions. I start from a cognitive interpretation of economic and social interaction, with a single exogenous variable: a limited cognitive capacity for learning that results in knowledge accumulation as well as distribution of knowledge in society. Individual agents accumulate knowledge for behavioural purposes: it enables them to respond to challenges and opportunities in their environment. For the purpose of this chapter, knowledge can be split in two categories: knowledge used for production of goods and knowledge used to settle conflicts among agents. The first produces consumables, the second re-allocates consumables among individuals. I aim to demonstrate in this chapter that the interaction between both technologies determines the architecture of political and property rights (incentives) and the level of economic development (deadweight losses) in society.

The structure of this chapter is as follows. In the next section I develop the baseline scenario, with conflict and production technology as fully shared public goods, and examine its economic consequences in terms of deadweight losses and incentives. In the subsequent section I introduce unequally distributed conflict technology and, in the next section, unequally distributed production technology – or division of labour. Part II explained at length how unequally distributed production technology is a consequence of the limited cognitive resources that we have. Unequally distributed conflict technology, by contrast, is caused by economies of scale in the production and use of conflict technology. For instance, an individual person can use a gun to defend his personal property. But there is usually no point in owning a tank or jetfighter to defend your backyard. Tanks and jetfighters represent heavy investment costs that require a much larger domain to defend in order to be economical. Because of these economies of scale, unequally distributed conflict technology results in territorial monopolies, or to use a more political terminology, dictatorship. Dictatorship has an economic advantage, however (as I will show in this chapter), because it reduces deadweight losses in society. On the other hand, it does not provide production incentives. I will demonstrate in this chapter why we need a combination of distributed production technology, through division of labour, and a monopoly on conflict technology, or a monopoly on violence, in order to generate secure private property rights at low transaction costs and strong production incentives. I discuss some implications of this model in the concluding section.

Before we start, a brief note on semantics. I use fairly belligerent language in most of this text: conflict, military technology, violence and coercion. The application of these conflict models is not limited to violent conflict and situations of life and death, however. In most of our daily lives, conflicts are fortunately of much lower intensity. Still, they can be very decisive in determining the allocation of resources. The most frequently used conflict technology is verbal and social pressure. Weapons consist of words (expressed at various levels of loudness), behaviour (from friendly talk to active shunning and aggressive acts) and attitudes often barely noticeable to outsiders but very effective in influencing the behaviour of insiders. Various means of signalling and threatening (posturing) with sophisticated social retaliatory measures are often very effective. This wide interpretation of the word 'conflict' illustrates the importance of Barzel's (2001) emphasis, in his definition of the state as the 'ultimate' holder of a monopoly on violence. We all have means of violence or conflict at our disposal; only some means are more effective than others. Most daily conflicts can fortunately be settled through the force of words, voice and mime. Stronger conflict may require an appeal to social organisations, procedures and third-party judges. If push comes to shove, plaintiffs can always climb up the hierarchical ladder of conflict settlement technology and 'ultimately' invoke the monopoly of the state on the most dominant conflict technology, in order to enforce a court ruling.

Production versus conflict

The model that I propose in this section integrates the voluntary cooperation models (Chapter 8) as well as the need for coercion to achieve enforceable property rights (Chapter 9) with conflict theory. A small but interesting literature on conflict theory was pioneered in the 1990s by Skaperdas (1991; 1992; 1995), Hirshleifer (1991; 1996), Grossman and Kim (1996) and Neal (1995; 1997), amongst others. These models show how property rights institutions are produced by the underlying distribution of conflict technology and how that technology affects the deadweight loss of conflict in society. Conflict theory models neglect incentives, however. To introduce that aspect, I will combine them with agency theory models of delegation and asymmetric knowledge. This combination links the state of institutions to the division of knowledge, or the division of labour. Whereas the predatory and contractual models of the state in North (1981), North and Weingast (1989), Weingast (1997), McGuire and Olson (1996) and Barzel (1997; 2001) produce institutional outcomes in function of exogenous variables such as the ruler's time preference or the ability to achieve collective action, the approach followed in this chapter endogenously generates both economic and institutional outcomes as a function of the distribution of conflict and production technology. The division of labour thereby becomes the exogenous variable that solves Barzel's (2001/2000) problem of indeterminacy in predatory and contractual models of the state. It also permits the construction of likely and less likely trajectories of institutional and economic development. These trajectories explain the evolution of institutions, from social norms to private property rights, in function of conflict technology and the distribution of knowledge.

I start from a simple set-up, whereby individual agents seek to maximise the quantity of consumables at their disposal, subject to a cognitive resource constraint: the capacity to accumulate knowledge and use it for behavioural purposes. Agents can allocate this scarce cognitive capacity between two types of knowledge, one for the production of consumer goods and the other for the extraction of consumer goods from other agents. In other words, the first contains production technology, the second conflict technology that (re-)allocates property rights.

Knowledge of production and conflict technology are just two different ways of coping with the challenges and opportunities of the environment. The first seeks to profit from events in the natural environment, the second seeks to profit from the resources already accumulated by other persons. In fact, much of our knowledge may have a dual use. Guns serve for hunting (production) as well as conflict (re-allocation) purposes. It is only in more advanced stages of technological development that a functional differentiation between the two technologies occurs. Still, even when both technologies remain functionally undifferentiated, the choice problem analysed in the game described below is still present: agents need to choose between use of their scarce cognitive capacity for production or for conflict.

The decision matrix for a game with two players is presented in Table 10.1, and is identical to the game presented in Table 8.2. Although it superficially resembles Axelrod's (1984) Prisoners' Dilemma game, it is nevertheless fundamentally different. Axelrod-type games have exogenously determined institutions or property rights allocations. Decisions on production and conflict (responses to others' behaviour) are taken in a sequential order: first production, than retaliation in a subsequent round if other players turn out to be defectors. As such, Axelrod-type games, and indeed most of the games that have been experimentally tested in laboratory settings, follow the standard von Neumann-Morgenstern scenario with perfect information on player's range of actions (production) but no information on responses (conflict) (Thompson and Faith 1981). Axelrod's innovation consisted of opening up an indirect communication channel between the players to communicate likely responses to actions through repeated rounds of play. More communication increased the chances of moving away from a Nash to a Pareto equilibrium. The game situation analysed in this chapter diverts from the von Neumann-Morgenstern assumption and introduces simultaneity of decisions on production actions and conflict responses. The choice here is not either cooperate (produce) or defect (conflict) but an appropriate mix of both. Players should determine a mixed strategy of conflict and production.

To determine the Nash equilibrium strategy outcome, we need to examine the properties of the conflict and production functions. In this baseline scenario, I start from the assumption that knowledge of conflict and production technologies is a public good, available to all players in a

Table 10.1 Consumption through conflict and production

	Player A chooses conflict	Player A chooses food production
If Player B chooses conflict	A: 0	A: 0
	B: 0	B: 10
If Player B chooses food production	A: 10	A: 10
	B: 0	B: 10

group.[1] This assumption will be gradually relaxed in the next sections. As a consequence, all players have equal productivity in each technology. Each player has just one resource, a fixed amount of time (T), that can be allocated either to production (Tp) or to conflict (Tc), so that Tp + Tc = T. Time invested in production yields consumable outputs, with constant returns to scale so that output Q = a Tp. However, the return to investment in conflict depends not only on how much the other players invest in conflict, but also on the specification of the conflict production function. In this baseline scenario, I assume a proportional or indecisive Conflict Success Function (CSF) (Hirshleifer 1991; Skaperdas 1992) of the following type:

$$S_i = Tc_i / (\Sigma_i \, Tc_i) \text{ and } (\Sigma_i \, S_i = 1$$

where S_i is the share of total private goods output allocated to player i as a result of conflict between i and the other players in the group. Tc_i are the time units allocated to conflict production by players.[2] This conflict production function yields decreasing returns to conflict for each player, for a given investment in conflict by the other player, but increasing returns for one player to decreasing investment in conflict by other players. This type of CSF is usually labelled as 'indecisive conflict technology' (Hirshleifer 1991) because the shares in total output are proportional to inputs in conflict – contrary to a CSF of the 'winner takes all' type, that I will discuss in the next section.

Finally, we assume that the actions undertaken with both technologies are fully observable *ex-post* by all players, at zero information costs. In other words, there is no *ex-post* asymmetric information between the players. However, there is no direct communication channel between the players, either: they can observe each other's actions but they cannot communicate in advance what strategy they will play. All players make their allocation decisions at the same time and without communication between them. They observe the outcomes of their decisions in the next period. Without any advance communication between the players, the players will opt for their safest bet, a Nash strategy. The Nash equilibrium is not a pure but a mixed strategy equilibrium in this case: a combination of conflict and production. A pure conflict strategy whereby both players allocate all their resources to conflict technology would result in zero consumption and thus starvation for both players. It is too risky. On the other hand, the Pareto optimal outcome whereby each player invests all his resources in production and none in conflict technology, is very risky too: a small allocation of resources to conflict by any one player would allocate all consumable output to that player. Consequently, the safest bet is somewhere in between both strategies.

The properties of a Nash equilibrium strategy mix are analysed by Garfinkel and Skaperdas (2000a). An equilibrium occurs when the allocation of resource inputs (time) between conflict and production is such that the marginal rate of substitution between both technologies, in terms of consumption, is the same for both players. First, since this baseline scenario assumes that both players have the same production functions for conflict and food production, that equilibrium point should be the same for both players. Consequently, at that point, total consumable output should be equally divided (50/50) between both players. Second, in equilibrium, the marginal individual gain from allocating another unit of resources to conflict (in terms of increased share of total output) should be undone by the marginal overall loss (in terms of reduced total output). That point is reached when resources are allocated equally (50/50) between conflict and production. To see why this is so, consider the case where player B chooses a 40/60 allocation between conflict and production, while A sticks to a 50/50 allocation. B's marginal return to conflict, in terms of food consumption, will be higher than A's because his loss of output from switching resources to conflict will be compensated by an increase in his share of total production. Consequently, he will benefit from allocating more resources to conflict. For a formal proof of these conclusions, see Garfinkel and Skaperdas (2000a). Hirshleifer (1996) calls this outcome a 'stable anarchy': it offers stability of property rights among a group of equally armed and productive agents, without there being a leader or without imposed rules.

This leads us to three important conclusions.

First, the social deadweight loss in a society where all individuals have equal productivity in conflict (in the absence of clearly defined and enforced property rights) as well as in production of consumables, amounts to 50 per cent of GDP (that part of production capacity invested in deadweight conflict technology), compared to a society where enforcement of property rights is cost-free (no investment in conflict). The latter Pareto-optimal reference point is, of course, utopian. No society can costlessly enforce property rights; investment in coercion has a positive opportunity cost.

A second conclusion is that total consumable output will be shared equally in these societies. In an earlier study of the California gold rush, Umbeck (1981) went a step further. He demonstrated that, with equal productivity in conflict technology but unequally distributed productivity in production technology,[3] total consumable output would still be shared equally among the players, by modulating the allocation of production factors (in this case, land) among the players. Players with lower labour productivity in production will allocate relatively more resources to conflict and thereby increase their consumption. Players with higher labour productivity in production will do the reverse. Umbeck (1981) generalises this result in the following formulation: With equally distributed conflict technology among n players, each player will get a 1/n share of total output, irrespective of the distribution of production technology. In other words, conflict technology dominates production technology: with equally distributed conflict technology, consumables are equally shared, irrespective of productivity in the production of consumables.

This brings us to a third conclusion, namely that equally distributed conflict technology not only results in high deadweight losses but also weak production incentives. Equal sharing, irrespective of productivity, violates the basic economic rule of efficient allocation (marginal revenue equals marginal product) and thereby deprives producers of an incentive to exert effort. If they were to exert effort, any gain in output would be distributed equally among all players. In the case of n players, $(n-1)/n$ of a producer's additional output would be reallocated to others as a result of externalities imposed on him through conflict technology. Clearly, that is not a sound institutional basis to build an economically successful society on.

Sharing norms

This sheds new light on the puzzling phenomenon of sharing norms (Mauss 1924; Posner 1980; Platteau 2000). Their origin is usually traced back to highly uncertain natural environments with highly variable productivity and few opportunities for storage and trade of goods. Sharing norms provide an insurance mechanism against resource volatility. They are considered to be an advantage in poor societies (Posner 1980), where they act as an insurance mechanism across families and communities: if one person or family has bad luck and faces resource problems, others will share their surplus with them. The origin of trade and property rights has been explained by some authors in terms of sharing norms and their insurance properties (Mauss 1924). Some empirical evidence for the link between sharing norms and environmental uncertainty has emerged from experimental economics (Smith 1997). Players who earn a windfall profit, purely by luck and not by skill or effort, are expected to share this profit with other players. On the other hand, players who earn revenue through skill and effort are usually allowed to privately appropriate these revenues: 'they deserve it'. By contrast, in the game-theory analysis presented above, sharing norms and egalitarian standards are not the result of inherent resource uncertainty. Rather they are the result of equally distributed conflict technology, independent of the properties of the natural environment or volatility in productivity. A non-egalitarian distribution can occur only when conflict technology varies across players.

Sharing norms constitute a disincentive to effort, and may explain why poor societies remain poor. Ellickson's (1991) story of *Order without Law* in Shasta County is a good example of a society that gets stuck in a low productivity sharing equilibrium. Potential conflicts between farmers and ranchers are settled through intensive social interaction, whereby allocations of additional costs and benefits are often settled on an equal sharing basis. While formal law may allocate rights in a particular way between farmers and ranchers, the potential costs that could be imposed through social conflict technology makes farmers and ranchers refrain from claiming their full rights, and settle more 'amicably' for sharing. Equal distribution is, in fact, not the result of friendly neighbourliness, but rather of equally distributed social conflict technology whereby no player can impose a decisive victory in case his rights are trespassed. Hirschleifer (1996) calls this type of society a 'stable anarchy'. Societies in many developing countries exhibit similar properties. Because appeal to formal legal systems is often very costly and unreliable, and the potential costs of local conflict and social pressures are far more immediate and tangible, citizens prefer to adapt their behaviour to prevailing informal institutions or social norms and the pressures of local conflict technology. Since that technology is fairly equally distributed and the outcomes of local actions are easily observable, the baseline scenario applies: equal sharing of output prevails, independent of productivity differences. The prevalence of equal sharing norms, whether in Shasta County or in developing countries, reflects the presence of tightly knit societies where actions are easily observable and social conflict technology is equally distributed.

A special form of social pressure that may result in equality but also stable anarchy, is posturing. Posturing has always been an important element in conflict, among animals as well as humans. The threat of using violence is often sufficient to change the behaviour of others. Peter Berger (1970) and Robert Bates (2001) emphasise the role of honour in traditional societies. It revolves around the credibility of the threat to use violence if one's rights are trespassed. The more credible that threat, the more likely potential trespassers will shy away from trespassing. Even though individual conflict technology may not have been very decisive, the threat of sparking a fight raises the spectre of heavy costs and uncertain results for potential trespassers. That alone should be enough to avoid conflict.

Consider another real-life example: the introduction of more stringent private property rights legislation in developing countries. If a new law is introduced that allocates particular types of property (say, land) in accordance with marginal labour productivity, say under pressure from external donor agencies, it would ignore social reality by trying to impose the primacy of labour productivity over conflict technology. Donors may insist on such laws because they correspond to a reality in their home country, where conflict technology is monopolised in the hands of the state and used for the enforcement of formal laws, in accordance with third-party judgements. That may not be the case in the recipient country, where social conflict technology may be far more decentralised. Consequently, the new law will be trespassed or simply ignored in the recipient country. Donors would label this 'corruption'; recipients would just label it social reality. In fact, the situation is very similar to the one in Shasta County, as described by Ellickson (1991). Consider another example: a donor insists on the introduction of competition legislation that forbids pre-emptive allocation of outputs on the basis of social sharing norms and replaces it by allocation through competitive bids. In that case, the losing party would lobby against the law because it does not allocate them their 'fair due' as prescribed under the social sharing norm system. The losing party would label this competition legislation as 'corrupt' because it trespasses a prevailing social norm. Clearly, the opinion on fairness depends on whether one considers conflict technology as exogenous or endogenous.

Platteau (2000) explores a variety of possibilities that can move society away from sharing norms and into a more economic allocation of outputs, based on effort and skill. He explains how various forms of split social communities may achieve this. Alternatively, the introduction of insurance markets, for instance in the forms of social security and health insurance, may be a solution to overcoming sharing norms, provided that they found their origin in environmental uncertainties. However, if sharing norms emerged from equally distributed conflict technology, then insurance systems may not be an appropriate solution.

Here, I would like to explore another road away from social sharing norms: the neutralisation of conflict technology. In Axelrod-type Prisoners' Dilemma games, that move is achieved through repeated rounds of the game, building up a credible track record and 'trust' between the players. In the more realistic Skaperdas-type game that we are considering here, however, players are unlikely to significantly improve upon the Nash outcome of the baseline scenario by repeated play so that investment in conflict can be scaled down and ultimately eliminated. Unlike in Axelrod's PD games, information about each other's likely behaviour is not the key to achieving Pareto optimality. Even if good past track records exist, there is no guarantee that players will abide by their past record in a future round of play. This is due to strongly increasing marginal returns to investment in conflict. Whereas in Axelrod-type PD games the returns to defection are constant, in this game the returns to conflict (defection) increase with total output of consumables. At one extreme, when other players invest zero in conflict, a single player can appropriate all output by investing just a single unit in conflict. Any diversion from the Nash equilibrium, for instance because of trust, becomes a very risky strategy. Resolving risk is the key to moving away from Nash equilibrium in a Skaperdas-type game. Solutions will have to neutralise these risks through the creation of credible commitment devices; for instance, by 'entrusting' property rights enforcement to a single and neutral third party. How that can be achieved is explored in the next sections.

Asymmetrically distributed conflict technology

The above 'stable anarchy' baseline scenario provides us with a welfare benchmark: a stable anarchy produces consumables (assumed to be the only factor in a social welfare function) at 50 per cent of its total capacity. We can now relax the assumption of fully shared knowledge of conflict and production technology and examine how this affects welfare, or total production of consumables. I first introduce asymmetrically distributed conflict technology (this section), and later (in the following section) asymmetrically distributed production technology. The former moves us away from output sharing norms, and establishes a vertical hierarchy in decision-making on property rights allocations: power prevails over productivity. The latter affects the assumption on fully observable production technology, introduces transaction costs and leads us straight into the division of labour. We can evaluate the impact of each of these changes on deadweight losses and production incentives in society, and consider the most efficient institutional response to minimise these losses.

One way to introduce unequally distributed conflict technology is to assume that all available technologies can be ranked according to their productivity in terms of appropriating a share of total output per unit of (time) input. It is not only the amount of resources allocated to conflict that determines the outcome, but also productivity differentials. A small difference in resources allocated to conflict may result in a vast difference in allocation of consumable output. In an extreme form, the format of the conflict production function changes from a proportional to a 'winner-takes-all' allocation. Hirshleifer (1996) examines various formats of the conflict production function and their impact on the decisiveness of conflict. Nuclear warfare with first-strike capability is a good example: whoever attacks first is the most likely winner. Hirshleifer discusses some historical examples too. The introduction of cannons in Europe in the early fifteenth century ended the indecisiveness of siege warfare. Only large cities could afford the improved but costly defences against cannon; smaller and less prosperous cities became part of larger empires. In a somewhat similar vein, Grossman and Kim (1996) split arms technology in offensive and defensive technology and examine the impact of various assumptions on conflict decisiveness. Relatively small investments in defence may substantially reduce the effectiveness of relatively large investments in offensive arms, depending on the technology involved. My point is that, with increasingly non-linear conflict production functions and more decisive conflict success functions, the likelihood of ending up in a 'winner-takes-all' situation increases, so that a single player appropriates all resources.

In terms of Table 10.1, decisive or disproportional conflict technology pushes the game into a corner solution: one player wins the conflict and appropriates all consumable resources.[4] The other players become slaves of the winner. The master has an interest in maintaining his asset, the slaves, by allowing them to retain a subsistence amount of consumables to survive and work. He can appropriate all remaining surpluses. As long as we stick to the assumption that all production technology is publicly shared knowledge and all actions are perfectly observable at zero cost, there is no need for the master to invest in slave supervision to monitor their production performance.

As long as the slaves get a lump-sum subsistence allocation of consumables, independently of their level of effort, they have no incentive to exert effort. Any increase in productivity is fully appropriated by the master. Barzel (1977/1997) argues that the master could gain by giving his slaves an incentive to work harder. For instance, he could allow the slaves to retain a share in additional output. Still, their marginal revenue would not equal marginal productivity; weak incentives would prevail. It may be more efficient for the master to introduce a negative incentive: punishment when the master observes outcomes of actions that do not correspond with the expected outcome, according to his knowledge of the production function. Retaliation imposes costs on slaves; they have an incentive to avoid it.

My basic argument here is that, while Hirshleifer's (1996) 'stable anarchies' with equally distributed conflict technology have hardly any production incentives to offer at all since additional output is equally shared, slavery societies with monopolised conflict technology may offer some forms of positive or negative incentives to exert effort. While the master is in a position to fully appropriate all surplus production (above subsistence level), he may re-invest part of that surplus in punishment or re-allocate it to his slaves, as a (weak) production incentive, thereby increasing effort and productivity above the level of an egalitarian 'stable anarchy'.

The social deadweight cost of slave societies consists of conflict and retaliation costs. Conflict costs should be considerably lower though with unequal distribution of conflict technology, compared to the stable anarchy situation. Only one individual has to invest in conflict technology; all others might as well do without since they cannot win a conflict anyway. This releases resources for production activities. Force, the over-whelming power of a comparative advantage in conflict technology, achieves what an equally distributed conflict technology was unable to do in the baseline scenario: move a stable anarchy society away from a Nash equilibrium and towards a more Pareto-optimal welfare level. Consequently, slavery societies may actually turn out to be economically more efficient than stable anarchies – provided that production technology is a public good and production activities are perfectly observable. Neal (1995) provides a formal proof of this finding.

Hirshleifer (1996) notes that unequal conflict technology introduces 'vertical hierarchy' in society, a two-level hierarchy with 1 master and $n-1$ slaves. Starting from this two-level hierarchy, one could easily imagine a multi-layered hierarchy when conflict technology is somewhat less extremely unequally distributed or less decisive, with intermediate conflict technologies and degrees of decisiveness occupying intermediate hierar-chical levels. This would be in line with Barzel's (2001) definition of the state as an agency with an 'ultimate monopoly on violence' within a terri-tory. The qualification 'ultimate' implies that there are lower hierarchical levels where autonomous violence is permitted and can be used to appro-priate benefits. This approach introduces a link between hierarchy and distribution of conflict technology – again provided that production tech-nology is a public good and production actions are perfectly observable.

Unequally distributed production technology

In this section I introduce unequally distributed production technology. Production knowledge is no longer a public good. Individuals specialise in the production of particular goods and start to trade truncated knowledge sets. Specialisation sets in and gainful trade of comparative advantages emerges. This has two consequences.

The first consequence of specialisation is that the observability of production efforts by agents decreases. It becomes increasingly costly to observe production behaviour, obtain and interpret the information required to evaluate agents' production efforts. The opportunity cost of obtaining information increases with the degree of specialisation or divi-sion of labour in society. Also, some actions are inherently more complex to understand than others. This introduces a new source of deadweight costs in society, besides the cost of conflict technology: transaction costs to obtain information on the production decisions and actions of agents.

For example, compare observability of production efforts by agricul-tural workers and traders. Agricultural output is relatively easily measurable and it can be readily assessed whether productivity corre-sponds to some standard technical norms. There is no need to control each input into the production process; output is a good indicator of effort. For trade, matters are more complicated. A supervisor cannot readily observe whether a trader obtained the best possible deal since he does not have all the market information that the trader has – unless of course he follows every move of the trader. That requires a costly monitoring process of all inputs, including those inputs that the trader may have omitted. Only then can a supervisor assess the optimality of a trader's decisions and efforts.

Assume for the time being that unequally distributed production technology is introduced after unequally distributed conflict technology, so that a slavery society with a dictator with a monopoly on violence already exists. The dictator is then forced to invest some of the surplus that he extracted in transaction costs. He needs to hire supervisors to observe his agents. In some cases, transaction costs may actually become prohibitive, for instance for trading activities. Unless the dictator is willing to invest his entire surplus and/or tolerate substantial residual uncertainty regarding the efforts of his slaves, only institutional change (shifting the transaction costs – residual uncertainty trade-off in Figure 6.2) can restore the equilibrium.

That institutional change requirement forces the dictator to decentralise production incentives. This move can be split into two steps.

Delegation of incentives

In order to reduce information costs, the dictator should give incentives to producers to reveal the required information or exert effort on their own initiative. Private property rights constitute such an incentive. They transfer residual uncertainty, and the corresponding claims on costs and benefits, from a central supervisor (the dictator or his supervisor) to a decentralised decision-maker with more complete information and thus better able to handle this residual uncertainty. Barzel (1977/2001) argues that slave owners decentralise (partial) property rights to their slaves when they feel more secure. Here, slaves receive property rights in function of the cost for the master to accurately control their activities.

In fact, the whole vertical integration literature, starting with Coase (1937) and Williamson (1975/1985) is about splitting up or integrating residual uncertainties and the corresponding residual claim rights, in function of transaction costs. That literature is so voluminous that it cannot possibly be summarised here. However, there are a few recent agency models that explain the need to decentralise and privatise property rights in an environment with increasingly distributed information.

Aghion and Tirole (1997) develop a model that explains the separation between formal and real authority as a function of increasing information asymmetry between a principal and his agents. Formal authority prevails when the principal is informed and makes his own choices in function of his preferences, for instance revenue maximisation. However, if agents are likely to be better informed than the principal about the various options, it is rational for the principal to accept the agents' proposals and rubber-stamp their decisions, for fear of picking a worse alternative. The agents then have real – but no formal – authority. Delegation of authority increases the agent's initiative and incentive to acquire more information, and thus increases his knowledge and further improves his decisions, provided that it is accompanied by an appropriate reward: a share in profits or an increased wage. However, even that does not exclude moral hazard and adverse selection. Aghion and Tirole's point is that the wider the knowledge gap between principals and agents, the further formal and real authority in an organisation will divert, with more authority being informally delegated to the agent. The problem in this model is that the situation remains ambiguous. The principal can, at any moment, revoke the authority that he informally delegated. This creates *ex-post* uncertainty for the agent, and he may refrain from making large investments in asset specificity, including knowledge assets. As such, informal delegation reduces the division of labour and knowledge accumulation.

Baker *et al.* (1999) avoid this ambiguity by making a clear distinction between informal and formal delegation of authority. Since informal delegation *within* an organisation can always be overturned by the principal, agents prefer formal delegation in order to have a credible incentive to pursue their investments in knowledge. This requires splitting up the organisation and establishment of private property rights for the agents: the principal/dictator should formally announce that he relinquishes control over certain assets and decisions, despite his ultimate monopoly on conflict technology. Furthermore, he should set up an independent third party to adjudicate any conflicts of interest between ruler and agents, and hand over the decision to use violence to enforce these decisions to that third party. It is in his own interest to do so because it does not only reduce monitoring costs but provides incentives for agents to reveal their true capacities and maximise effort, thereby enlarging the ruler's tax base and increase his overall tax revenue. In summary, the Baker *et al.* model provides the underlying organisational rationale for the emergence of private property rights from within an organisational setting. It is applicable to commercial enterprises as well as entire nations. Their model extends the logic of Barzel's (1997; 2001) delegation of rights and formalises that approach.

Cremer (1995) focuses on the principal's monitoring technology. He argues that an efficient monitoring technology lowers the information cost for the principal but, at the same time, lowers the agent's incentive to fully reveal his true capacities; it reduces his efforts. In line with Holmstrom (1982), he argues that principals/dictators may be their own worst enemies when their pursue their objective (revenue maximisation). Their agents are aware of this objective and know that additional production efforts on their part will be (at least partially) expropriated by the principal. This weakens the agents' incentives and thus their efforts. If the principal could credibly commit not to extract (too much) of the additional effort, he would provide a stronger incentive. One way of doing so would be for principals, in case they cannot have full information on an agent's behaviour, to deliberately choose a much less efficient monitoring technology and prefer to have little information so as to give an incentive to the agent to reveal his full production capacity.

Holmstrom (1982) points out that there is a fundamental incompatibility here. If the dictator relinquishes his authority and hands it over to a third party, he undermines his own objective (surplus maximisation or maximisation of his own revenue). On the other hand, if he doesn't do so, he also undermines his own objective because he will have only poor incentives to offer to his agents and run into high transaction costs in monitoring their efforts. This points to a key issue: the positive link between the observability of agents' efforts and the possibility of centralised control of an economy. The less observable these efforts are, the more the dictator's powers to pursue his surplus maximisation objective are eroded. In the end, he will have to give up his residual property rights on surplus production, and become a salaried civil servant (a president or prime minister with a fixed salary, rather than a claim on the entire surplus). As such, a successful dictator will ultimately make himself useless, at least under conditions of increasing division of knowledge in society. Dictators can only thrive and survive in relatively easily controllable economies, for instance economies that rely mainly on mineral extraction (Ross 2001).

Miller (2000) uses Holmstrom's (1982) 'Incompatibility Theorem' to explain the emergence and role of public administrations in this institutional transition process. The problem of a dictator is how to make a credible commitment not to expropriate his agents if they produce a surplus. To achieve this, he can delegate management of his estate to an intermediary who has other objectives and does not pursue surplus maximisation. Public administrations are such an intermediary. Civil servants do not aim to maximise a country's surplus; they aim to maximise their career perks: salary, promotions, security of employment, pensions and other benefits. They have no claim on residual property rights. Private agents will have more trust in these administrators than in the dictator to leave residual rights in private hands. Miller notes that this conclusion goes somewhat against the grain of principal-agent theory. That theory perceives misalignment of objectives between principals and agents as the cause of moral hazard and adverse selection. However, the Holmstrom theorem demonstrates that strong alignment of objectives may also cause adverse selection: it may be better for the principal to hire an agent whose objective is not in line with his own, so that he can escape from his own surplus maximisation trap.

The above line of reasoning has many common elements with Congleton's (2001) 'king and council template'. Congleton observes that dictatorships are rarely, if ever, one-man shows. The king or dictator usually has a 'council', a group of advisers and participants in the decision-making process. Congleton casts the interaction between king and council in an agency model of the state (though he does not use that terminology) whereby the king is the principal and his agents form a council. In line with the models discussed above, he explains the power balance between king and council in function of the information asymmetry between the two poles. When the king has a relatively easy job collecting all relevant information for his decisions, the balance shifts to his side. The reverse is true when information is hard to observe. He combines this informational dimension of decision-making with a military or conflict dimension. Weaker parties in society may not be able to dominate stronger parties, but the cost of conflict is high for both. Implicitly, the Congleton model assumes that conflict technology is not very decisive. All parties have a tendency to avoid conflict, provided a reasonable compromise can be found. Consequently, weaker parties will consent to be ruled provided some of their interests are taken into account. That approach may increase welfare for stronger as well as weaker parties. Congleton justifies his choice for this type of model by referring to historical examples of regime changes in Europe. Many changes were gradual and did not depend on revolutionary events.

Congleton's model contains no explicit mechanism for the emergence of a monopoly on violence, vested in the state, and changes in conflict technology are not taken into account. He concentrates on the informational dimension which, by itself, is sufficient to explain some shifts in the balance of power. The model is also rather weak in terms of driving forces. Congleton acknowledges the existence of a historical trend, away from principal (king)- dominated governance and towards agent (council and parliament)- dominated models of governance. He attributes this trend to exogenous technological changes that increase the complexity of policy analysis and make more representative governments informationally superior, and to exogenous shifts in ideology that affect the costs of control and resistance. The model that I present contains more explicit mechanisms to trace the impact of changes in conflict and production technology on political decision-making mechanisms. It also brings production incentives into the picture in order to account for the evolution of property rights regimes.

Collective action

The decentralisation movement is not the end of the story, however. While the cost of monitoring and the need for incentives act as a decentralising force with increasing division of labour, the need for collective action to rein in externalities induces a countervailing force that brings decision-making power back to the ruler.

As explained in Chapter 6, unsolicited externalities (residual or secondary uncertainties) are the inevitable consequence of advancing specialisation and complexity of production. Agents can invest more in *ex-*

ante transaction costs to assign property rights for *ex-post* events (see Figure 6.2) but that is an inefficient solution. Another solution is for agents to agree among themselves on more sophisticated *ex-ante* property rights (general laws) that allocate the cost of residual uncertainties to the parties that can modify these, thereby giving them an incentive to invest in reducing uncertainty. Agents may set up their own third-party judgement authorities to enforce the agreed collective action within the context of social organisations. Such agreements amount to efficiency-enhancing changes in the institutional technology of a society. However, as Barzel (2001) remarked, private agreements among a group of agents do not have the coercion technology to impose sanctions for single-round exchanges outside these communities. Anonymous exchange, outside social organisations and with third-party judgement and enforcement, requires access to the use of violence. That crucial piece in the institutional architecture is, however, monopolised by the ruler. The ruler cannot tolerate any competition in this domain and cannot allow private organisations to set up their own enforcement authorities. The ruled thus need the ruler's consent to provide effective enforcement of the institutional arrangements that they have agreed upon, with the help of his monopoly on violence. So, despite the fact that the ruler decentralises residual rights to individuals, he is called upon to use his monopoly on violence for the protection of these individual rights (and not for the purpose of his own direct objective to raise tax revenue). This opens up a new bargaining round between the ruler and the ruled and affects the institutional equilibrium.

The more the ruled appeal to the ruler's monopoly on violence to settle disputes regarding their own externalities, the more power the ruler can appropriate to intervene in these disputes. He may set up his own centralised administration of disputes, establish rules, regulations and other types of institutions and, in general, use his administrative discretion in the application of these institutions to influence property rights allocations for his own benefit. In short, this demand for his enforcement services may act as a back door through which he could continue to pursue his own surplus or taxation-maximising objective. Again, however, his credibility is at stake. If he uses his enforcement powers as a lever for discretionary behaviour in his own favour, he will lose credibility and create a disincentive for effort by his citizens. Likewise, the delegation of enforcement authority to a third party, with other objectives – such as an established judiciary that pursues career prospects rather than surplus maximisation – may be a solution.

Climbing Mount Improbable, starting from stable anarchy

So far, I assumed that the introduction of unequally distributed production technology followed a sequence, starting with conflict technology first and then moving on to production technology. But that assumption may not necessarily be true. Let us examine the consequences of a reversed sequence: starting from the baseline scenario with stable anarchy and equally distributed conflict technology, we introduce unequally distributed production technology first. 'Stable anarchy' was already characterised by high deadweight costs as a result of considerable investments in conflict technology and the absence of productivity-enhancing incentives as a result of sharing norms. To these, we now add the information costs induced by the division of labour or specialised knowledge. This is unlikely to make society more efficient.

As a thought experiment and in order to illustrate the problem, imagine producing and selling technologically complex portable PCs and state-of-the-art software, produced by highly specialised engineers working in highly distributed knowledge networks, in a society where the state of the art in conflict technology has not evolved beyond bows and arrows, or even machine-guns. Furthermore, assume that this conflict technology is equally distributed among the population: everybody has a bow and arrows, or a machine-gun for that matter. In contemporary vocabulary, we would call such a society a 'failed state': there is no centralised state authority that enforces collective action.

The introduction of a very specialised technology that is not a public good, for instance PCs, makes it costly for citizens to observe the qualities of these goods. It is difficult to find out what exactly the producer is selling. Indeed, the seller may not have perfect information on the technical properties of the PC that he is selling. When a disagreement emerges, conflict technology is highly decentralised and conflict settlement is costly. It would be very difficult to settle a disagreement with my software supplier in Redmond. Although there are high-speed internet connections between us, there is no single overarching authority that could impose the judgement. We do not belong to the same social circles and peer group pressure would be ineffective. There would be no central state with a monopoly on violence that covers both locations, not even two states with a trade agreement between them. The supplier would have to open a representative office in many locations, mainly for the purpose of letting his representative act as a hostage until further settlement. Few representatives would be operational in these circumstances. One could consider a return to the medieval community responsibility scheme, described by Greif (2000). However, taking into account the quantity of software packages that Redmond sells all across the world, citizens of Redmond would soon become *persona non grata* in most of the world. The asset value of the owner of the Redmond software company would not exceed the value of my local grocery store.

Greif (2000) explains why voluntary cooperation schemes, such as the community responsibility system, are unworkable in these circumstances. With growing number of traders and trade deals, the risk of being caught up in retaliatory actions increased, not only because of the growth in numbers but also because cities became more anonymous places where social control diminished. In the end, the community responsibility system and its retaliatory action scheme had to be abandoned and replaced by enforcement systems that were not based on social control. Social control turned out to have high transaction costs, worsened by larger communities and asymmetric information between traders. Milgrom *et al.* (1990) explain how the law merchant did away with the necessity of repeated interactions between any pair of traders; it made reputations portable across the community of traders and thereby overcame the problem of situational asymmetry. However, it still required repeated interaction within a limited group. Indeed, the system was limited to a single market place where a single law merchant could keep track of all trade disputes.

In short, the reverse sequence (specialised production technology before unequally distributed conflict technology) is unlikely to occur. Or, in other words, societies with equally distributed conflict technology are unlikely to develop a significant degree of specialisation. They run into very high transaction costs that make specialised exchange uneconomical, and they have no efficient means to settle the disputes that are inherent to exchange of incomplete or highly asymmetric knowledge packages. The combination of high deadweight losses (equally distributed conflict technology) and high transaction costs (division of labour) makes it improbable that such a society would exist at all.

Policy implications of the model

As Barzel (2001) points out, the key to explaining the evolution of states is to explain the evolution of residual claims on property rights. In this chapter I presented an approach that is based on two driving factors: the distribution of conflict technology and the distribution of production technology. When both are equally distributed, an inefficient but 'stable anarchy' emerges. With the introduction of unequally distributed conflict technology, a monopoly on violence for the holder of the most powerful technology occurs, who can use it to extract all surplus from society. However, he needs to give his citizens some sort of production incentive, if only a negative one (punishment for insufficient effort). Dictatorships are economically more efficient than stable anarchies, provided the deadweight losses of monitoring and punishment are less than the deadweight loss of conflict technology in anarchies. With the introduction of unequally distributed production technology, the observability of production effort declines, thereby making monitoring and incentive costs prohibitive. The only solution is to decentralise residual claim rights to producers, giving them a stronger incentive to produce. The only credible way to do so may require the dictator to relinquish decision-making privileges to intermediaries who do not pursue a surplus-maximisation objective.

The most important conclusion from the above discussion, from the point of view of the wider argument in this book, is that increasing division of labour and knowledge in society increases the pressure on a dictator to privatise his residual property rights to his agents and allow for decentralised decision-making. This establishes a clear link between the cognitive, economic and institutional development of society, and endogenises institutions in a wider cognitive-economic model – our main purpose in this chapter.

There are a number of other implications too, however.

Roads to prosperity

The above-presented framework endogenously generates political institutions (the power to make allocative decisions) as well as property rights themselves (allocative decisions) from a combination of conflict and production technologies. These two variables allow us to predict the output allocation mechanism, the deadweight loss and the efficiency of production incentives in society.

Table 10.2 summarises the different scenarios. Starting from the baseline scenario in the northwest quadrant, there are several roads that could lead societies to the prosperity of the southeast quadrant. The road through the northeast quadrant looks more like an uphill battle: increasing transaction costs, no central monopoly on conflict technology, resulting in high deadweight costs, and no incentives because of the absence of a property rights mechanism that allocates consumables in function of efforts. The road through the southwest quadrant seems like an easy downhill stroll from the northwest quadrant, once innovation and unequal distribution in conflict technology emerge, but it may become a tough uphill struggle again to move onwards to the southeast quadrant and get the dictator to relinquish his prerogatives. Still, there are incentives to move in the right direction and the going shouldn't be too difficult if deep entrenchment in slavery and dictatorship can be avoided.

Is there a straight road from the northwest to the southeast quadrant, avoiding the labours of the northeast quadrant and the ugliness of the southwest quadrant? That requires careful sequencing of innovation in conflict and production technology. In this model, dictatorship occurs when innovation in conflict technology outpaces innovation in production technology. The reverse is unlikely to occur.[5] The 'sequence' of technological change is critical: it is the *combination* of a high degree of division of labour and a monopoly on violence that produces a liberal market economy. Both are essential and none can be omitted. Desynchronisation between the two may lead to lock-in situations that are not easily overcome.

Table 10.2 explains why the combination of highly developed conflict technology and low division of labour or production technology (the southwest quadrant) is likely to generate dictatorship and weak economic

Table 10.2 Endogenous states of institutions

	Low division of labour	*High division of labour*
Indecisive, decentralised conflict technology	STABLE ANARCHY Sharing, weak incentives High deadweight losses	MOUNT IMPROBABLE High deadweight and transaction costs, weak incentives
Decisive, monopolised conflict technology	SLAVERY AND DICTATORSHIP Weak negative incentives Low deadweight losses	CAPITALIST DEMOCRACY Private property incentives Low deadweight losses, high transaction costs

performance. Unfortunately, that combination is a common occurrence in the real world. Developing countries (low degree of division of labour) with sufficient financial resources can buy advanced conflict technology (centralised violence) on world markets and use that to control a non-specialised population at home. In these circumstances, citizens have no informational counterweight powers at their disposal that enable them to negotiate with an armed ruler. They have no lever to force him to concede private (property) rights.

Transferability of institutions

This brings me to a related issue regarding the transferability of institutions between countries. Economists' traditional prescription for developing countries and transition economies for 'improving' their political and property rights institutions is simply to 'adopt' more efficient institutions.[6] Such prescriptions are usually rooted in the neo-classical economic model that is based on exogenously defined property rights institutions and does not consider the endogenous equilibrium situation between ruler and ruled that defines institutional outcomes. A particular situation such as 'stable anarchy' may be considered efficient from the point of view of technology in society, though more efficient social arrangements can be conceived from an external observer's point of view. External economic observers come with the prejudices of their own habitat, usually a developed country with centralised state enforcement powers and a fairly high degree of specialisation or division of labour. Developing countries, on the other hand, may satisfy none of these institutional preconditions. They may have a low degree of specialisation and/or a high degree of observability of production efforts (agriculture, mining industries for instance). In that case, rulers have no incentive to decentralise residual rights. Alternatively, they may only have a weakly centralised monopoly on violence, in which case 'stable anarchy' would be a more appropriate description. Transposing First-World institutions to such a society would be at best unworkable, at worst counterproductive.

With endogenously determined institutions, the search for '(more) efficient' institutions (North 1981; 1990) is in fact difficult to interpret. Institutional efficiency can only be compared between societies with similar conflict technology and degrees of specialisation. Although institutions may generate inferior economic outcomes, they may still be efficient within the context of the society that generated them. Even if a particular institution generates development in one country, it does not guarantee a successful 'import' into another economy.

Much of the development and transition economics literature that has been produced in the wake of the fall of the Berlin Wall assumes that institutions are exogenous to societies. Especially at the start of the transition wave in Eastern Europe in the early 1990s, it was assumed that ex-communist countries could simply import Western 'capitalist' economic institutions such as property rights, commercial and bankruptcy laws and competition regulations, and so on. If the exogenous institutions assumption were correct, exporting the economic institutions of, say the US, to less developed countries would automatically turn them into prosperous nations. That is obviously not the case. The endogenous institutions framework in this chapter demonstrates that economic development and institutions are the joint product of conflict and production technology; one cannot operate without the other.

Predatory and contractual governance

Much of the institutional economics literature is dominated by the juxtaposition of two models of evolution of formal institutions: the top-down 'predatory state' model and the bottom-up 'contractual' model. In the first type, the state or the ruler has a monopoly on conflict technology and can dictate his will. The ruler maximises his own return, constrained only by transaction costs (Levi 1988). He may have an 'encompassing interest' (McGuire and Olson 1996) in promoting economic development because it enhances his tax base and his revenue. But his policy stance is usually determined by his time preference, a security-related exogenous variable (North 1981; Barzel 2001). The problem is that these models can work both ways: a short-term threat may induce a ruler to be generous with his citizens in the hope that they will support him, or it may trigger a clampdown. These models focus on taxation by the ruler, not on the supply of institutions by the ruler. In the bottom-up contractual models, rulers are 'invited' by citizens to rule over them, based on a contract (Barzel 2001; Weingast 1997; North and Weingast 1989). It is hard to see how such a contract can constitute a credible commitment device without the necessary conflict technology to back it up. Indeed, most of the historical examples of contractual institutional change (Magna Carta, the Glorious Revolution) are the outcome of conflict between an armed ruler and an armed elite, not unarmed citizens. Contracts are not the cause but the outcome of the balance of power between the contracting parties. Neither top-down predatory nor bottom-up contractual models of governance can explain the close correlation between property rights institutions and economic performance. Przeworski and Limongi (1993) point out that there is a missing exogenous variable: if both economics and politics are endogenous, then there must be a third exogenous variable to explain the state of the system. The approach proposed in this research introduces such an exogenous variable: knowledge accumulation and distribution, in production and conflict technology.

Table 10.2 may help to explain some of the puzzling empirical findings in the institutional economics literature. While there is an overwhelming amount of empirical evidence (for instance, World Bank 1997) regarding the strong correlation between the quality of property rights institutions and economic performance, there is no conclusive empirical evidence that allows us to extrapolate these findings to the democratic qualities of political institutions. Przeworski and Limongi (1993) note that many studies have produced very conflicting or inconclusive evidence on the link between democracy and economic performance. That is not surprising in the context of Table 10.2. Indeed, there are two endogenous states of institutions that could be associated with fairly democratic and open political regimes, stable anarchy in the northwest quadrant and liberal democracy in the southeast quadrant. The first reflects a situation of low and inefficient economic development while the second reflects a well performing economy. Dictatorship or absence of democracy is situated in the southwest quadrant and could be a transition phase, bordering both the low and the high economic development stages.

Conclusions

In this chapter, I developed a framework that endogenously and simultaneously generates institutions and states of the economy. The model is driven by knowledge accumulation in two technologies, one for production of consumables and another for conflict. Continued knowledge accumulation or learning will result in an unequal distribution of knowledge or division of labour. Extant models, based on voluntary and involuntary cooperation, in predatory and contractual states, turn out to be special cases of this more general framework.

We can conclude that the emergence of a division of labour in production technology as well as specialisation in conflict technology are necessary ingredients for the emergence of private property rights. Such rights are unlikely to occur in a simple agrarian economy without division of labour. Another consequence of the model is that the deadweight losses from conflict technology investments can only be reduced through monopolisation of conflict technology. Societies with equally distributed conflict technology are likely to suffer more from deadweight losses and transaction cost inefficiency. Cost-efficient societies with strong private property rights – the Western model – can only emerge at the confluence of monopolised conflict technology and decentralised knowledge and decision-making.

Notes

1 Introduction

1 'Cognition' is an ability, 'knowledge' and 'behaviour' are the results of that ability.
2 The link between the closely related but distinct concepts of information and knowledge is explained in Chapter 4.
3 All these terms are used as synonyms in this book.

2 The uneasy relationship between knowledge and economics

1 It should be pointed out here that the diminishing returns and convergence issue is not limited to the production or supply side of economic systems. The Harrod-Domar/Solow approach to growth theory has strongly emphasised the supply side. The demand side comes in only as a market for products and a supplier of savings surpluses to fuel investment. However, the same problems of decreasing returns and slower growth appear on the demand side. One can easily see how ever more production of the same basket of consumer goods must necessarily run into diminishing marginal utility in a convex utility space, and thus diminishing marginal expenditure and increasing savings. Economies of scale and corresponding price reductions can slow down this process but cannot fundamentally change it. Growth of consumption is not sustainable without qualitative changes or changes in the composition of output. This problem has apparently not been discussed yet in the convergence debate.

3 The role of distributed knowledge in economics

1 I use 'knowledge' and 'information' as related though not synonymous concepts. The exact relationship between these variables is explained in Chapter 4.
2 This definition excludes international trade related uses of the concept of division of labour because there it refers to differentiation or specialisation among countries or sectors, not among individuals. I do not use the concept of division of labour in this book in an international trade related way.
3 Comparative advantage can of course be based on a geographical and/or legal monopoly. Oil producing countries have a geographical monopoly on oil wells within their border. Railway infrastructure operators have a geographical monopoly on railway tracks. In many countries, public utility companies have

legal monopolies on telecommunications, postal services, water, gas and electricity supply, garbage collection, etc.

4   Agent-wise differentiation may still occur if we assume different age profiles for agents, so that they are at different stages in their learning curves.

4   Knowledge and the principle of cognitive economy

1   This is true for chaotic systems whereby the slightest deviation from the original conditions produces a large change in the final result. For less chaotic systems, this conclusion will be weakened and ultimately disappear for fully deterministic systems where the outcome is fixed with probability 1.

2   There is a debate in the relevant literature on what 'fully random' actually means. See Gell-Mann (1995).

3   For an introduction to graph theory, see for instance Harary (1969).

4   In connectionist networks, these links can vary in intensity. However, to simplify the mathematics, we exclude that possibility here.

5   I make a distinction here between the knowledge graph H, which is a set of nodes and their links, and a measure of that knowledge graph v(H), that is defined as the product of I and d(H).

6   The reader should be aware that the term 'distributed knowledge' has different meanings for different authors. For Rummelhart and Norman it means 'distributed within the brain'. In that context, distributed knowledge representation models are often considered synonymous to connectionist models and neural network representations. Zhang (see further) uses it in the sense of 'distributed between internal and external representations'. I will introduce my own usage of this term in the next chapters, where 'distributed' stands for 'distributed across several persons'. The latter is the general sense in which this term will be used mostly in this book.

7   Goody (1986) notes that early predecessors of modern writing systems emerged in response to the need for securing agreed trade deals in the form of a contract. The number of objects of a deal, for instance the number of livestock, was represented by the number of stones in a closed clay cylinder that could be broken once the deal was carried out. This excluded cheating and 'forgetting' and thereby reduced uncertainty. The security function of an external representation is a feature derived from its memory storage function.

5   Communication and distributed knowledge

1   The Boyd and Richerson model is situated on the borderline between the neo-Darwinian view of sociobiology (that allows for phenotypic learning, within the confines of a genotypic 'leash', but not transmission of that learning) and a Lamarckian view that allows for unlimited learning and transmission of learned behaviour. Since neo-Darwinism was in part a reaction to Lamarckism, it is understandable that Darwinists are not happy with the idea that Lamarck is being vindicated. Whether the B&R model invalidates Darwinism in mimetic development depends on the point of view one takes regarding individually learned behaviour: the orthodox Darwinian view of learning (a set of randomly generated behavioural variations) as advanced for instance by Plotkin (1994), or the Lamarckian view (a set of purposively designed trials). The Lamarckian viewpoint would be valid if learning is an active and purposeful internal activity of the mind. The Darwinian viewpoint would be valid if learning is an external environmental selection mechanism on which internal mental

processes have little influence.
2   Errors in imitation processes could also result in declining fitness.
3   In the absence of pure 'curiosity' as a driving force for learning.
4   The larger the share of spare capacity used for additional learning, the larger the quantity effect.
5   There are circumstances whereby private individuals may be induced to supply public goods, once their private valuations of the benefit/cost ratio exceeds one, for whatever reason (Bergstrom *et al.* 1986). The recent literature on Open Source Software has elaborated on this theme, and compared the relative advantages and disadvantages of private provision of knowledge goods (such as software packages) without intellectual property rights protection (Johnson 2001). The issue of undersupply of research efforts remains a problem in most cases.
6   Restricting knowledge transmission to imitation only is a strong abstraction from reality. In practice, not all knowledge can be or is communicated through imitation, or not even through symbolic means. Some knowledge is inevitably retained by the learner; this constitutes his comparative advantage over imitators. The imitators or beneficiaries of that knowledge will have to induce the learner to let them participate in the benefits, for instance by offering him economic advantages.

6 The economy as a knowledge communication system

1   In modern computer parlance, 'object oriented programming' aims to achieve the same objective. There is no longer any need to know all the technical details of an object. It is enough to have a standardised protocol regarding the key features of the interface in order to allow the transfer and use of an 'object' between different software packages.
2   The non-communicated part of a truncated knowledge set should not be confused with tacit knowledge, a concept that is often used in the economics literature on knowledge and innovation. Polanyi (1967) originally defined tacit knowledge as a sort of unconscious knowledge. However, the meaning of tacit knowledge quickly shifted to 'not codified' knowledge, i.e. knowledge that has been left unspecified and is therefore not readily transmittable to others. Cowan *et al.* (1999) show that the borderline between codified and uncodified knowledge is endogenously determined as a function of costs and benefits. However, while imitation and symbolic systems can transfer codified knowledge only, exchange of knowledge embodied in goods and services can also transfer tacit or uncodified knowledge incorporated in the good. That tacit knowledge cannot be extracted (reverse-engineered or 'decompressed') from these goods and transferred to the brain of the recipient; it is usually lost in the formatting of the product.
3   Arrow does not explain how the division of labour increases output compared to individual agents in autarky. He does enumerate some advantages and disadvantages, though: 'total output is much greater than can be attributed to individuals' but it also 'increases the cost of cooperation'. The latter is attributed to 'different life experiences' and the resulting cost of communication.
4   In modern economic jargon, 'dexterity' could be translated as productivity gains.
5   Langlois and Metin (1996) have demonstrated how total production costs are shared between producers and consumers. Consumers spend opportunity costs of processing time to achieve a transaction: costs for scanning advertisements

and listening to salesmen, time spent on transport to shopping places, etc. Any additional costs borne by the producer to facilitate a transaction will reduce consumer transaction costs but not necessarily total transaction costs. However, a producer may benefit from strong economies of scale and thus a comparative advantage in taking some of these costs on board and into his sales price, rather than leaving them to the consumer. In any case, an empirical analysis of transaction costs is incomplete without the consumer side.

6 The concept of secondary uncertainty was first introduced in social science by the German sociologist Ulrich Beck (1986) in his book *The Risk Society*. Beck emphasises the environmental risks generated by technological developments that are meant to overcome natural constraints to human development. He did not as such relate the concept to transactions or exchanges of embodied knowledge.

7 A detailed discussion of transaction costs is presented in the next section.

8 This statement is true only for trade based solely on compared advantages. Trade can of course also be based on geographical and legal monopolies that exclude other parties from the property rights to the resources required for a particular trade. I exclude trade based on these types of monopolies, for the time being. Property rights will be brought back into the picture in Part III of this book.

9 Institutions do of course exist prior to economic exchange. Societies without trade also have institutions that put constraints on human behaviour, both individual and in social interaction. As such, institutions are not caused by the emergence of specialisation. The reverse is true however: specialisation and trade can not emerge without institutions that reduce the secondary uncertainty that they generate.

7 Economies of scope

1 On the relationship between economies of scale and scope, and the role of knowledge in these, see Langlois (1997) and Edwards and Starr (1987). Langlois argues that both scale and scope involve the re-use of knowledge, either over time (diachronic) or in parallel within a given time period (synchronic). In this chapter, the interpretation of economies of scope is slightly different. Here, it does not refer to the re-use of existing knowledge for a given activity, but rather for the acquisition of additional knowledge in learning processes.

2 Bresnahan and Gambardella (1998) present a model of General Purpose Technologies, specialised knowledge that creates economies of scope, not within a sector but across sectors. This overcomes the limits to the extent of the market within a sector and uses markets across sectors and economy-wide. In Baumgardner's (1988) model of specialisation, the extent of the market is affected by the elasticity of demand.

9 The state's monopoly on violence

1 Barzel (2000) adds a small but important qualification to that definition: 'ultimate' monopoly on violence. There may be several levels of decentralisation of a monopoly on violence, towards lower and sub-territorial authorities, or even towards non-authorised entities whose use of violence is somehow 'tolerated'.

2 Contrary to modern conflict theory (Hirshleifer, Skaperdas), Dudley does not distinguish between economies of scale in the cost of military technology (one

expensive fighter plane can cover a larger territory than a cheaper tank) and the decisiveness of military technology (infantry and guns are less decisive than tanks and bombs, city walls make infantry less decisive, artillery reduces the effectiveness of walls).

10 Endogenous institutions

1 Note that when production technology is a public good, there can be no trade because players have no comparative advantages. This is not a model of voluntary trade, only of production and involuntary redistribution.
2 Note that in this formulation of the CSF, S_i is badly defined if $Tc = 0$ for all i.
3 In Umbeck's gold mining example, unequal productivity was not the result of unequal knowledge or technology, but rather of unevenly distributed quality of another production factor, land.
4 Note that the Axelrod PD game is not resistant to unequally distributed technology, either. That would also produce a corner solution and make all attempts at repeated play to achieve a Pareto solution futile.
5 Two illustrations of this argument: Baumol's (1990) story of the Roman glassmaker who proudly told his emperor that he had invented an unbreakable glass and was promptly beheaded. Gleeson's (1999) story of the invention of porcelain in seventeenth-century Europe shows the lengths and costs to which even a dictator would go to appropriate property rights on specialised knowledge.
6 The neo-classical model, with exogenously defined property rights institutions, does not consider the trade-off between production and conflict or the internal equilibrium situation in which both ruler and ruled are trapped.

Bibliography

Acemoglu, D., Johnson, S. and Robinson J. (2001) 'The colonial origins of comparative development: an empirical investigation', *American Economic Review*, vol. 91(5), 1369–401.

Aghion, P. and Howitt, P. (1992) 'A model of growth through creative destruction', *Econometrica*, vol. 60(2), 323–51.

——(1998) *Endogenous growth*, MIT Press, Cambridge MA.

Aghion, P. and Tirole, J. (1997) 'Formal and real authority in organisations', *Journal of Political Economy*, vol. 105(1), 1.

Alchian, A. (1950) 'Uncertainty, evolution and economic theory', *Journal of Political Economy*, vol. 58, 211–21.

Arrow, K. (1962) 'The implications of learning-by-doing', *Review of Economic Studies*, vol. 29, 155–73.

——(1977/1994), 'The division of labour in the economy, the polity and society', reprinted in J. Buchanan and Y. Yoon (eds) (1994) *The return to increasing returns*, University of Michigan Press, Ann Arbor.

Arrow, K. and Debreu, G. (1954) 'The existence of an equilibrium for a competitive economy', *Econometrica*, vol. 22, 265–90.

Axelrod, R. (1984) *The evolution of cooperation*, Basic Books, New York.

Babbage, C. (1835) *On the economy of machinery and manufactures*, reprinted by Kelly, New York (1963).

Baker, G., Gibbons, R. and Murphy, K. (1999) 'Informal authority in organisations', *Journal of Law, Economics and Organisation*, vol. 15(1), 56–73, April.

Barkai, H. (1969) 'A formal outline of a Smithian growth model', *Quarterly Journal of Economics*, vol. 83, 396–414.

Barkow, J., Cosmides, L. and Tooby, J. (1992) *The adapted mind: evolutionary psychology and the generation of culture*, Oxford University Press, New York.

Barro, R. (1997) *Determinants of economic growth: a cross-country empirical study*, MIT Press, Cambridge MA.

Barro, R. and Sala-I-Martin, X. (1992) 'Convergence', *Journal of Political Economy*, vol. 100(2), 223–51, April.

Barzel, Y. (1977) 'An economic analysis of slavery', *Journal of Law and Economics*, vol. 20, 27.

——(1985) 'Transaction costs: are they just costs?', *Journal of Institutional and Theoretical Economics*, vol. 141, 4–16.

——(1997) [1977] *An economic theory of property rights*, Cambridge University Press, Cambridge, 2nd edn.

——(2000) 'Property rights and the evolution of the state', *Economics of Governance*, vol. 1(1), 25–51, February.

——(2001) *A theory of the state*, Cambridge University Press, Cambridge.

Bates, R. (2001) *Prosperity and violence*, Norton, London.

Bates, R., Greif, A. and Singh, A. (2001) 'Organising violence', mimeo.

Baumgardner, J. R. (1988) 'The division of labour, local markets and worker organisation', *Journal of Political Economy*, vol. 96(3), 509–27.

Baumol, W. (1990) 'Entrepreneurship: productive, unproductive, destructive', *Journal of Political Economy*, vol. 98(5), 893.

Beck, U. (1986) *Risikogesellschaft* ('Risk society') Suhrkamp, Frankfurt am Main.

Becker, G. (1964) *Human capital: a theoretical and empirical analysis with special reference to education*, NBER General Series no. 80, New York.

——(1976) *The economic approach to human behaviour*, University of Chicago Press, Chicago.

Becker, G. S. and Murphy, K. M. (1992) 'The division of labor, coordination costs, and knowledge', *Quarterly Journal of Economics*, vol. 107(4), 1137–60.

Berger, P. (1970) 'On the obsolescence of the concept of honour', *European Journal of Sociology*, vol. xi, 339–47.

Bergstrom, T., Blume, L. and Varian, H. (1986) 'On the private provision of public goods', *Journal of Public Economics*, vol. 29(1), 25–49.

Borland, J. and Yang, X. (1992) 'Specialisation and a new approach to economic organisation and growth', *American Economic Review*, vol. 82(2), 386–91.

Boulding, K. (1966) 'The economics of knowledge and the knowledge of economics', *American Economic Review*, vol. 56, 1–13.

——(1978) *Ecodynamics: a new theory of societal evolution*, Sage, Beverly Hills.

Boyd, R. and Richerson, P. (1985) *Culture and the evolutionary process*, University of Chicago Press, Chicago.

——(1995) 'Why does culture increase human adaptability?', *Ethology and Sociobiology*, vol. 16, 125–43.

Bresnahan, T. and Gambardella, A. (1998) 'The division of labour and the extent of the market', in E. Helpman (ed.) *General purpose technologies and economic growth*, MIT Press, Cambridge MA.

Brewer, A. (1991) 'Economic growth and technical change: John Rae's critique of Adam Smith', *History of Political Economy*, 23(1), 1–11.

Brooks, D. and Wiley, E. (1986) *Evolution as entropy*, University of Chicago Press, Chicago.

Buchanan, J. M. and Yoon, Y. J. (eds) (1994) *The return to increasing returns*, University of Michigan Press, Ann Arbor, ix, 382.

Burkhart, R. and Lewis-Beck, M. (1994) 'Comparative democracy: the economic development thesis', *American Political Science Review*, vol. 88(4), 903–10.

Caldwell, B. (1997) 'Hayek and socialism', *Journal of Economic Literature*, vol. 35, 1856–90.

Callebaut, W. and Pinxten, R. (eds) (1987) *Evolutionary epistemology: a multiparadigm program*, Reidel, Dordrecht.

Cheung, S. (1970) 'Transaction costs, risk aversion, and the choice of contractual arrangements', *Journal of Law and Economics*, vol. 13, 49–70.

——(1998) 'The transaction cost paradigm', *Economic Inquiry*, vol. 36, 514–21.

Choi, Y. B. (1993) *Paradigms and conventions: uncertainty, decision making and entrepreneurship*, University of Michigan Press, Ann Arbor.

Coase, R. (1937) 'The nature of the firm', *Economica*, vol. 4(4), 386–405.

——(1960) 'The problem of social cost', *Journal of Law and Economics*, vol. 3, 1–44.

Cole, M. and Griffin, P. (1980) 'Cultural amplifiers reconsidered', in M. Olson (ed.) *The social foundations of language and thought*, Norton, New York.

Congleton, R. (2001) 'On the durability of king and council: the continuum between dictatorship and democracy', *Constitutional Political Economy*, vol. 12, 193–215.

Conlisk, J. (1996) 'Why bounded rationality?', *Journal of Economic Literature*, vol. 34, 669–700, June.

Cooter, R. and Ulen, Th. (2000) *Law and economics*, 3rd edn, Addison-Wesley, Reading MA.

Cowan, R., David, P. and Foray, D. (1999) 'The explicit economics of knowledge codification and tacitness', mimeo.

Cowan, R. and Foray, D. (1996) 'The economics of codification and the diffusion of knowledge', mimeo.

Cremer, J. (1995) 'Arm's length relationships', *Quarterly Journal of Economics*, vol. 110(2), 275–95.

Dahlman, C. (1979) 'The problem of externality', *Journal of Law and Economics*, vol. 22, 141–62.

Damasio, A. (1989a) 'The brain binds entitities and events by multiregional activation from convergence zones', *Neural Computation*, vol. 1, 123–32.

——(1989b) 'Time-locked multiregional retroactivation: a systems level proposal for the neural substrates of recall and recognition', *Cognition*, vol. 33, 25–62.

——(1994) *Descartes' error*, Avon Books, New York.

Dawkins, R. (1976) *The Selfish Gene*, paperback edn, Oxford University Press, Oxford, 1989.

——(1982) *The extended phenotype*, Oxford University Press, Oxford.

Deacon, T. (1997) *The symbolic species*, Norton, New York.

Demsetz, H. (1967) 'Towards a theory of property rights', *American Economic Review*, vol. 57, 347–59.

——(1968) 'The cost of contracting', *Quarterly Journal of Economics*, vol. 82, 33.

——(1986) 'The core disagreement between Pigou, the profession and Coase in the analyses of the externality question', *European Journal of Political Economy*, vol. 12, 565–79.

Denison, E. F. (1967) *Why growth rates differ*, Brookings Institution, Washington DC.

——(1969) 'Some major issues in productivity analysis: an examination of the estimates by Jorgenson and Griliches', *Survey of Current Business*, vol. 49, 15–31.

Dixit, A. (1996) *The making of economic policy: a transaction cost politics perspective*, MIT Press, Cambridge MA.

Dixit, A. and Stiglitz, J. (1977) 'Monopolistic competition and optimum product diversity', *American Economic Review*, June, 297–308.

Domar, E. (1946) 'Capital expansion, rate of growth and employment', *Econometrica*, vol. 14, April.

Donald, M. (1991) *Origins of the modern mind*, Harvard University Press, Cambridge MA.

Dosi, G. and Nelson, R. (1994) 'An introduction to evolutionary theories in economics', *Journal of Evolutionary Economics*, vol. 4(3), 153–72.

Downs, A. (1957) *An economic theory of democracy*, Harper, New York.

Dudley, L. (1991) *The word and the sword: how techniques of information and violence have shaped our world*, Blackwell, Cambridge MA.

Durham, W. (1991) *Coevolution: genes, culture and human diversity*, Stanford University Press, Stanford.

Durkheim, E. (1893) *The division of labour in society*, with an introduction by L. Coser, Macmillan Press, London, 1994.

Easterly, W. (2001) *The elusive quest for growth*, MIT Press, Cambridge MA.

Easterly, W. and Levine, R. (2000) 'It's not factor accumulation: stylised facts and growth models', mimeo, November 2000.

Edwards, B. and Starr, R. (1987) 'A note on indivisibilities, specialisation and economies of scale', *American Economic Review*, vol. 77(1), 192–4, March.

Eggertsson, Thráinn (1990) *Economic behaviour and institutions*, Cambridge University Press, Cambridge.

Ellickson, R. (1991) *Order without law*, Harvard University Press, Cambridge MA.

Elman, J., Bates, E. and Johnson, M. (1996) *Rethinking innateness: a connectionist perspective on development*, MIT Press, Cambridge MA.

Elmslie, B. (1994) 'The endogenous nature of technological progress and transfer in Adam Smith's thought', *History of Political Economy*, vol. 26(4), 649–63.

Eltis, W. (1975) 'Smith's view of economic growth', in S. Skinner and T. H. Wilson (eds) *The market and the state: essays in honour of Adam Smith*, Clarendon Press, Oxford.

Esanov, A., Raiser, M. and Buiter, W. (2001) 'Nature's blessing or nature's curse: the political economy of transition in resource-based economies', Working Paper no. 65, European Bank for Reconstruction and Development.

Festinger, L. (1957) *A theory of cognitive dissonance*, Stanford University Press, Stanford.

Findlay, R. (1996) 'Towards a model of territorial expansion and the limits of empire', in M. Garfinkel and S. Skaperdas (eds) *The political economy of conflict and appropriation*, Cambridge University Press, Cambridge.

Fisher, R. A. (1930) *The genetic theory of natural selection*, Oxford University Press, London.

Furubotn, E. and Richter, R. (1997) *Institutions and economic theory : the contribution of the new institutional economics*, University of Michigan Press, Ann Arbor.

Garfinkel, M. and Skaperdas, S. (eds) (1996) *The political economy of conflict and appropriation*, Cambridge University Press, Cambridge.

——(2000a) 'Contract or war: on the consequences of a broader view of self-interest in economics', *The American Economist*, vol. 44(1), 5.

——(2000b) 'Conflict without misperceptions or incomplete information', *Journal of Conflict Resolution*, vol. 44(6), 793.

Gell-Mann, M. (1995) *The quark and the jaguar*, Freeman, New York.

Georgescu-Roegen (1971) *The entropy law and the economic process*, Harvard University Press, Cambridge MA.

Gleeson, J. (1999) *The Arcanum*, Warner Books, New York.

Goody, J. (1977) *The domestication of the savage mind*, Cambridge University Press, Cambridge.

——(1986) *The logic of writing and the organisation of society*, Cambridge University Press, Cambridge.

——(1987) *The interface between the written and the oral*, Cambridge University Press, Cambridge.

Greif, Avner (1989) 'Reputation and coalitions in medieval trade: evidence on the Magribi traders', *Journal of Economic History*, vol. 49(4).

——(2000) 'The community responsibility system', in M. Aoki and Y. Hayami (eds) *Communities and markets in economic development*, Oxford University Press, Oxford.

——(2001) 'Historical institutional analysis', mimeo, Stanford University.

Griliches, Z. and Jorgenson, D. (1966) 'Sources of measured productivity change: capital input', *American Economic Review*, vol. 56, 50–61.

——(1967) 'The explanation of productivity change', *Review of Economic Studies*, vol. 34, 249–83.

Grossman, S. and Hart, O. (1986) 'The costs and benefits of ownership: a theory of vertical and lateral integration', *Journal of Political Economy*, vol. 94(4), 691–719.

Grossman, H. and Kim, M. (1996) 'Predation and production', in M. Garfinkel and S. Skaperdas (eds) *The political economy of conflict and appropriation*, Cambridge University Press, Cambridge, ch. 4.

Hahlweg, K. and Hooker, C. (eds) (1989) *Issues in evolutionary epistemology*, State University of New York Press, Albany.

Harary, F. (1969) *Graph theory*, Addison-Wesley, Reading MA.

Harrod, R. (1939) 'An essay in dynamic theory', *Economic Journal*, vol. 49, March.

Hayek, F. von (1945) 'The use of knowledge in society', in Hayek, *Individualism and economic order*, Routledge and Kegan Paul, London, 1949.

Higgins, E. T. and Sorrentino, R. (1990) *Handbook of motivation and cognition*, 3 vols, Guilford Press.

Hirschleifer, J. (1991) 'The technology of conflict as an economic activity', *American Economic Review*, vol. 81(2), 130–4.

——(1996) 'Anarchy and its breakdown', in M. Garfinkel and S. Skaperdas (eds) *The political economy of conflict and appropriation*, Cambridge University Press, Cambridge, ch. 2.

Hoebel, E. A. (1964) *The law of primitive man: a study in comparative legal dynamics*, Harvard University Press, Cambridge MA.

Hoffman, E., McCabe, K. and Smith, V. L. (1998) 'Behavioural foundations of reciprocity: experimental economics and evolutionary psychology', *Economic Inquiry*, vol. 36, 335–52, July.

Holcomb, H. (2001) *Conceptual challenges in evolutionary psychology*, Kluwer, Dordrecht.

Holland, J. (1995) *Hidden order*, Addison-Wesley, Reading MA.

Holloway, R. (1996) 'Evolution of the human brain', in A. Lock and C. Peters (eds) (1999) *Handbook of human symbolic evolution*, Blackwell, Oxford, ch. 4.

Holmstrom, B. (1982) 'Moral hazard in teams', *Bell Journal of Economics*, vol. 13, 324–40.

Holmstrom, B. and Milgrom, P. (1991) 'Multitask principal-agent analysis: incentive contracts, asset ownership and job design', *Journal of Law, Economics and Organisation*, vol. 7(special), 24–52.

Huntington, S. and Dominguez, J. (1975) *Political development*, Addison-Wesley, Reading MA.

Hutchins, E. (1995) *Cognition in the wild*, MIT Press, Cambridge MA.

Ingold, T. (1999) 'Social relations, human ecology and the evolution of culture', in A. Lock and C. Peters (eds) *Handbook of human symbolic evolution*, Blackwell, Oxford.

Ippolito, R. A. (1977) 'The division of labour in the firm', *Economic Inquiry*, vol. 15, 469–92.

Jensen, M. C. and Meckling, W. H. (1976) 'Theory of the firm: managerial behavior, agency costs and ownership structure', *Journal of Financial Economics*, vol. 3(4), 305–60.

Johnson, J. (2001) 'Economics of open source software', mimeo, MIT.

Jones, C. H. (1995) 'R & D models of economic growth', *Journal of Political Economy*, vol. 103 (4), 759 - 84.

Jones, C. H (1999) 'Growth: with or without scale effects' *American Economic Review*, vol. 89 (2), p139 - 144

Kagan, J. (1994) *Galan's prophecy*, Basic Books, New York.

Kahneman, D. and Tversky, A. (1979) 'Prospect theory: an analysis of decision under risk', *Econometrica*, vol. 47(2), 263–91.

Karmiloff-Schmit, A. (1992) *Beyond modularity: a developmental perspective on cognitive science*, MIT Press, Cambridge MA.

Kaufmann, D., Kraay, A. and Zoido-Lobaton, P. (2002) *Governance matters: updated indicators for 2000/01*, World Bank Policy Research Working Paper no. 2772, World Bank, Washington DC.

Kenny, C. and Williams, D. (2001) 'What do we know about economic growth? Or, why don't we know very much?', *World Development*, vol. 29(1), 1–22.

Keynes, J. M. (1936) *The general theory of employment, income and money*, Macmillan, London.

Klaes, M. (1996) 'Transaction costs and measurability', mimeo, Department of Economics, Edinburgh University, October.

Knight, F. (1921/1971) *Risk, uncertainty and profit*, University of Chicago Press, Chicago, 1971.

Krugman, P. (1979) 'Increasing returns, monopolistic competition and international trade', *Journal of International Economics*, vol. 9, 469–79.

——(1994) 'Complex landscapes in economic geography', *American Economic Review*, vol. 84(2), 412–16.

Kuhn, T. (1962) *The structure of scientific revolutions*, University of Chicago Press, Chicago.

Laffont, J. J. and Tirole, J. (1993) *A theory of incentives in procurement and regulation*, MIT Press, Cambridge MA.

Langlois, R. (1997) 'Scale, scope and the reuse of knowledge', paper for the conference in honour of Brian Loasby, mimeo, University of Connecticut, Department of Economics.

Langlois, R. and Metin, C. (1996) 'The organisation of consumption' in M. Bianchi (ed.) *The active consumer*, Routledge, London.

Levi, Margaret (1988) *Of rule and revenue*, University of California Press, Berkeley.

Li, C H. (2000) 'Endogenous versus semi-endogenous growth', *Economic Journal*, vol 110, March 2000, .c109 - c122

Lipset, S. M. (1988) *Democracy in developing countries*, Lynne Rienner, Boulder.

Loasby, B. (1999) *Knowledge, institutions and evolution in economics: the Graz Schumpeter Lectures*, Routledge, London.

Locay, L. (1990) 'Economic development and the division of production between households and markets', *Journal of Political Economy*, vol. 98, 965–82.

Lock, A. and Peters, C. (1999) *Handbook of human symbolic evolution*, Blackwell, Oxford.

Lowe, P. (1975) 'Smith's view on economic equilibrium', in S. Skinner and T. Wilson (eds) (1976) *The market and the state: essays in honour of Adam Smith*, Clarendon Press, Oxford.

Lucas, R. (1988) 'On the mechanics of economic development', *Journal of Monetary Economics*, vol. 22, 3–42, July.

Lumsden, C. and Wilson, E. O. (1981) *Genes, mind and culture: the co-evolutionary process*, Harvard University Press, Cambridge MA.

Maddison, A. (2001) *The world economy: a millennial perspective*, Development Economics Centre, OECD, Paris.

Malmgren, H. (1961) 'Information expectations and the theory of the firm', *Quarterly Journal of Economics*, vol. 77, 399–421.

Mankiw, N., Romer, D. and Weil, D. (1992) 'A contribution to the empirics of economic growth', *Quarterly Journal of Economics*, vol. 107, 407–37, May.

Mantzavinos, C. (2001) *Individuals, institutions and markets*, Cambridge University Press, Cambridge.

March, J. and Simon, H. (1952) *Organisations*, Wiley, New York.

Marschak, J. and Radner, R. (1972) *Economic theory of teams*, monograph, Cowles Foundation for Research in Economics at Yale University, Yale University Press, New Haven, 22.

Marshall, A. (1890) *Principles of economics*, 3rd edn, Macmillan, London, 1920.

Masten, S. and Williamson, O. (1999) *The economics of transaction costs*, Edward Elgar, Aldershot.

Maturana, H. and Varela, F. (1980) *Autopoeisis and cognition: the realisation of the living*, D. Reidel, London.

Mauss, M. (1924) 'Essai sur le don', reprinted in Marcel Mauss, *Sociologie et anthropologie*, Presses Universitaires de France, Quadrige, 1995.

Maynard Smith, J. (1970) 'Time in the evolutionary process', *Studium Generale*, vol. 23, 266–72.

McGuire, M. and Olson, M. (1996) 'The economics of autocracy and majority rule: the invisible hand and the use of force', *Journal of Economic Literature*, vol. 34, 72–96.

Milgrom, P., North, D. and Weingast, B. (1990) 'The role of institutions in the revival of trade: the law merchant, private judges and the champagne fairs', *Economics and Politics*, vol. 2(1), 1–23.

Miller, G. (2000) 'Above politics: credible commitment and efficiency in the design of public agencies', *Journal of Public Administration Research and Theory*, vol. 10(2), 289–327.

Mirowski, P. (1989) *More heat than light: economics as social physics: physics as nature's economics*, Historical perspectives on modern economics, Cambridge University Press, Cambridge.

Mithen, S. (1996) *Prehistory of the mind*, Thames and Hudson, London.

Mokyr, J. (1990) *The lever of riches: technological creativity and economic progress*, Oxford University Press, New York.

——(1993) *The British industrial revolution: an economic perspective*, Westview Press, Boulder.

Neal, H. (1995) 'The initial resource distribution in an economic model of conflict', University of British Columbia, Department of Economics, working paper.

——(1997) 'Equilibrium structure in an economic model of conflict', *Economic Inquiry*, vol. 35(3), 480–94.

Nelson, R. and Winter, S. (1982) *An evolutionary theory of economic change*, Belknap Press of Harvard University, Cambridge MA.

Nonneman, W. and Vanhoudt, P. (1996) 'A further augmentation of the Solow model and the empirics of economic growth for OECD countries', *Quarterly Journal of Economics*, August, 944–53.

North, D. (1981) *Structure and change in economic history*, Norton, New York.

——(1990) *Institutions, institutional change and economic performance*, Cambridge University Press, Cambridge.

——(2000) 'Non-ergodicity', mimeo.

North, D. and Thomas, R. (1973) *The rise of the western world*, Cambridge University Press, Cambridge.

North, D. and Wallis, J. (1986) 'Measuring the transaction sector in the American economy 1870–1979', in S. Engerman (ed.) *Long term factors in American economic growth*, University of Chicago Press, Chicago, 95–148.

——(1994) 'Integrating institutional change and technical change in economic history: a transaction cost approach', *Journal of Institutional and Theoretical Economics*, vol. 150(4), 609–24.

North, D. and Weingast, B. (1989) 'The evolution of institutions governing public choice in seventeenth century England', *Journal of Economic History*, vol. 49(4), December.

Olson, M. (1965) *The logic of collective action*, Harvard University Press, Cambridge MA.

Ostrom, E. (1991) 'Rational-choice theory and institutional analysis: towards complementarity', *American Political Science Review*, vol. 85(1) (March) 237–50.

Ostroy, J. (1984) 'A reformulation of the marginal productivity theory of distribution', *Econometrica*, vol. 52(3), 599–630.

Papandreou, A. (1994) *Externality and institutions*, Clarendon Press, Oxford.

Pejovich, S. (1998) *Economic analysis of institutions and systems*, Kluwer, Amsterdam.

Phelps, E. (1966) 'Models of technical progress and the golden rule of research', *Review of Economic Studies*, vol. 33, 133–45.

Pigou, A. (1932) *The economics of welfare*, 4th edn, Macmillan, London.

Platteau, J. P. (2000) *Institutions, social norms and economic development*, Harwood Academic Publishers, Reading.

Plotkin, H. (1994) *Darwinian machines and the nature of human knowledge*, Harvard University Press, Cambridge MA.

——(1997) *Evolution in mind: an introduction to evolutionary psychology*, Allen Lane, London.

Poggi, G. (1978) *The development of the modern state*, Stanford University Press, Stanford.

Polanyi, M. (1967) *The tacit dimension*, Routledge and Kegan Paul, London.

Popper, K. (1959) *The logic of scientific discovery*, Basic Books, New York.

Posner, R. (1980) 'A theory of primitive society, with special reference to law', *Journal of Law and Economics*, vol. 23, 1–53.

Prigogine, I. (1987) 'The meaning of entropy', in W. Callebaut and R. Pinxten (eds) *Evolutionary epistemology: a multiparadigm program*, Reidel, Dordrecht, ch. 2.

Prigogine, I. and Stengers, I. (1979) *La nouvelle alliance*, Editions Gallimard, Paris.

Pritchett, L. (1984) *Order out of chaos: man's new dialogue nature*, Bantam Books and Fontana Paperbacks, London.

—— (1995) *Divergence, big time*, World Bank Policy Research Working Paper no. 1522, World Bank, Washington DC.

——(1996) *Where has all the education gone?*, World Bank Working Paper no. 1581, World Bank, Washington DC.

Przeworski, A., Alavarez, M., Cheibub, J. and Limongi, F. (2000) *Democracy and development: political institutions and well-being in the world 1950–1990*, Cambridge University Press, Cambridge.

Przeworski, A. and Limongi, F. (1993) 'Political regimes and economic growth', *Journal of Economic Perspectives*, vol. 7(3), 59.

Rae, J. (1834) *Statement of some new principles on the subject of political economy*, reissued 1964 by Kelly, New York.

Reid, G. Clydesdale (1989) *Classical economic growth: an analysis in the tradition of Adam Smith*, Blackwell, Oxford UK and Cambridge MA, xiv, 210.

Ricardo, D. (1815) *Principles of political economy and taxation*, reprinted 1996 by Prometheus, Amherst NY.

Rodrik, D., Subramanian, A. and Trebbi, F. (2002) 'Institutions rule: the primacy of institutions over geography and integration in economic development', NBER working paper no. 9305, Cambridge MA.

Rogers, A. (1988) 'Does biology constrain culture?', *American Anthropologist*, vol. 90, 819–31.

Romer, P. (1986) 'Increasing returns and long-run growth', *Journal of Political Economy*, vol. 94(5), 1002–37.

——(1987) 'Growth based on increasing returns due to specialisation', *American Economic Review*, vol. 77(2), 56–62, May.

——(1990a) 'Are non-convexities important for understanding growth?', *American Economic Review*, vol. 80(2), May.

——(1990b) 'Endogenous technological change', *Journal of Political Economy*, vol. 98(5), 71–102.

——(1994) 'The origins of endogenous growth', *Journal of Economic Perspectives*, vol. 8(1), 3–22.

——(1995) 'Comment on Gregory Mankiw, "The growth of nations" ', Brookings Papers on Economic Activity, part 1, Brookings Institution, Washington DC, 313–20.

Rosch, E. (1978) 'Principles of categorisation', in E. Rosch and B. Lloyd (eds) *Cognition and categorisation*, Lawrence Erlbaum Associates, Hillsdale NJ, ch. 2.

Rosen, S. (1978) 'Substitution and division of labour', *Economica*, vol. 45(179), 235–50.

——(1983) 'Specialisation and human capital', *Journal of Labor Economics*, vol. 1(1), 43–9.

Rosenberg, N. (1976) 'Another advantage of the division of labour', *Journal of Political Economy*, vol. 84(4), 861–8.

Ross, Michael (2001) 'Does oil hurt democracy?', *World Politics*, April.

Rummelhart, D. and Norman, D. (1988) 'Representation in memory', in R. Atkinson, R. Herrnstein, G. Lindzey and R. Luce (eds) *Stevens' handbook of experimental psychology*, vol. 2, Wiley, New York, ch. 8.

Sala-I-Martin, X. (1997) 'I just ran two million regressions', *American Economic Review*, vol. 87(2), 178–83.

——(2002) '15 years of New Growth Economics: what have we learned?', mimeo, Universitat Pompeu Fabra, June.

Samuelson, P. (1954) 'The pure theory of public expenditures', *Review of Economics and Statistics*, vol. 36(4), 387–9.

Schneider, J. and Ziesemer, Th. (1995) 'What's new and what's old in New Growth Theory', *Zeitschrift für Wirtschafts und Sozialwissenschaften*, vol. 115(3), 429–72.

Schumpeter, J. (1934) *The theory of economic development*, reprinted 1983, Oxford University Press, London.

Segerstrom, P., Anant, T. and Dinopoulos, E. (1990) 'A Schumpeterian model of the product life cycle', *American Economic Review*, vol. 80(5), 1077–91.

Shannon, C. and Weaver, W. (1947) *Mathematical Theory of Communication*, University of Illinois Press, Urbana-Champaign.

Shell, K. (1967) 'A model of inventive activity and capital accumulation', in K. Shell (ed.) *Essays on the theory of optimal growth*, MIT Press, Cambridge MA.

Simon, H. and March, J. (1968) *Organisations*, Wiley, New York.

Skaperdas, S. (1991) 'Conflict and attitudes toward risk', *American Economic Review*, vol. 81, May.

——(1992) 'Cooperation, conflict and power in the absence of property rights', *American Economic Review*, vol. 82(4), September, 720–39.

——(1995) 'Risk aversion in contests', *Economic Journal*, July.

Skinner, S. and Wilson, T. (eds) (1976) *The market and the state: essays in honour of Adam Smith*, Clarendon Press, Oxford.

Smith, Adam (1762) *Lectures on rhetoric and belles lettres – reported by a student 1762–63*, ed. J. Lothian, Carbondale, 1971.

——(1776/1993) *The wealth of nations*, selected edn with an introduction by K. Sutherland, Oxford University Press, Oxford, 1993.

Smith, V. L. (1997) 'The two faces of Adam Smith', Southern Economic Association Distinguished Guest Lecture, Atlanta, 21 November.

Solow, R. (1956) 'A contribution to the theory of economic growth', *Quarterly Journal of Economics*, vol. 70, 65–94.

——(1957) 'Technical change and the aggregate production function', *Review of Economics and Statistics*, vol. 39, 312–20, August.

Stern, N. (1991) 'The determinants of growth', *Economic Journal*, vol. 101, 122–33.

Stigler, G. J. (1951) 'The division of labor is limited by the extent of the market', *Journal of Political Economy*, vol. 59(3), 185–93, June. Reprinted in *The essence of Stigler*, eds K. R. Leube and T. G. Moore, Stanford University, Hoover Institution Press, 1986, 13–24.

——(1976) 'The successes and failures of professor Smith', *Journal of Political Economy*, vol. 84(6), 1199–213.

Stokey, N. (1991) 'Human capital, product quality and growth', *Quarterly Journal of Economics*, vol. 106, 587–616, May.

Tamura, R. (1991) 'Income convergence in an endogenous growth model', *Journal of Political Economy*, vol. 99(3), 522–40.

Teilhard de Chardin, P. (1958) *Le phenomène humain*, Editions du Seuil, Paris.

Thompson, E. and Faith, R. (1981) 'A pure theory of strategic behavior and social institutions', *American Economic Review*, vol. 71(3), 366.

Tirole, J. (1982) 'On the possibility of speculation under rational expectations', *Econometrica*, vol. 50, 1163–81.

——(1986) 'Hierarchies and bureaucracies: on the role of collusion in organisations', *Journal of Law, Economics and Organisation*, vol. 2, 181.

——(1999) 'Incomplete contracts: where do we stand?', *Econometrica*, vol. 67(4), 741–81, July.

Ullmann-Margalit, E. (1977) *The emergence of norms*, Clarendon Press, Oxford.

Umbeck, J. (1981) 'Might makes right', *Economic Inquiry*, vol. 19, 38, January.

Uzawa, H. (1965) 'Optimum technical change in an aggregative model of economic growth', *International Economic Review*, vol. 6, 18–31, January.

Von Weizsäcker, C. Chr. (1991) 'Antitrust and the division of labor', *Journal of Institutional and Theoretical-Economics*, 147(1), 99–113, March.

——(1993) 'The division of labour and market structure', *Empirica*, 20(3), 241–4.

Wallis, J. and North, D. (1994) 'Integrating institutional change and technical change in economic history: a transaction cost approach', *Journal of Institutional and Theoretical Economics*, vol. 150(4), 609.

Weber, M. (1924) *Gesammelte Aufsätze zur Soziologie und Sozialpolitik*, Mohr Verlag, Tübingen.

Weingast, B. (1997) 'The political foundations of democracy and the rule of law', *American Political Science Review*, vol. 91(2), 245–63.

Wen, U. (1994) 'An analytical framework with consumers-producers, economies of specialisation and transaction costs', working paper, Department of Economics, Monash University, Australia.

Williamson, O. (1975) *Markets and hierarchies*, Free Press, New York.

——(1985) *The economic institutions of capitalism*, Free Press, New York.

Wilson, E. O. (1975) *Socio-biology: the new synthesis*, Harvard University Press, Cambridge MA.

World Bank (1997) *World development report: the state in a changing world*, World Bank, Washington DC.

Wuketits, F. M. (ed.) (1984) *Concepts and approaches in evolutionary epistemology: towards an evolutionary theory of knowledge*, Reidel, Dordrecht.

Yang, X. and Borland, J. (1991) 'A micro-economic mechanism for economic growth', *Journal of Political Economy*, vol. 99, 460–82.

Yang, X. and Ng, Y. K. (1993) *Specialisation and economic organisation: a new classical microeconomic framework*, North-Holland, Amsterdam.

Young, Alwyn (1993) 'Invention and bounded learning by doing', *Journal of Political Economy*, vol. 101(3), 443.

Zhang, J. (1997) 'The nature of external representations in problem solving', *Cognitive Science*, vol. 21(2), 179–217.

——(2000) 'External representations in complex information processing tasks', in A. Kent (ed.) *Encyclopedia of library and information science*, Dekker, New York.

Zhang, J. and Norman, D. (1994) 'Representations in distributed cognitive tasks', *Cognitive Science*, vol. 18, 87–122.

Index